Thinking
Better

Thinking Better

DAVID LEWIS AND
JAMES GREENE

RAWSON, WADE PUBLISHERS, INC.
NEW YORK

Library of Congress in Publication Data

Lewis, David, 1942–
    Thinking better.

    Bibliography: p.
    Includes index.
    1. Thought and thinking.   2. Problem solving.
3. Success.   I. Greene, James.   II. Title.
BF455.L43   153   80-5994
ISBN 0-89256-168-8   AACR2

Published simultaneously in Canada by McClelland
and Stewart, Ltd.

Composition by American-Stratford Graphic Services, Inc.,
Brattleboro, Vermont.
BOMC offers recordings and compact discs, cassettes
and records. For information and catalog write to
BOMR, Camp Hill, PA 17012.
Designed by Jacques Chazaud

The order of the authors' names is a difficult issue to decide for any book which is the product of a coauthorship. James Greene is the principal author of this book and supplied the bulk of the information contained herein. However, the order of names on the cover was decided by the flip of a coin. James Greene called the toss and apparently fell prey to the Guesser's Disadvantage—a misfortune which you, the reader, can avoid by following our instructions in Section Three of Step Five in this book.

To our many colleagues in the Mind Potential Study Group who have helped us in the research on which this program is based, and to our even greater number of volunteer subjects who allowed us to put theory into practice and practice to the test, this book is gratefully dedicated.

Contents

Brains well prepared are the monuments
Where knowledge is most surely engraved.

—JEAN JACQUES ROUSSEAU

Part One

HOW YOU CAN THINK BETTER AT ANY AGE

Five Steps
to Successful Thinking

This is a book about *your* brain and ways of making it work at peak efficiency. In five easily mastered steps you will learn how every major aspect of intellectual performance can be substantially increased. We will show you how to assess your individual styles of learning, problem solving, and decision making and then explain how such knowledge can be used to enhance the speed and efficiency of all kinds of thinking.

The techniques we are going to reveal will allow your brain to function more effectively no matter how well or poorly you may feel it is working at present. If your mental performance is highly efficient right now, this course could make you even smarter and allow fresh intellectual challenges to be dealt with successfully. If you have any doubts about your present level of intelligence, do not be discouraged by the damaging belief that setbacks in the past must inevitably predict failures in the future. As you will shortly discover, your mind possesses a remarkable natural talent for excellence and this potential may be realized by anyone at any age.

What benefits can you expect by investing your time in this training course? Most people identify four main areas of enhancement after following our program; they report they can:

• Make decisions more quickly and easily, even those where there is a high degree of risk and uncertainty, and later find their choice was correct.

• Learn any new material rapidly, accurately, and with a minimum of effort, whether the study involves working for examinations, a conference speech, lines of poetry, or a foreign language.

• Become more creative when thinking about solutions for problems that demand an original approach, and use their powers of imagination more fully in all areas of life.

• Reduce the amount of mental and physical stress experienced when working under pressure so that it becomes possible to do more high-quality work in less time.

We can say with confidence that all this, and much more besides, lies within the reach of every reader of this book because, during the past six years, we have been teaching men, women, and children of all ages and from all walks of life to do just that. We have been training them to think better by providing the skills and insights needed to exploit the previously under-used powers of their minds. The training did not give them anything that they did not already possess, since they arrived at the seminars with the potential for efficient thought already locked away inside their brains.

What we were able to give them, and what through this book we now pass on to you, is the key needed to unlock that power so that your mental abilities can be more fully and effectively utilized.

By thinking better it will become possible to undertake intellectual activities with greater ease and confidence than ever before and to achieve goals which might, at the moment, seem beyond your intellectual capacity. They could be goals at work: more rapid promotion, a career offering greater fulfillment, the additional skills needed for continued success, the ability to solve complex problems or make vital decisions more rapidly. Alternatively they might be goals connected with your leisure activities, family, or home: learning another language to make travel more enjoyable, studying for a demanding hobby, acquiring the knowledge needed for a sport, helping your children through their educational programs, or working toward academic qualifications in your spare time for the pleasure of learning. Whatever your goals may be, this training course can help you realize them with less effort and in a shorter space of time than might now seem possible.

When people attend our workshops we ask them what they hope to achieve through their training and how they would like their ability to think better to help them in life. By setting themselves clear targets in this way, motivation and interest are sustained and subsequent achievement may be assessed more objectively. Furthermore, by examining these initial goals and comparing them with the results actually obtained, we are able to get a clear picture of the gains made by thinking more effectively.

Surveying the aims and achievements of some three hundred past students, we found the following pictures of goals and attainments:

I want to acquire new skills so that I can get ahead faster in my company or switch to a more mentally stimulating career 34%
Those reporting complete success in their ambitions 80%
Those reporting a good degree of attainment 11%

I want to be able to solve problems more efficiently and improve my decision-making skills 20%
Those reporting complete success in their ambitions 90%
Those reporting a substantial improvement in this area 8%

I want to be able to understand my children's school assignments better so that I can help when they run into difficulties 10%
Those reporting complete success in their ambitions 80%
Those reporting substantial improvement in this area.....12%

I want to return to full-time (or part-time) education as a mature student and feel I can hold my own with younger minds 10%
Those reporting complete success with their ambitions 75%
Those reporting a high level of attainment in their goal 8%

I want to take up a mentally demanding leisure activity for the pleasure of keeping my mind active 6%
Those reporting a high measure of success in this ambition
....87%
Those reporting a good measure of attainment 11%

As you can see, the reasons for embarking on a course of better thinking are varied, but the overall success rate, when our techniques are consistently practiced, is extremely high. Of course, motivation is a very important factor in such success, but we generally find that people who are sufficiently interested to want to find ways of thinking better are among the most motivated and ambitious members of society. If, in the past, they have been forced to abandon some intellectually demanding pursuit, it was usually because confusion arising from the inefficient use of the brain undermined self-confidence, increased anxiety, and so made whatever was being attempted appear needlessly difficult and complex. When your mind has been trained to think correctly about any task, confidence remains high and anxiety stays low, while difficulties, confusion, and complexities are far more readily resolved.

In many cases, too, people gave up an ambition or decided they would be unsuccessful before even starting, because they had come to believe one or more of three myths about mental abilities, pieces of widely accepted folklore that can quickly cripple the intellect and stunt the development of mental skills. Let's run through them briefly so you can decide if such false beliefs have tended to hold you back in the past:

Myth Number One—"I just wasn't born smart."

But you were! This myth is popular because it shifts responsibility for failure away from an individual and onto the genetic blueprint from which the brain was constructed. Students who get poor grades can excuse their marks by thinking: "I wasn't born smart enough to cope with studying!" Incompetent teachers can justify poor grades by complaining: "How can we teach kids who were born to fail?"

Ulrich Neisser, one of the world's foremost specialists in the field of mental functioning, sets the record straight when he explains: "Human cognitive activity would be more usefully conceived of as a collection of acquired skills than as the operation of a single, fixed mechanism."[1]

In other words, "intelligence" is something we acquire from experience rather than an inborn ability. This does not mean that inheritance has no role to play in establishing levels of intellectual ability. Few would argue against the fact that the upper limits of human intellectual capacity are to a great extent determined by the physical structure of the brain and this, like every other structure in the body, develops directly from "blue prints" contained in the genes. It is also fair to assume that these upper limits will vary from one individual to the next, depending on the instructions contained in those "blue prints." Even the most effective and best-organized genetic building plans will be constrained by the characteristics of the biochemical processes which translate those designs into a working brain. For example, just as it will take a small, but measurable, amount of time for a pain signal to reach your brain after you have stubbed your toe, so too must a certain delay occur in passing messages from one part of the brain to another, although we should also point out that strong evidence exists to show that the speed of neural transmission can be considerably improved with practice.

Our contention is, however, that these genetically determined upper limits are of no practical significance to the person seeking to increase mental ability substantially. There are many reasons for supposing that we never come anywhere near these limits and that man's ability to reason, to remember, and to learn expands as the need arises. Our brains are not significantly different, in biological terms, from the gray matter which filled the skulls of our Bronze Age forebears, yet they are capable of exploring space, constructing computers and comprehending complex abstract scientific concepts. The harder your brain is obliged to work, the greater will be its capacity for work. The more efficiently you allow your brain to function, the greater will be its ability to function with speed, accuracy, and confidence no matter what the intellectual challenge.

Of key importance in imposing restrictions on this functioning, however, is the manner in which an individual comes to view his or her intellect. This is why the myth of inborn mental inferiority is so damaging. Believe it, and you place your brain behind bars to serve out a life sentence of inadequacy. Change those beliefs, and you can free it to work better than you might ever have considered possible. A study which vividly illustrates this point was performed not many years ago in a New England school by researchers Richard Rosenthal and Leonore Jacobson,[2] who were able to change students' perceptions of themselves, and the way in which the teachers viewed those youngsters' abilities, through the use of a fake IQ test.

At the end of the summer term, teaching staff were informed that certain children had been identified as "spurters" who could be expected to do well over the coming months. These youngsters had, in fact, been selected at random from among their classmates and showed no such indications of special potential. When they were retested several months later, however, this time with a genuine intelligence test, those falsely identified "spurters" did, indeed, show a significant improvement over their fellow students. This result can be explained by the fact that because the teachers expected them to do well, their perceptions of each student's ability rose and those children's own self-image was enhanced. If you regard yourself as bright, and others support and confirm this belief, then you are much more likely to realize your brain's true potential.

The tragedy is that believing yourself to be born dumb matters so much because the brain is such a superb learning device. Any negative perception it acquires, and these can be learned extremely quickly, influences the way it functions. If you limit your intellectual growth by developing a damaging self-image where mental activities are concerned, the brain can never perform at peak efficiency.

Myth Number Two—"I have a terrible memory."

This equally widely held belief is just as false as the first myth. Your brain has the capacity to hold billions of items of information, and research has shown that the millions of facts acquired from infancy and then apparently forgotten are actually indelibly imprinted on the mind. Any problems which occur when you try to recall something you have just seen or heard arise not from an inability to retain information, but from difficulties of retrieval.

The astounding dimensions of human memory began to be revealed in the late fifties in the course of brain surgery performed by Dr. Wilder Penfield at the Montreal Neurological Institute, in an attempt to cure epileptics by electrical stimulation of certain areas of the brain.[3] Because the brain is insensitive to pain the patients required only a local anesthetic to deaden the nerves of the scalp as their heads were opened up for examination, and Dr. Penfield was able to probe the cerebral tissue of people who were conscious and alert. As he started to stimulate the gray cells with his electric probe, Wilder Penfield was astonished to find that the slight current evoked precise and vivid memories from his patients.

"I see a guy coming through the fence at the baseball game," cried one man, as soon as Penfield touched the upper part of his front temporal lobe. "It's the middle of the game, and I'm back there watching him."

Exactly what memory appeared depended on which part of the cortex, the outer layer of brain cells, happened to be stimulated. When Penfield's fine electrode touched one particular spot, a woman patient recalled a detailed image of the office in which she had worked as a stenographer, and this was followed by memories of watching a play in a theater. Another point evoked clear scenes of the lumber yard where she had played as a child. At the slightest touch from the surgeon's electrode the brain came alive with sights and sounds, long lost to awareness, each as detailed and powerful as if they had been taking place at that very moment. With the addition of nothing more drastic than a mild electric current, the brain was transformed into a haunted house of apparently long forgotten yet still perfectly remembered incidents.

We now know that even this slight stimulation is not always needed in order to help people bring perfectly to mind information which they believed was lost forever, or perhaps not even remembered in the first place. The police forces of several countries are turning to hypnosis in order to increase the depth and accuracy of recall among witnesses to some major crimes. In Israel, the authorities called in a hypnotist to help them identify a car used in a bomb attack. Witnesses to the incident believed they had told everything they could remember. But under hypnosis far more detailed and accurate information emerged. One man was able to recall the scene so vividly that he "read" the car's license plate number from the image in his mind and passed it on to the police. That vital clue enabled them to track down the people responsible. But, although the witness had the strongest desire to be helpful, he could not have pried that knowledge from the archives of his brain unaided.

Perhaps the most convincing pieces of evidence in the psychologist's detective-like search for an understanding of memory function have been produced by two American investigators, Robert Reiff and Martin Sheerer.[4] Once again the key that unlocked the storehouse of the mind was hypnosis. This time it was used not in the pursuit of wrongdoers but to take subjects on an eerie journey through time to the years of their childhood. Using a technique called *hypnotic age regression,* adults were able to recall any day of any year in their school lives. Not only could they describe in great detail the classrooms in which they sat, the companions around them and the lessons taught, they could even bring into sharp focus the names of the textbooks read. In related studies, Robert True of the University of Vermont College of Medicine, made use of the same technique to explore people's memories of specific days in the past.[5] He found that 93 percent of his subjects were able to name the day of the week on which their tenth birthday fell, while

69 percent could recall the day they celebrated their fourth birthday.

Child psychologists have estimated that as many as 20 percent of young children possess what is termed an eidetic memory (more popularly known as a photographic memory) that allows them to retain anything they have seen with the precision of a mental snapshot.

These youngsters are able to describe every feature of the scene held in their minds, down to the smallest and most trivial detail. Most children gradually lose the skill as they enter their teens, and it is found in very few adults. But this does not mean the ability has been lost forever. As psychologist Neil Walker[6] has demonstrated, this supermemory lies dormant in every adult who possessed it in childhood. By means of hypnotism he was able to regress his adult subjects to the age of seven, a time in life when the photographic memory is at its most powerful. He found that a significant percentage of his subjects regained their skill while under hypnosis, although they lost it as soon as they were taken out of their trances.

One example of a memory so prodigious that it almost defies description was that of the Russian journalist Solomon Veniaminoff whose life and mental powers have been meticulously studied and graphically described by the great Soviet psychologist Alexander Luria.[7] Veniaminoff had a memory so perfect that he could recall in complete detail a railway timetable he had only glimpsed twenty years earlier. His powers first came to light when an editor admonished him for never taking notes, and Veniaminoff defended himself by repeating verbatim a lengthy interview which had just taken place. Impressed and astonished, the editor allowed him to discard his notebook and rely on a memory which was in many ways far more reliable than any written record.

We now know that the memory possessed by Solomon Veniaminoff is latent in many people. Evidence in support of this rather startling claim comes from numerous observations of a peculiar form of supermemory which can suddenly occur in men and women who have never previously exhibited an exceptional power of recall. Termed *hypermnesia* by psychologists, it produces an almost photographic retention and recall of some situation. During periods of hypermnesia, subjects are able to describe everything observed in great detail, down to the expressions on the faces of those involved, what sounds they heard, the smells around them, and the feel of things held or touched. Often this is achieved years after the event, although the clarity of the memory is such that it might have happened only a few moments before.

In one of the major studies of hypermnesia, G. M. Stratton[8] of the University of California interviewed 225 adults, selected at random, and discovered that one in ten reported occurrences of this unexpectedly powerful recall of some incident from their past. Researchers have found that the situations remembered most vividly were those which held an emotional importance for the person concerned: a period of danger, some shocking or frightening event, a moment of great joy or tremendous unhappiness.

We clearly all possess a much better memory than most people realize, or can usually gain access to. The sights and sounds of yesterday should be regarded as mislaid rather than missing. Recent scientific experiments have shown that by using a simple technique, which we will describe during Step Three of our program, anyone can generate a mental state very close to that of hypermnesia in order to enhance massively the ability to remember any type of information. With this procedure you will find that recall for learned material *increases* over a period of time, rather than suffering the normal decline and decay.

Myth Number Three—"You can't teach an old dog new tricks."

One of society's most harmful misconceptions about brain power is that it gets worse as you grow older. Research has proved that any decreases in the intellectual skills of the elderly are mainly due to the adoption of stereotyped roles. Just as a child who sees himself as dumb and is regarded as slow-witted by adults starts to act out that part, so too do many older men and women slip into the trap of living *down* to popular expectations.

It is a vicious circle of decline which, once started, may prove hard to stop. Because they regard themselves as incapable of meeting new intellectual challenges many older people get into a mental rut. They live unstimulating lives where few unfamiliar problems ever present themselves to challenge their brains back into shape.

The mind, just like other organs in the body, must work hard in order to sustain the capacity for hard work. Take too little physical exercise and your muscles will quickly go weak, your stamina decline, and your strength fade. It is the same with the brain. Remove the necessary stimulation of a demanding job, take away the need to solve difficult problems and make tricky decisions, absolve the person from having to use his or her memory with the excuse, "All old people are absentminded," and you quickly undermine intellectual performance.

One reason why this myth gained ground so readily and was so widely accepted, even by those who suffered most as a result, was a belief that brain cells die off progressively as we age since such cells, unlike others in the body, cannot regulate themselves.

Marian Diamond,[9] the eminent California neuroanatomist, examined this notion in a series of animal studies and clearly showed that though there is a *small* decrease in the number of brain cells as animals mature to adulthood, from then on such decline remains absolutely minimal.

Do we find it harder to learn something new or solve problems as we grow older? Not according to the findings of Geoffrey Naylor and Elsie Harwood of the University of Queensland, Australia,[10] who conducted a six-month study to investigate the ability of a group of senior citizens to learn German. Their classes contained some of the most mature students in the history of education, with a total age approaching a thousand years! But the fact that every pupil was more than sixty years old did not prevent them from working hard or mastering the unfamiliar language successfully. Each had to attend a two-hour weekly class and work at least one hour at home. In just half a year many students reached a standard only attained by the average high school senior after two years of continuous study.

Dr. Naylor commented: "Far from being unreliable and forgetful, the majority of our elderly students have shown a dogged resolution worthy of students fifty years younger."

Similar results were reported at the University of San Diego[11] where senior citizens were brought onto the campus for an intensive program of classes in various academic subjects together with physical training sessions. Their response was described by one of the project's organizers as "absolutely phenomenal," with a performance which more than matched that of far younger undergraduates. Overall they were found to have attained a standard of excellence "far beyond expectation."

Everything that we have said here applies to you. When we talked about a brain of almost unlimited memory capacity and problem-solving ability we were describing your own brain.

It is very likely that you have already experienced something of the excitement and the sense of supreme confidence that comes from being able to harness the stupendous intellectual driving force of the human mind. The pioneering studies of the late Professor Abraham Maslow of Brandeis University,[12] the founder of humanistic psychology, showed that almost everyone has been able to make contact with this power at some time in their lives. According to Professor Maslow, we make contact with this inner intellectual force during what he termed "peak experiences," moments when mind and body perform with total excellence and we *know* that whatever is attempted will be accomplished. Nearly everyone has enjoyed at least a few peak experiences and, if you reflect back, we are fairly certain that you will be able to recall, perhaps very vividly, such moments for yourself. They were times when all doubts were resolved, all obstacles disappeared, and you knew for certain you could give the performance of a lifetime. "There are signals from inside," Maslow said. "There are voices that yell out 'By gosh, this is good, don't you ever doubt it.' "

As Maslow pointed out, performance does dramatically improve during such experiences. After interviewing thousands of men and women from all over the United States, he reported that peak experiences are most likely to occur during such intellectually demanding tasks as learning, problem solving, and decision making. Students talked of the time when they took an exam *knowing* they were answering every question near perfectly and being so confident of getting a maximum grade they never endured a moment's doubt before the marks came out; businessmen and women recounted occasions when they made important decisions completely and justifiably confident that the choices made would turn out right; scientists spoke of suddenly gaining insight into a previously intractable problem and being absolutely certain their ideas were correct.

Even if you are unable to recall a peak experience right now, you should take a little time at some point during the day to think about any moment when you were inspired by the knowledge that everything was going to go your way. All at once, as if blinkers had fallen from the mind, you understood how to solve a problem, knew what was needed to reach a decision, found that previously difficult information could be learned with ease. It was the time you discovered a small part of what the brain can achieve when used correctly, the kind of moment we try to make an almost routine part of everyday thinking through the techniques we have developed.

If you visited our laboratory at the Mind Potential Study Group in London, you would find it looks unlike most other research establishments. Instead of work benches and banks of electronic equipment, there are easy chairs, potted plants, and a coffee machine. It is true we have a computer tucked away in a back room, and the cupboards around the place contain such items of equipment as a tachistoscope for measuring reaction times, biofeedback apparatus for monitoring stress levels, and various kinds of recording devices for obtaining an audio or video record of experimental sessions, but we still aim to produce an atmosphere more like a lounge than a lab.

During a typical experiment, insofar as any experiment can be said to be typical, a subject will sit comfortably in an easy chair and watch a TV screen. Although it resembles the kind of domestic receiver found in every home, the images generated on our set come mostly from a computer. Problems of various kinds, material to be learned, or situations demanding some kind of a decision appear on the screen, and the person helping us has to complete the task as best he or she is able. They may be asked to speak their thoughts aloud as they work toward a solution, read a decision, or attempt to commit something to memory; they may respond by touching an electronic pen to the TV screen or by tapping out their answers on a keyboard. Depending on the type of study being undertaken, the computer will either store their responses for later analysis or else react to their replies in a specific way. In one series of experiments we have been running over the past few years, adults and older children are confronted with a whole series of math problems. As they type in their solutions, the computer scrutinizes the logic being employed, identifies faults in the reasoning, and might either print out an analysis of their thinking or automatically provide a further series of problems designed to strengthen weaknesses in that individual's mathematical knowledge. Before long we expect such electronic teachers to be regular members of a school's faculty, providing an endlessly patient and highly perceptive coach for any students whose math ability is letting them down.

If you called on another day, you might see a different group of subjects watching a video recording on a TV monitor with five wires snaking from head and body to instruments monitoring such physiologic responses as electrical activity in the brain, variations in skin conductivity due to anxiety, and increases in heart rate, blood pressure, and muscular tension associated with varying levels of stress. On one occasion our subjects may be a group of company directors; on another, we will be studying housewives, teachers, or manual workers. They watch scenes acted on the TV screen and are then asked to make a decision in order to resolve the dilemma each one presents. Such decisions may be made almost instantly by pressing buttons, or only after long discussions among group members. Sometimes the situations involve serious scenarios where a wrong decision might mean the difference between life and death for the actors and actresses on screen, at other times the situations will be trivial. All are designed to help answer fundamental questions about how and why decisions are made, in the broader context of trying to learn more about intellectual performance in general.

Author David Lewis became involved in this research after graduating with honors degrees in psychology, neurology, and communications studies. His initial work, in the area of clinical psychology, was concerned with the effects of stress on physical and mental performance, and he became involved in treatment programs for people with anxiety and phobic difficulties. In an effort to discover which aspects of child development resulted in this type of difficulty in adulthood, he began a detailed investigation of the first five years of life, exploring such crucial developmental features as nonverbal communication between infants, the effects of early experience, pair-bonding, the acquisition of social skills, and the role of parents, peers, and siblings in cognitive performance. Later, studying older children and young adults, he examined the ways in which physical tension is related to mental confusion and the part played by anxiety in either enhancing or, as more usually happens, undermining intellectual function. Finally, he considered the influence exerted by various self-fulfilling prophecies and the way these often led to intellectual incompetence and negative attitudes of the kind already discussed.

Equally negative attitudes in offices, industry, and education were encountered by James Greene in his work as a consultant in psychological assessment and instructional technology in the United States and Europe. An American psychologist, now living and working in London, he began to research techniques for enhancing learning, decision making, and problem solving some ten years ago. His present work brings together psychology, computer science, and mathematics to create "adaptive teaching systems." These are sophisticated computer programs which diagnose individual needs, carry out personalized teaching, and modify their own functioning as they themselves learn from each student how best to present the material being taught.

We began working together to develop techniques, based on our own research and that of other specialists in universities and research establishments around the world, which would make people think better about their abilities by being able to think better about the mental tasks confronting them. Only in this way is it possible to improve self-image, reduce anxiety, and transform negative attitudes. Initially we worked with school-age children, but the interest of their parents in our procedures soon led us to the conclusion that adults could, and would, benefit just as greatly from these techniques.

In 1975 we set up the Mind Potential Study Group, a nonprofit organization based in London's West End, the purpose of which is to bring together people from all areas of study concerned with mental performance. Today our group includes teachers, psychologists, psychiatrists, computer scientists, and mathematicians, as well as interested business persons and industrialists. In the same year the first experimental training workshop was organized to teach and assess our new procedures for mental growth. Since then we have constantly been updating these techniques as more and more knowledge was gained into how anyone at any stage of life can learn to think better.

This book represents a long-held ambition on our part to make the training, previously available only through seminars, available to the widest possible audience. Use the procedures in your own home and work at your own pace to discover just how well your brain is able to work if given the chance to do so. In just five simple steps you can learn how to think better about every significant intellectual activity, from learning to problem solving and decision making to logical reasoning. Your mind has a tremendous untapped potential for growth just waiting to be realized. Why keep it waiting any longer?

How to Realize Your Brain's Real Potential

The problem that Ed brought to one of our workshops was typical of the kind of difficulty that arises when you try to use your brain in an unsystematic manner. He complained that, while he could solve difficulties at work if given time to think about all the major aspects of the problem, he found it impossible to come up with a satisfactory solution against an urgent deadline. "When I am pressed to find an answer my mind just goes blank," he told us. "I seem to think of everything *except* the subject I'm supposed to be focusing on. The result is I become anxious, confused, and incompetent. I never sell myself as a good problem solver, even though I can cope with this kind of task perfectly well if given time to think things over." Ed blamed his brain for these failures, and felt that his lack of problem-solving skills was preventing him from achieving the promotion he deserved.

Anne had a rather different kind of mental block; she couldn't make decisions in her personal life. "I have no trouble about being decisive in the office," she assured us. "But when the choice is close to home I find it almost impossible to see what to do for the best and often make bad decisions as a result." Like Ed, Anne saw her difficulties as arising from some basic fault in her mental makeup. "My mind wasn't designed to make intimate decisions," she said.

Just as common a complaint against the brain is its inability to retain and retrieve information when needed. If you have ever apologized for some oversight by remarking: "I'm sorry, I've got a terrible memory," then you will feel some sympathy for the large number of people who attribute their lack of success to just this kind of mental failing—people like Phillipa, a twenty-three-year-old biochemistry student who thought she would fail her final examinations because she found it so hard to recall facts and figures. "I've got a memory like a sieve," she said miserably.

Ed, Anne, and Phillipa were all aware of *where* they were going wrong and eager to put things right. But they weren't helping themselves at all by identifying the culprit as some sort of mental weakness, although their excuses were typical of the way most of us respond if something goes wrong with the mechanisms of thought. All too often when we are unable to come up with the correct answer, find it almost impossible to reach the right decision, or forget something that has just been carefully learned, we immediately place the blame on our brains. The self-criticisms we offer and the explanations we provide, both to ourselves and others, reflect the widely held view that intellectual success or failure arises from aspects of the way in which that organ is constructed, rather than the manner in which it is being made to work. "My brain can't cope with that kind of situation," said Ed. Anne feels that her mind was not designed to make good personal decisions. "My memory is hopeless," Phillipa tells us.

By making statements like this, they are advancing the popular notion that mental ability depends on specific structures inside the brain and that these are determined by inheritance. They believe that intellect is laid down by the parental blueprint, as written into the genes, and that this predetermines both their strengths and their weaknesses.

Such a view is both mistaken and misleading. By focusing on the physical attributes of thinking—the brain cells themselves—it diverts our attention from the real cause of all intellectual success and failure, the way in which thinking occurs. By asserting that levels of mental ability are more or less immutable, a self-fulfilling prophecy of failure is created which restricts the growth of the intellect and raises those barriers to progress which we discussed in the introduction. In a moment we will be looking at some of the research which has led many psychologists to see intellegence in this way. For the moment we ask you to accept what you will soon prove for yourself.

Your brain has a potential for brilliance and can attain almost any intellectual goal you care to set.

The only restrictions on achievement are those which are created through a failure to understand what good thinking is all about. By learning how to make your brain function more efficiently you will quickly and easily enhance every aspect of mental performance.

Why the "Stupidity" of Computers Can Help Make Us More Intelligent

On July 22, 1962, a single hyphen cost American taxpayers $18.5 million. A Mariner I rocket, rising from the launching pad at the start of a mission to Venus, veered so wildly off course that the ground controllers had no choice but to destroy the errant missile. The reason for this costly failure was later discovered to be a symbol this trivial, "-", which had been omitted from the program controlling the navigational computers. Without that tiny but crucial symbol the instructions proved meaningless and the rocket went out of control.

Computer sciences have come a long way since the early sixties, but the need for meticulous care when designing and creating programs—the sets of commands that tell the machine how to function—remains as great as ever. However superintelligent computers may appear to the uninitiated, they are basically simpleminded creations whose ability to solve complex problems and make good decisions depends entirely on the skill of those constructing the programs. They can only perform in a meaningful way when the information they need has been provided in a precise and systematic manner. It is, therefore, hardly surprising that in order to make a computer function intelligently it must be given an extremely intelligent program. To write intelligent programs demands a detailed understanding not only of the tasks to be accomplished but also of the ways in which the human brain would carry out the same activity. Intensive studies into techniques which allow computers to think more successfully have revealed equally effective procedures for enabling men and women to make better use of their minds.

Suppose, for example, you are interested in creating a computer program that will allow a particular kind of problem to be solved electronically. The essential starting point is to analyze every aspect of that task, identify the different stages that have to be gone through, and ensure that the logic involved is flawless. You will then organize these logical stepping-stones, from the problem statement to the ultimate solution, into an exactly ordered sequence of instructions. In effect, you will spell out each and every stage of the answer-finding process with precision before translating the completed program into a special language which the computer can "understand." Exactly the same meticulous procedure has to be gone through if you want a computer to make a decision. Available options must be identified and a detailed analysis of the task carried out as the preliminary to creating commands suitable for allowing the situation to be accurately assessed and the best possible decision advocated.

Once the program has been created, it can, of course, be used to deal with any number of similar problems or arrive at decisions in related areas rapidly and reliably. With electrons passing through its circuits at the speed of light, the computer is capable of processing a vast quantity of information in a very short space of time without ever getting bored, fed up, or careless.

What happens when the human brain is provided with a thinking program that is as logical and systematic as that demanded by the computer? It begins to work with the same efficiency and often almost the same tireless speed as the machine. You start to employ previously under-used or ineffectively utilized areas of the mind to good purpose. If there were previously confusions surrounding the task, these tend to disappear. If you were making numerous errors, they are either greatly reduced or vanish completely. If you had to think long and hard before coming up with a decision, the information needed seems to appear almost instantly in the majority of cases. The task has not changed and neither, of course, has the brain. What is different is the way in which you are making the mind function. It is as if, by freeing the thinking processes from the shackles imposed by disordered commands, the total power of your brain suddenly surged into action.

We can best illustrate this idea of the difference between brain and brain programs by considering that most elementary of all problem-solving gadgets—the pocket calculator. If you kept on producing wrong answers when using one, there could be two possible explanations for such persistent failure. It might be that the device itself was faulty, as a result of poor design, faulty manufacture, or accidental damage. If there was no evidence for this and it worked fine when somebody else used it, however, one might reasonably conclude that it was your technique of operation rather than the equipment itself which was at fault. In order to produce the answer required, you must key in all the numbers and the mathematical operations to be carried out correctly and in the proper sequence. Any failure at this point will inevitably result in errors.

In the language of computer science, the physical circuits of the calculator are known as the *hardware,* while the instructions which "tell" it what to do with any information are termed *software.* One can only expect 100 percent efficiency provided both these components are themselves entirely efficient.

Brain research during the past few years has revealed that human thinking is organized along surprisingly similar lines. The *hardware* consists of the billions of nerve cells and their myriad interconnections that constitute the physical matter of the mind. The *software* comprises previously acquired sets of instructions which determine exactly how information is to be dealt with and the final outcome of that mental processing.

These sets of instructions, the list of precise steps that have to be taken in order to solve problems, make decisions, or carry out a learning task, are called *programs* and many of the world's foremost psychologists and neurologists now believe that intellectual activity is based on the interaction between an enormous number of such programs in the mind.

"The lives of human beings ... are governed by sets of programs," says the eminent neuroscientist J. Z. Young of London University. "Some of these may be called practical or physiological and they ensure that we breathe, eat, drink and sleep. Others are social, and regulate our speaking and other forms of communication, our agreeing, and our loving or hating. . . . Perhaps the most important programs of all are those used for the activities that we call mental, such as thinking, imagining, dreaming, believing and worshipping."[13]

Programs in the Mind

To get the basic principles clear from the start, let's return to that pocket calculator and look at a simple mathematical problem that could be more easily tackled by using one.

Suppose you are asked to convert a set of temperature readings from centigrade to fahrenheit. This can be done by the simple process of multiplying the figure in ° C by 9, dividing it by 5, and then adding 32. If you only had to do the calculation a couple of times there would be no problem in keying each figure and operation into the device. But suppose you were asked to do the same conversion on a year's weather records. Now a much better method would be to use a "programable" calculator, that is, one with a memory that can store instructions and execute them automatically on command. Having keyed-in the necessary steps you could make your conversions simply by putting in each centigrade reading and ordering the calculator to run its program.

The steps needed to perform this task can be represented graphically by means of a technique used in computer science called a flowchart. This makes each instruction explicit and, rather like a road map, allows you to discover the best route between two points. A flowchart for the centigrade to fahrenheit conversion task looks like this:

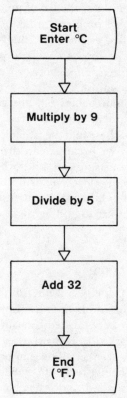

You will see that the flowchart is drawn from the top of the page to the bottom, representing the flow of instructions. Different shapes are used to indicate various aspects of the program with oblongs containing instructions about how information is to be processed. In a moment we will use a diamond shape to mark decision steps at which a single input can produce either of two outputs.

Now let us look at the kind of program your mind might operate when solving problems and making decisions in everyday activities. We have chosen situations which must be familiar to almost every driver—the problem of getting a car to start on a cold, damp morning and the decisions to be taken when, having gotten the car moving, one is driving in traffic.

These programs are not intended to be a complete list of all the possible factors that might have to be considered when starting or driving a car, since such a program could easily run to many pages. All we are doing here is offering a general illustration of the sequence of instructions the brain is likely to follow under these circumstances.

After trying to get the motor running without success, you stop turning the ignition key and start thinking about what could have gone wrong. You carry out some checks, make an adjustment under the hood, and manage to start the car. Now you can drive onto the main road. Coming up behind a slow-moving truck, you pull out, judge whether or not you can pass, and, when you feel it is safe, make that maneuver. If all your decisions are sound, you will arrive at your destination safely. These may appear to be very mundane and routine pieces of thinking, but by analyzing them we can start to appreciate the way programs are used to solve problems and make decisions.

If you had spoken your thoughts aloud while trying to start the motor, they might have followed this sequence: "Is the battery dead? If it is, I could use jump cables. The starter motor sounds okay, so it can't be the battery. Is there fuel in the tank? If not, it'll mean a walk to the filling station with a can. No, the gauge shows the tank is half full. I'd better take a look under the hood. It could be a block in the fuel line or an electrical problem. I'll check the electrical system first. If the plugs are firing, then I'll examine the fuel lines. There's no spark from the plugs when the starter motor turns over. The leads look pretty damp. I'll dry them and try again. If the car still doesn't start, I'd better call the garage. Okay, it's running at last. That's solved the problem."

As you drive along the road you come up fast behind a truck and think along these lines: "I'll edge out to get a good view. Not safe to pass yet . . . I'll pull back and try again in a moment. Okay, now the way is clear."

We are not suggesting that you are necessarily aware of all these thoughts. Once any complex skill, such as driving a car, has been perfected, the programs required to perform it run so smoothly and automatically that the mind is left free to concentrate on other thoughts. It is only when the situation changes and you have either to modify or replace a familiar program that active consideration of the instructions is again necessary. If, for example, you switched from an automatic to a manual transmission, additional instructions would have to be incorporated into your *car driving program* to cope with the changed requirements of the task. After a short time, of course, the new instructions are firmly established and thinking switches back to a routine process once again.

When written out in the form of a flowchart, the partial program for getting your car started might look like this:

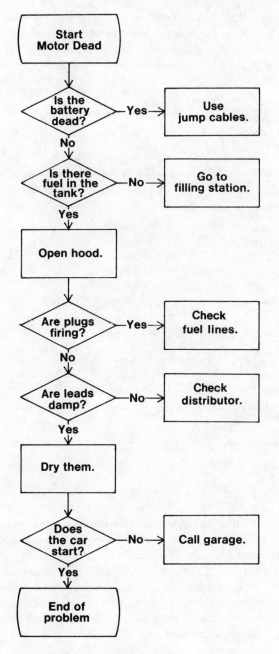

The program for deciding whether or not it is safe to pass the truck contains a *loop*, which means that the brain continues to run the same instructions until the incoming information—that is, visual data about road conditions—changes in such a way as to close the circle of instructions.

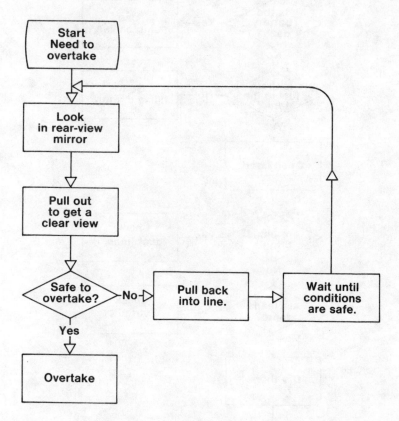

By stating the different steps in this formal way it becomes easier to review the program as a whole and come to important conclusions about the essential qualities which it should possess.

First of all it is clear that to be successful the program must be *complete*. No vital step can be missed if the required solution is to be found. For example, if the "check fuel tank" instruction were forgotten, time and effort could easily be wasted in searching for a nonexistent mechanical fault.

At the same time it must be as *concise* as possible in order to avoid any waste of time in tracking down the answer. People very often make use of programs which, while they do produce a satisfactory answer or lead to a correct decision, take much longer than is necessary to do so. This means they find it especially hard to think efficiently under pressure, can fit less mental activity into the working day, and are far more prone to errors. The mistakes are made because, by giving the brain more instructions than are absolutely essential, it becomes increasingly likely that some of them will be missed or misinterpreted.

Furthermore, since each instruction produces further information for the brain to process—as you can see from the flowchart, a single input to a decision step produces two possible outcomes—the more steps there are, the more information will be generated. This places a greater strain on a storage system in the brain known as the *working memory,* a sort of mental "in box," which provides a temporary store for information actively being processed by the mind. Unlike the capacity of *long-term memory* which, for all practical purposes, seems unlimited, *working memory* quickly fills up. If any attempt is made to add items beyond this point, earlier information will be lost. Keeping within the capacity of working memory is essential to the success of any mental activity. In practice, we tend to off-load working memory from time to time by taking written notes at different points in the thinking process. This prevents working memory overload by providing just the right amount of intermediate information. In Step One of the course, we will show you how this can be done and the freedom which it allows you to solve problems of considerable complexity in your head.

The final requirement is that each program be as *flexible* as possible so that it can be applied to tasks that are similar to, yet in important respects different from, the original activity. This enables you to perform a wider range of intellectual functions with a smaller number of programs.

Most of the programs we use were acquired in a haphazard manner. We are never taught *how* to think, only *what* to think. We are never told *how* best to make decisions, only given decisions to make. We are expected to learn a whole range of things from the first days of formal education, yet never provided with *lessons in how to learn.* Because of this we tend to use our minds in an unsystematic and often ineffective manner.

To be truly efficient, any program must take two key factors into account. The first is your personal thinking style. As we will explain, there are important differences in the way individual brains prefer to operate and these preferences should be identified before creating any program. You will be shown how to analyze your personal styles for the major activities of problem solving, decision making, and learning.

The second component of a successful program is to be found in the task itself. Before any organized thinking can take place we need to know the nature of the information available and establish its relationship to an inner structure which all mental tasks possess. This structure must be revealed through special techniques of analysis since it is seldom explicit and often well concealed. How such an analysis is carried out will also be fully explained during the course.

Better thinking, it will be seen, depends on acquiring programs that the brain can run best because they match its natural style of functioning. It depends on the use of programs that are capable of taking the mind from the starting point to the goal of solution finding, decision making, or learning by the shortest yet most complete route. Only in this way can errors and waste of time be avoided.

The purpose of our training is to allow you to equip yourself with such programs and learn how to use them to best effect. "The mind is a mansion," says British psychologist Dr. William Michaels, "but most of the time we are content to live in the lobby."[14]

Our five-step course in better thinking will enable you to move out of that lobby and into the mental mansion that is your natural birthright.

Part Two

THE FIVE-STEP PROGRAM

Thinking Better
by Thinking Clearly

We are going to start our course by providing you with a simple but, we confidently anticipate, convincing demonstration of how, by using an efficient brain program, you can allow your mind to work at peak efficiency. Before turning the page, try and answer the following questions. When doing so, you should time yourself to see exactly how long it takes you to come up with the answers:

Mary wants to spend her vacation in Europe but her husband can't get her to decide which country she would like to visit. When it comes to stating her preferences she tells him:

I like Germany less than Spain,
But I would sooner go to France than to Italy.
I don't like the idea of going to Portugal as much as I like going to Germany,
But I think Spain is less interesting than Italy.

Which country is she most likely to visit and which one does she want to go to least?

When you've worked out the answer (which will be found at the end of this section), notice how long it took. After you have found out how to think better by thinking more clearly you will come to the right choice in reasoning tasks like this in less than six seconds per question.

How to Banish Confusions of Choice

The task we are going to look at in Step One of this course may strike you initially as rather a trivial sort of problem, the kind you might expect to find in a puzzle book or the quiz page of a newspaper, unrelated to everyday mental activities. In one sense this is true, as this kind of question is a favorite with compilers of popular brain-teasers, but you should not allow the apparent slightness of the problem to mislead you as to its importance. The reasoning you use when trying to come up with the answer plays a crucial role in real decision making because it is concerned with selecting options, making comparisons between choices, and juggling a relatively large amount of information around in your memory. All these are essential skills when making major choices and we will be looking at them in far greater detail in Step Five, when we consider how to think better about decisions. Our main purpose in using this task as the starting point for the training course is to enable you to discover for yourself how an efficient brain program can cut away confusion and lead effortlessly to the correct solution. If someone told you he did not enjoy playing golf as much as he liked swimming, would sooner play tennis than swim, and thought baseball was a better sport than tennis you could probably work out quite easily that his favorite activity is baseball and he likes golf the least. Psychologists call the process by which such an order of preference is established *transitive inference* and it is often a good deal harder and more confusing than the example above might suggest. In fact, *transitive inference* problems can rapidly become so complex that most people get them wrong on their first attempt, and quite frequently on their second and third tries as well. Even if you are only considering three preferences, with relationships between them fairly clearly stated, it is still easy to become confused and blurt out an incorrect answer. In researching such problems we have found that if someone is asked to say which is preferable, given the fact that A is preferable to B and B is better than C, there is a one-in-three chance he will say that C is the first choice if asked to choose between A and C. Where there are more than three preferences to rank, or the relationship is described in a roundabout manner, faulty reasoning becomes even more likely. Yet when it comes to making decisions in real life, we frequently have to manipulate a large number of options that are related to one another in ways that are often complex.

Try your hand at this transitive inference task and you will see what we mean.

A customer wants to buy a new car in his favorite color. The salesman tells him that as it may not be possible to provide that particular model in a specific color it would help to have a short list of those colors that would be acceptable.

The customer then tells him:
I dislike red less than white.
I don't dislike blue as much as green.
I like blue less than white.
I don't like red as much as black.

What color car does the customer most want and which would he be least likely to accept?

Take a few moments to think about this problem and try to come up with the solution. As you are working out the order of preference, give a little thought to the way your mind is tackling the task.

Before we provide the answer, reflect on the method you used to search for it. Perhaps your approach was to form a mental image of the different-colored cars, maybe imagining a number painted on each one which represented its place in the order of preference. You might also have gone to work on the words, changing the phrases so as to make their meaning more explicit. "I dislike red less than white," for instance, might have been transformed into the far less confusing: "I like red better than white."

Most people adopt both tactics to some extent, although there are those who concentrate entirely on either images or words. The former have a mainly visual approach to reasoning, while the latter think best if working with words. Any of these methods *could* produce an answer, provided that the transitive inference problem is not too complex. But such thought processes quickly become unreliable if the number of choices rises beyond a certain point. This, as we have already explained, overloads the working memory and so causes important intermediate steps in the program to be forgotten. You may not always be able to off-load working memory by writing down the different stages in your reasoning, either because there is just not enough time to do so or because you are obliged to try and find the answer in your head. Even if you are able to make notes, there is no point in doing so unless absolutely necessary, since it slows down the time taken to come up with an answer and offers no guarantee against faulty reasoning. A far better method is to provide your brain with a program which produces no more intermediate information than working memory can easily handle, while taking you to the right choice by the fastest and most direct route.

We have developed the following program to handle any type of transitive inference program. We call it the *if . . . then* process since these are the only two points you need to resolve when tackling each line of the problem. Incidentally, if you have written computer programs, you will recognize that statement as one of the commands that can be given to an electronic brain. It works just as well in this type of reasoning situation when programmed into the human brain.

Stage One

Start by looking at the first line and find an answer based on the information available. This provides you with what we call the tentative solution. That is the answer which can be allowed to stand unless further information is provided that disproves it. Here, the first line tells us: "I dislike red less than white." In other words *if* nothing else arises to contradict our conclusion, *then* the solution to that problem will be *red.* For the moment, therefore, RED becomes the tentative answer and may be held temporarily in working memory. Put a check beside the line to show that this statement has been processed and move on to . . .

Stage Two

Consider the second statement. If your tentative answer (in this case RED) is *not* contained in that statement, then simply ignore it and pass on to the next one.

Stage Three

Continue in this way through each of the statements, ignoring them as long as your tentative answer is *not* mentioned. If you reach the last line and the tentative answer has not been mentioned again, then it becomes your final answer.

Stage Four

If the tentative answer is mentioned in a later statement, notice whether the information causes you to come up with a different answer. In the problem above, the last statement tells us: "I don't like red as much as black." So we replace the tentative answer RED by BLACK and again place a check against that statement.

Stage Five

Return to the first unchecked statement and reevaluate your tentative answer as before. If it is not mentioned then, the line can be ignored as it was earlier. In the example we see that both statements ignore BLACK, which, therefore, becomes the *correct* answer.

Although this may sound slightly complicated on first reading, the program is in fact the fastest and easiest approach once you have mastered its use. Indeed, given a transitive inference problem containing a large number of statements, it is the *only* approach that will allow you to solve it automatically.

The efficiency achieved when this program is used was demonstrated during our research. When subjects relied on their normal problem-solving tactics to tackle the choice of car colors, they needed an average of 90 seconds and achieved only a 60 percent success rate. By using the program we describe, however, they took an average of 12 seconds and achieved 100 percent accuracy. This method works whether your personal style for this type of problem involves images or word manipulations or a combination of the two, because it operates at a more fundamental level of thinking. With other kinds of problems, as you will discover in Step Four, personal mental style must be considered more closely when creating a program.

Check your understanding of this procedure by discovering what color car the customer is *least* likely to purchase. (The answers are at the bottom of this page.)

Now we would like you to try your hand at a more difficult transitive inference problem, identifying, as before, the first and last choices. Before starting, check the time so that you can see how long it takes to come up with the answers using our *if . . . then* program. You might also like to see how much time someone without such a program needs to come up with the correct solutions. The result is likely to be a convincing demonstration of just how well the brain can function if given the right kind of commands. In our research we have found that people who attempt to solve this problem using the usual, haphazard approach require 60 seconds thinking time and even then come up with both answers correct in only 50 percent of cases. With the *if . . . then* program to eliminate confusion and restrict demands on your working memory, it will take you about 10 seconds and you should be 100 percent correct. That is a reflection of how your brain wants to function and is able to work when freed from unsystematic thinking processes.

What Will George Do Tonight?

George has a problem about what to do with his spare time this evening. There's a pro football game on TV, friends have invited him to a party, he has free tickets to see the ballet, and the cinema near his apartment is showing a movie he has been looking forward to seeing. To make his dilemma even more acute he has just reached the last chapter of a gripping novel and is about to discover the murderer. What will George do tonight given that he . . .

Likes parties less than movies.
Dislikes reading less than sports.
Doesn't like the ballet as much as parties.
Dislikes reading more than the ballet.

When you have found out what he *will* choose, find out what he is least likely to have chosen.

Answers:

Mary is most likely to go to France and least likely to go to Portugal. The customer is most likely to buy a black car and least likely to want a green car. George will go to the movies and is least likely to watch football on TV.

STEP TWO

Thinking Better
About Intelligence Tests

Why IQ Tests Are Important to You

In this part of the training course we are going to show you how to increase your score substantially on any type of IQ test by providing your brain with the right programs for handling the problems they involve. The gains that can be expected once the mind is allowed to work efficiently on such problems vary from one person to the next and depend to some extent on the original starting point. If you normally obtained a slightly above-average IQ score of, say, around 110, then you could reasonably expect to boost this by up to 50 percent, giving you a rating of 160 or more. As you will see a little later, when we show how IQ's are distributed among the population, this is a score so high that only one person in five hundred would normally be expected to attain it. You should be able to do so consistently and quite easily, however, once you have mastered the necessary mental programs. Even if your IQ score is normally in the high range, it is very likely that certain kinds of test items prove harder than others and a failure to complete these successfully lowers your overall total. By learning fast, effective programs for tackling such items you will remove this obstacle to success, while also finding that even those problems which you solved correctly before can now be answered far more rapidly, a considerable advantage since IQ tests usually have to be completed against the clock. Remember that however smart you are at present there is always unrealized potential in your brain and ample opportunity to be smarter still!

There are three major reasons why we believe it is important to perform well in intelligence tests. The first, and perhaps most obvious, is that obtaining a high score could prove a considerable advantage to you in some circumstances. Despite complaints about their validity and concern over their usefulness, such tests are still widely used by employers, promotion boards, colleges, government departments, and the armed forces as a means of assessment. Your ability to do exceptionally well on such a test might considerably enhance the chances of obtaining a sought-after job, opportunities for promotion, a place at a prestigious college, or selection for officer training. While it is most unlikely that such a test will be the *only* form of assessment used, your score could still exert a powerful influence over your chances of success in these and many other important areas of endeavor.

But even if you never need to take an IQ test, the programs you are going to acquire will still play a crucial part in helping you to think better about all types of problems. The initial benefit comes from being able to prove to yourself just how efficient your mind can be if given the chance to function properly. In a moment we are going to ask you to take an intelligence test and, at the end of this part of the course, to complete a second test of similar difficulty. The difference between your two scores must then represent an objective measure of the improvement in mental performance gained after only a few hours effort. We have found that such clear proof of their true intellectual capacity increases people's motivation to go on and learn even more about making their brains work better.

The final advantage of taking these tests and discovering how to tackle the problems they contain is that it provides useful practice in analyzing and organizing information effectively. During Step Four, when you begin to consider real-life problems and discover how your personal problem-solving style should be used to improve performance even further, this basic training on simpler tasks should prove extremely helpful. As we explained earlier, all problems contain a hidden structure which has to be clearly identified in order to solve them efficiently. The less complex the problem, the easier it becomes to analyze the structure and learn how such knowledge can be used to find the fastest route to the correct answer.

The First IQ Test

Now we would like you to set aside *thirty minutes* to complete the first of our two IQ tests. Try to find a time and a place where you can work without distraction and finish the whole assessment at one sitting. After exactly half an hour you must stop, even if you are in the middle of a problem and others remain to be done. There is no need to worry if you have been unable to finish because the test has been designed so that it is *virtually* impossible to complete it correctly in the thirty-minute period. The only materials needed are a pen or pencil and some writing paper.

How to Take the Test

The IQ test you are about to take contains three different types of problems and we want you to familiarize yourself with each of them on the practice questions below before starting. This will avoid any waste of time when tackling the same questions in the test. Remember that you must stop after exactly thirty minutes if the result is to provide a meaningful comparison for your increased ability after learning the procedures in this part of the course.

Word Questions
Here you will be asked to select the appropriate word from a choice provided.
For example: BLACK is to WHITE as RISE is to   ?
(a) night   (b) snow   (c) increase   (d) dark   (e) fall.
The correct answer here is (e) fall.

Number Questions
Given a series of numbers you will be asked to work out the missing one.
For example: 2 4 6 ? 10
The correct answer here is 8.

Spatial Questions
You are given a series of shapes and asked to complete the sequence by selecting an appropriate design from the choice provided:

For example:

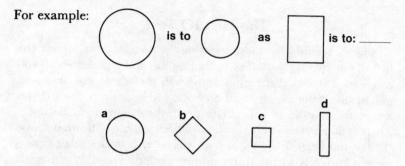

Here the correct choice is (c).

When you are ready, note the time. Remember to work for thirty minutes only, then stop at whatever point in the test has been reached.

THE FIRST IQ TEST—NOTE THE TIME NOW AND STOP AFTER EXACTLY THIRTY MINUTES

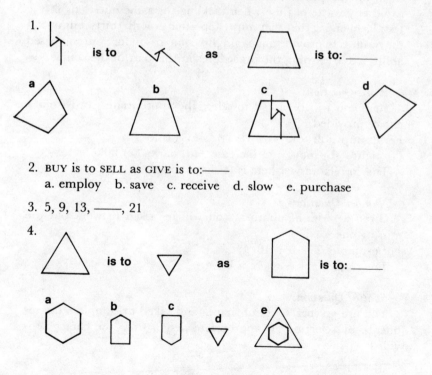

1.

2. BUY is to SELL as GIVE is to:——
   a. employ b. save c. receive d. slow e. purchase

3. 5, 9, 13, ——, 21

4.

5. PREFER is to LIKE as SAFE is to:——
   a. valuables b. secure c. keep d. spend e. want

6. 33, 26, 19, 12, ——

7.

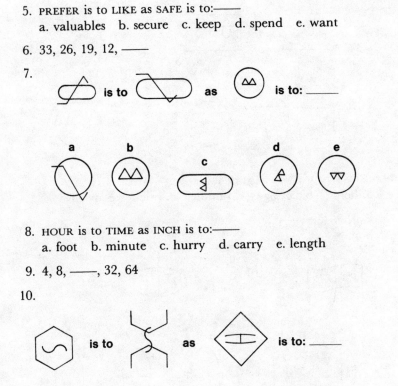

8. HOUR is to TIME as INCH is to:——
   a. foot b. minute c. hurry d. carry e. length

9. 4, 8, ——, 32, 64

10.

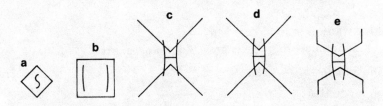

11. SEED is to PLANT as CHILD is to:——
    a. boy b. play c. human d. adult e. toy

12. 1, ——, 9, 27, 81

13.

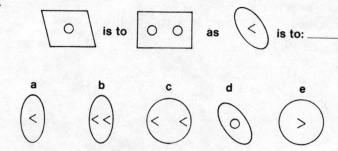

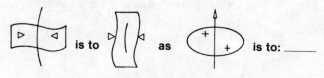

14. OCEAN is to POND as MANSION is to:——
   a. home   b. cottage   c. puddle   d. bricks   e. dwell

15. 2, 4, 7, 11, ——, 22

16.

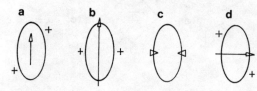

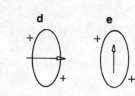

17. EWE is to SEED as ONE is to:——
   a. number   b. sell   c. grow   d. does   e. get

18. 3, 5, 9, 15, ——, 33

19.

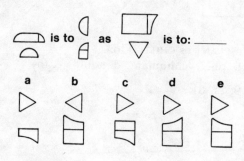

20. RED is to GREEN as LIME is to:——
    a. apple   b. tree   c. stem   d. eat   e. fruit

21. 0, 3, 9, ——, 30, 45

22.

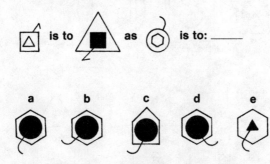

23. RUNNY NOSE is to HANDKERCHIEF as SHIVER is to:——
    a. cold   b. shake   c. sniff   d. heater   e. omit

24. 4, 7, 11 17, ——, 39

25. Complete the series by filling in the blank.

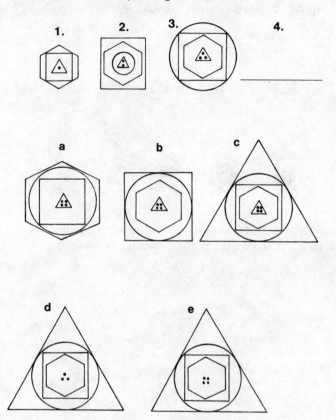

26. SLIGHT is to EXCESSIVE as LENIENT is to:——
    a. easy b. futile c. surrender d. find e. severe

27. 58, 35, ——, 11, 6, 3

28. Find the figure that belongs in the empty box.

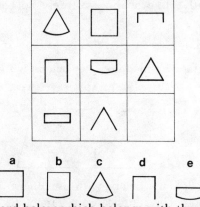

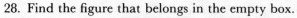

29. Find the word below which belongs with the others.

SKILL, KNOWHOW, ABILITY, ——

a. capacity b. implementation c. success d. product
e. desire

30. 4, 7, 12, 21 ——, 71

31.

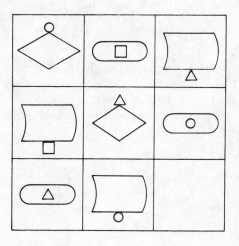

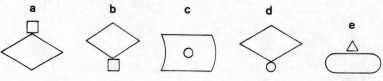

32. Find the word which does not belong with the others.
    a. frequently b. probably c. rarely d. sometimes e. often

33. 2, 4, 6 10, 16, ——

34. Find the *one* figure which does not belong with the others.

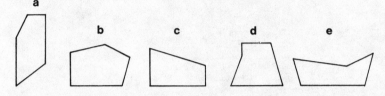

35. Which word does not belong with the others?
    a. once more b. duplicate c. renewal d. numerous e. replica

36. 7, 8, 15, 23, ——, 61

Answers

(1) d (2) c (3)17 (4) c (5) b (6) 5 (7) e (8) e (9) 16 (10) d
(11) d (12) 3 (13) c (14) b (15) 16 (16) e (17) d (18) 23
(19) e (20) a (21) 18 (22) b (23) d (24) 26 (25) e (26) e
(27) 20 (28) b (29) a (30) 38 (31) a (32) b (33) 26 (34) e
(35)d (36) 38

Total your score and refer to the chart below to find the IQ equivalent. The items in this test are arranged in the sequence Spatial Problems, Word Problems, Number Problems. You might like to note whether any specific type of question proved especially difficult.

Your Score	IQ Equivalent	Your Score	IQ Equivalent
12	88	23	130
13	93	24	133
14	96	25	137
15	98	26	140
16	100	27	144
17	105	28	147
18	109	29	151
19	114	30	155
20	118	31	159
21	122	32	163
22	126		

This is what the different IQ scores mean in terms of different levels of mental ability:

IQ Score	What It Means ...
88– 99	Although this score is below average, you should not be discouraged by such a result. As we explained in the introduction, anxiety and one's attitude toward any mental task can interfere with effective mental functioning. It could be that a lack of familiarity with such tests made you more nervous than would otherwise have been the case. The techniques you are going to learn will help increase not only your intellectual performance on such tests but, just as vital, the confidence with which you confront all types of mental challenge.
100–109	This is an average score. Some of the comments we made above probably apply here as well. You certainly ought not to feel discouraged by such an outcome. If you follow the training course diligently, the next score you obtain will certainly be substantially higher.
110–119	This score is above average. Your level of IQ is found in the top twenty-five percent of the population. A certain anxiety over the task and a lack of the correct mental programs for tackling some of the items probably combined to bring down your total score. With training you should be able to lift your performance by at least one if not two categories.
120–129	Your score is well above average. This level of test performance is found in the top ten percent of the population. The brain programs you will soon be acquiring are going to remove any confusions and boost your confidence so that most of the questions that caused you difficulty can be solved with ease.
130–150	This level of superior intelligence is found in only the top two percent of the population. You are obviously good at solving problems and can have found little

difficulty with the test. Our better thinking techniques can still help to make your reasoning ability and decision-making skills even more effective.

150+ Only about one person in five hundred can expect to attain a score this high; it indicates a very high level of mental ability. There is still scope for even greater efficiency in your thinking, however, since there is unrealized potential in the best of brains. If any of the problems caused you greater difficulty than the rest, we suggest you look at the programs dealing with this type of question with particular interest.

With the first intelligence test completed it is now time to consider how your brain can be programmed to tackle the kind of problems such assessments contain in the fastest, easiest, and most consistently reliable manner. We will be describing the techniques for dealing with spatial, number, and word problems based on our own extensive research into this type of problem solving and drawing on studies carried out by psychologists in the United States. We will also tell you how to handle one-on-one IQ tests and provide some useful general advice for taking tests.

But let us start by looking briefly at the nature of such assessments, how they are constructed, and what the designers hope to achieve when selecting problems for their tests.

SECTION ONE

How IQ Tests Are Put Together

When creating items for intelligence tests, psychologists try to devise problems that will explore some fundamental aspect of mental ability, such as logical deduction or clear reasoning, rather than general knowledge or educational attainment. There *are* tests which include such questions but these are generally of a more specialized nature and intended to assess *attainment* more than ability. In any general IQ test you have to take, it will not be the amount or type of information you possess that is being investigated but your skill in manipulating the information presented by the problems. Because of this you will find IQ tests have questions involving fairly simple and straightforward concepts. However complex some of them may appear, your brain is easily capable of coming up with the right answer in a short time, provided your thinking is correct.

Test constructors also strive to construct items that can be termed "culture free" because they do not depend on knowledge of the social or cultural norms and expectations of a particular group. If such a bias existed, the problems would clearly favor those who were most familiar with those norms and expectations, while working against equally intelligent individuals from other cultures or social classes.

Twelve of the questions in the test you have just taken were examples of items that most psychologists believe are relatively culture free. At least in theory, one's place of birth and upbringing ought not to make any difference when attempting to identify the correct design match. Because of this, spatial and matrix items (those in which a missing shape has to be fitted into an oblong frame) are popular with psychologists and are found in a wide range of tests. We are going to start Step Two of the course by showing you exactly how to tackle this popular item most effectively.

To make the learning as effortless as possible, we have adopted a procedure of programmed instruction at different points in this part of the course. This produces active involvement with the material being studied by helping you to ask yourself questions about what has been read a few minutes before. Studies have shown that such an approach organizes key ideas more systematically in your mind and so ensures easier and more accurate recall.

SECTION TWO
Thinking Better About Spatial Problems

is to   as   is to:

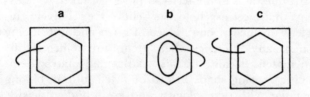

a   b   c

Figure 1

Here is a spatial problem typical of those you might meet in an IQ test. As you now know, the task involves deciding which of the lower figures should be fitted into the blank space.

All spatial problems are concerned with the relationship between different portions of a design. Solving them correctly requires the ability to visualize the changing nature of this relationship and as a result people who do well on them tend to have a strong visual imagination. They are likely to be talented in areas where such an ability is especially important, for example, in architecture, graphic design, technical drawing, engineering, and so on. But, in addition to this rather specialized intellectual skill, spatial problems also assess general mental functioning by testing the ability to focus attention on the *relevant* aspects of a problem and to think in a logical fashion.

The correct solution in the problem above is shape (c). If that was your answer, pause for a moment and try to work out what led you to make that choice.

Most people approach the task with no specific strategy in mind, but simply study the various options and make comparisons on a trial-and-error basis. Such a haphazard approach does of course produce the right answer now and again. But it is clearly much more sensible to have a mental program that enables you to deal with spatial problems swiftly, consistently, and correctly.

The Program for Spatial Problems

To investigate the factors involved in spatial tasks, James Pellegrino and Robert Glaser of the University of Pittsburgh made a careful study of the way volunteers set about solving them.[15] In a series of controlled laboratory experiments, the complexity of the problems was varied by changing some aspects of the design while holding the remainder constant.

By timing their subjects and then analyzing the results statistically the two psychologists discovered that almost all the errors made and time lost could be accounted for by a failure either to identify the key parts of the design or to realize how these changed between designs.

They also found that, although the range of possible designs is enormous, the majority of spatial problems contain no more than three key parts. Furthermore, while test constructors have at their disposal a total of ten different ways in which they can change these key parts, it is rare for more than *three* to be employed in any one item.

No matter how dauntingly complex the problems may appear at first glance, therefore, one need only be able to identify the key parts and the way they change in order to solve them correctly.

How to Identify the Key Parts

The key parts in a spatial problem are those portions of the design which change in some way to determine the answer. They are easily identified after a little practice.

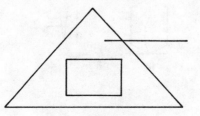

Figure 2

You can easily see that this design contains *three* key parts: a triangle, a square, and a line.

To make the task less obvious, test constructors often include deliberately confusing embellishments in their designs, but these need not make life any harder for you once you become skilled in key-part identification. To help you gain this experience here are sixteen typical spatial designs. Look at them and note down the

Practice Session One

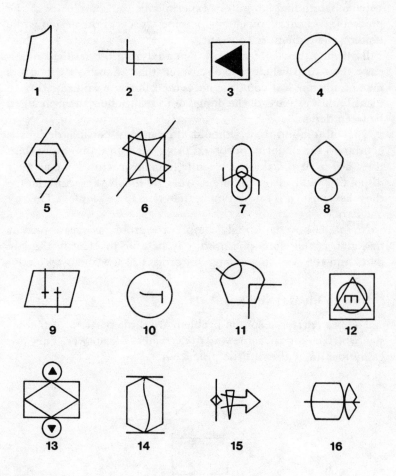

Figure 3

number of key parts each contains; there is no need to list them. Try to carry out the task as rapidly as you can because speed is important in an IQ test and you want to be able to reach a level of expertise at which correct identification requires no more than a brief glance at the design.

How to Identify the Changes

The only other skill you need master to succeed with spatial items is an ability to identify the changes that occur from one design to the next. If you turn back to the first illustration (Figure 1) you will see that the key parts of the first drawing (the oval, the diamond, and the zigzag) are changed in various ways to produce the second drawing. Consider what these alterations are before looking at the key parts in the third drawing. By applying the *same* changes to these, you produce a design identical to (c) in the group of possible answers provided.

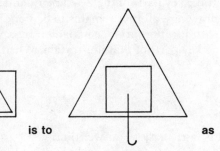

is to   as   is to:

c

a   b

Figure 4

Examine the drawing above. Your practice in recognizing key parts should allow you to spot that the first design consists of three elements:

a square
a triangle
a cane

Now what changes take place between the first two drawings? The statements below will guide you to the correct answers.

The triangle gets ....
The square remains ....
The cane ....

We expect what you said was:

The triangle gets larger—so much larger, in fact, that it now encloses the square.
The square remains the same size.
The cane swings around, like the hands on a clock until it points downward.

Having identified the three key parts of the two designs and seen how they vary between drawings, all that remains to be done is to match the third design with its appropriate companion by applying the same *changes* to the key parts of that illustration. When this is done we see that:

The oval will get ....
The six-sided box will ....
The flag is going to ....

We expect you found it fairly easy to answer that:

The oval will increase in size until it encloses the six-sided box.
The six-sided box will remain the same size.
The flag will swing around so that it points downward.

Now which of the three designs offered as possible solutions meets *all* these requirements? Clearly, drawing (a) is quickly ruled out. Although the key parts change, they do not obey the rules laid down by the relationships within the first two drawings. The same applies to (c), although here the test constructor has tried to trap you by making changes which are almost—but not quite—correct. The flag points left rather than right but has not moved around. So the correct choice has to be drawing (b).

You can provide your brain with a fast, consistently reliable program for solving all kinds of spatial problems by giving it just three instructions: *First* identify the key parts, *then* discover the changes occurring between the key parts of the first two designs before finally applying the same changes to the key parts of the third design. At this point the correct choice from the selection of designs provided becomes immediately clear.

Robert Sternberg of Yale University[16] has identified an important difference in the method of approach adopted by those who usually do well on spatial tasks and those whose performance is consistently below average. He found that people who scored high on spatial problems spent more time in identifying design changes between the first two drawings. It is this crucial step that makes success far more certain than failure. To help you become acquainted with this important skill, we suggest you practice counting key-part changes on the designs below. Start out by noticing how many key parts in one drawing change to produce another. Virtually every spatial problem you encounter will ask you to deal with no more than *three* key parts, while the number of possible changes in a particular problem varies from between one and three. This means you will almost always be dealing with a limited number of designs and a relatively small amount of variation in the relationship between them. You may like to time yourself while working through the second practice session so as to get an idea of how long it takes you to spot the changes. Dividing your total by 10 will then produce an average time per design. You can check your answers with those provided at the end of this section on spatial problems.

Practice Session Two

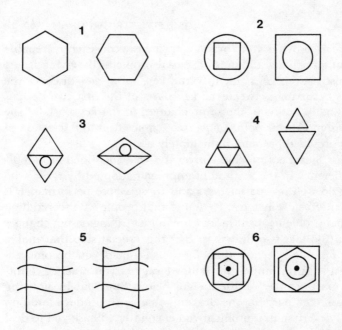

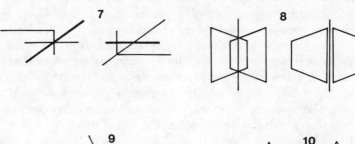

Figure 5

Now Practice Spotting Changes

The final skill you need to develop in order to tackle spatial problems is spotting *how* the key parts change. Paul Jacobs and Mary Vandeventer[17] of the Educational Testing Service in Princeton, New Jersey, studied twenty-two commonly used IQ tests in detail, examining more than 1,300 figural items and classifying them according to changes in the key parts.

Analysis of their results showed that there are only *ten* ways in which such changes occur in the vast majority of figural problems. Once you know what these are, it becomes an easy matter to identify variations between examples.

1. There Is a Size Change.

This is one of the most common types of change that IQ test designers are likely to throw at you. One of the key parts simply gets larger or smaller, as in the drawing below.

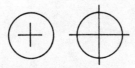

Figure 6

Here we have a situation in which the circle . . . . but the cross . . . .

(stays the same)
(gets larger)

2. There Is Spin.

The test constructor introduces a simple change by rotating one of the key parts in either a clockwise or counter-clockwise direction. We have already seen one example of this sort of variation in Figure 4 where first the cane and then the flag moved around like the hands of a clock. This is another very commonly used variation.

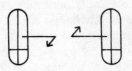

Figure 7

Here we have a situation in which the oval and cross . . . . while the broken arrow . . . .

(stay the same)
(moves half a turn clockwise)

3. They Bring in a Flip-Flop.

This is a slightly more subtle change, but one used fairly frequently by test constructors in an attempt to trap the unwary. It is as if one of the key parts had been picked up and flipped over to produce a reverse effect, as in the drawing below.

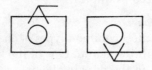

Figure 8

Here we have a situation in which the oblong and circle
.... while the arrow ....
   (stay the same)
   (flip-flops)

4. There Are Shading Changes.

Shading is often used in figure items because it gives the test designer more scope for altering the designs. Shading can be partially or completely changed or removed entirely between one figure and the next, as in the example below.

Figure 9

Here we have a situation in which the square remains
.... but the shading is ....
   (the same)
   (doubled)

5. There Are Shape Changes.

Variations do not necessarily have to be brought about by moving parts around between one design and the next. It is quite common for key parts to stay in place while their shapes alter.

Figure 10

Here we have a situation in which the circle and dot ....
while the .... in the first figure narrows to an .... in the second.
   (remain the same)
   (square)
   (oblong)

6. *They Use the Switcheroo.*

The key parts do not change, but their positions in the figure are switched around as shown below. The Switcheroo is a popular way of bringing in variations and you should keep a sharp eye out for it.

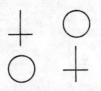

Figure 11

Here we have a situation in which the .... and the .... in the first design ....
    (circle)
    (cross)
    (switch places)

7. *They Bring in the Magic Act.*

Just like a professional magician trying to confuse you by making a rabbit appear from a hat or flowers disappear from under a silk handkerchief, the test construction causes the key parts to vanish or appear from nowhere between figures.

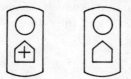

Figure 12

Here we have a situation in which the .... in the first design .... from the second.
    (cross)
    (disappears)

8. They Employ the Leap-Frog.

Ever eager to throw confusion into your mind, test constructors sometimes make key parts leap-frog from one part of the design to the next.

Figure 13

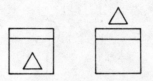

Here we have a situation in which the square . . . . while the triangle . . . . to a new position in the design.

(stays the same)
(leap-frogs)

9. There Is a Bust-Up.

Here a key part splits in half and the two parts undergo one of the changes already described. They might, for instance, leap-frog or switcheroo.

Figure 14

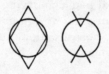

Here we have a situation in which the circle . . . . but the diamond first . . . . and then the parts do a . . . .

(stays the same)
(divides in two)
(flip-flops)

10. They Do a Double-Up.

This differs from the Bust-Up in that instead of the key parts splitting up and then changing, *they remain intact,* but—amoeba-like—one key part reproduces itself. These two duplicates may then undergo a further change of the kind described above.

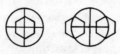

Figure 15

Here we have a situation in which the circle and cross
.... but the hexagon first .... and then ....
to the edges of the circle.

(stay the same)
(doubles up)
(leap-frogs)

Practice Session Three
Figure 16

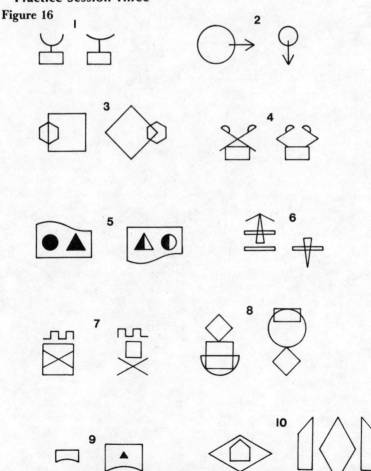

So that you can get used to spotting which particular change is taking place in a figure, here are some for you to practice on. Look at each in turn and jot down the *type* of changes which occur on a separate sheet of paper. Work as quickly as you can, then check your answers with those given at the end of this section.

Now you have all the skills needed to defeat any figure problems you are ever likely to meet. Remember the simple three-step procedure for finding the right match fast.

1. Identify the key parts in the first design provided. Then . . .

2. Notice which of the changes occur among these key parts on the second design. Finally . . .

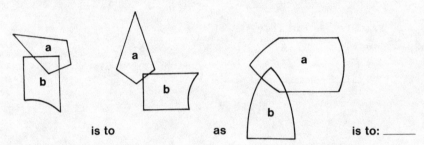

is to   as   is to: _____

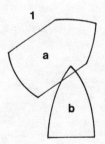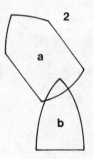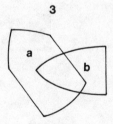

Figure 17

3. Apply the same changes to the key parts of the third design provided. This will tell you which of the choices offered is correct.

Obey these straightforward instructions and you cannot go wrong. What is more, you'll come to the correct choice in the least amount of time because unnecessary observations based on a haphazard search strategy have been eliminated.

In a moment we'd like you to carry out one final practice session on this type of IQ item. But, just to make certain the rules are clear, we will work through a couple of examples with you.

Step One
Identify the key parts.
This design has . . . . key parts.

(two—they are labeled "a" and "b" in the example)

Step Two
Observe the changes between the first and second design. When comparing the first design with the second it is clear that part "a" . . . . Part "b" has also . . . . around.

(spins)

(spun)

This is not the only change, however. One can also see that part "b" has played . . . . to hop from its initial position on the left of key part "a" to a new place on its right.

(leap-frog)

The changes can therefore be identified as:

Key part "a"—one alteration. It has *spun* a fraction clockwise.

Key part "b"—two alterations. It has *spun* around and *leap-frogged*.

This two-part, three-change problem is of about average difficulty compared with the ones you will face in most IQ tests.

Having carried out the first two steps of our strategy, we can proceed to the third design and apply the same changes to its key parts.

Step Three
Make similar alterations to the third figure. This will involve carrying out *one* change on key part "a" and *two* changes on key part "b."

Part "a" must be . . . .

(spun a fraction clockwise)

Carry out this change in your head and glance quickly at the choice of possible designs provided. You can immediately rule out (1) since it is obvious part "a" has been spun too far, even though the problem designer has cunningly turned it in the correct direction so as to introduce a note of confusion. Part "a" *has* been correctly turned in both remaining possibilities (2 and 3), so at this point it is impossible to make a final selection between them. This leaves us with some work to be done on "b."

Part "b" must undergo *two* alterations. It must be ....
and it must ....

    (spun; leap-frog)

When we look at the two possible designs, this rule makes it clear that (2) cannot be correct. Part "b" does a leap-frog movement all right, but it stays pointing in the same direction as before. If we rotate it one quarter-turn counter-clockwise in our minds, we arrive at a design identical to (3), which is the correct solution.

All this takes a great deal longer to read about than it does to think about once you have gained a familiarity with spatial problems. The secret of success is to not allow yourself to be thrown by any apparent confusion in the designs. Remember, it is a battle of wits between you and the psychologist who created the problem. At times he will try to trick you, especially in more difficult IQ tests, by introducing changes in the choice of possible designs which are almost but not quite correct. You must go through with

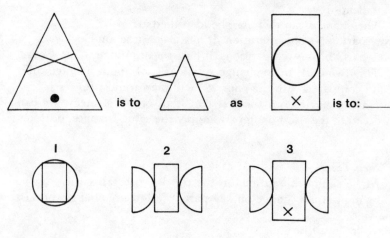

Figure 18

all the change rules identified from the sample designs and not be content with spotting just half of them.

Now that you've seen how to work through a problem in some detail, try your hand at another. We'll nudge you along in the right direction but won't provide a full explanation of what is being done.

Step One
First you . . . . the . . . .
    (identify; key parts)

Step Two
Next you . . . . how the key parts . . . . between de-signs.
    (notice; change)
The changes which take place are:
The triangle gets . . . .
    (smaller in *size*)
The double triangles, first . . . . and then do a . . . .
    (bust up; flip-flop)
The dot, does a . . . . and disappears.
    (magic act)
This is therefore a *three-part, four-change* problem and harder than most.

Step Three
Finally you make . . . . to the . . . . figure.
    (similar changes; third)
Start by making the oblong . . . . in size.
    (smaller)
Since the oblong becomes smaller in all the choices offered (the psychologist trying to trap you again), making this change does not provide us with any clue to the correct design.

So we must go on to consider the circle. This we see will have to undergo . . . . changes.
    (two)
First of all it must . . . . and then . . . .
    (bust-up; flip-flop)
Applying the same change rule to the third design we can imme-diately see that this happens only to (2) and (3). In the first figure

there is no change to the circle at all. Now we only have to identify
the design which also obeys change-rule three, the ....
which caused the "x" to do a .... and ....
     (magic act; disappear)

The essential change does not occur in (3) but it has been used in
(2), which must therefore be the correct answer.

As you become more practiced with spatial problems your brain
will move through the three-step program so rapidly you will
hardly be aware of the systematic strategy that is now being employed, but will simply arrive at the right solution in the shortest
amount of time and have good reason to know it must be correct.

Marcia Linn of Stanford University[18] has found that when subjects were taught to avoid two common mistakes there was an immediate increase of up to 50 percent in speed and accuracy. Our
program will ensure that you avoid these pitfalls, but it is still as
well to be aware of them. When dealing with spatial items make
sure that you:

1. Never select a design that is exactly the same as any of the
first two designs, since it cannot possibly be correct.

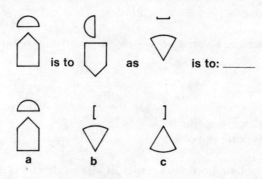

Figure 19

Avoid the temptation to choose (a) because it is identical to the
first design in the problem. By following your three-step program
you will see that the correct choice is ....
     (c)
2. Never choose a design that combines part of the third and
part of either the first or second figures in the problem statement.
This has to be incorrect as it is the *third* drawing transformed
which yields the answer.

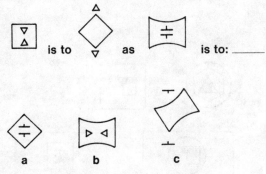

Figure 20

Here (a) and (b) must be wrong since they combine aspects of the first two designs with part of the third.

To complete work on spatial problems we suggest that you go through a final practice session. The ten designs below vary in the number of changes they involve and in their complexity. In the past it may have been that some would have defeated you, especially under the stress of a genuine test situation. With your three-step program for handling spatial items, there should be few, if any, difficulties. To get a measure of the time needed in an IQ test for these items you should time yourself on this session and divide by 10 to get an average for each problem.

Practice Session Four

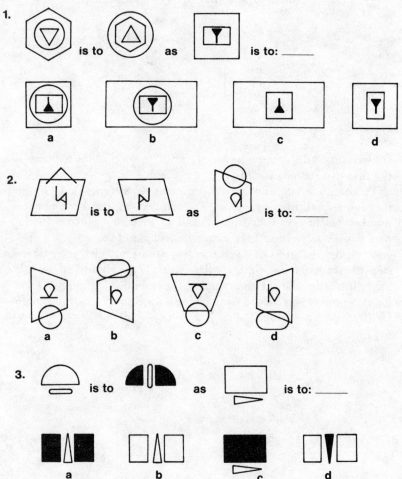

4.

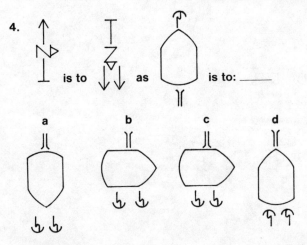

is to   as   is to: _____

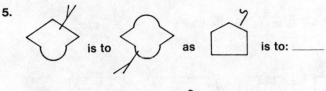

a   **b**   **c**   **d**

5.

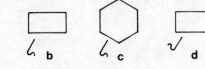

is to   as   is to: _____

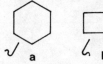

a   **b**   **c**   **d**

6.

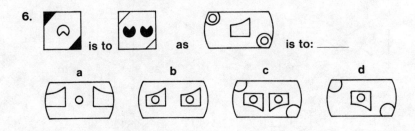

is to   as   is to: _____

a   **b**   **c**   **d**

7.

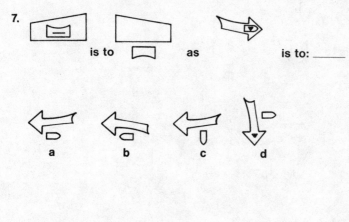

8.

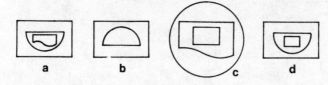

9.

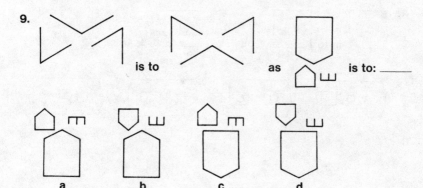

10.

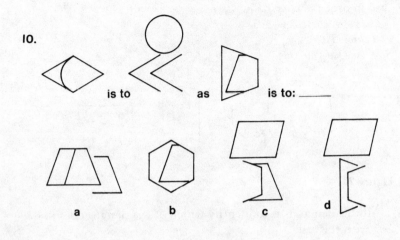

Figure 21

Four Further Teasers

In addition to the type of spatial problems we have already described, you may encounter one or more of the following variations on a theme. We included them in the IQ test you have just taken, so the items should be familiar.

Teaser One
Complete the Row

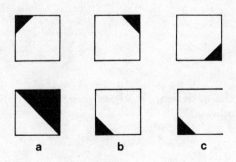

Figure 22

Given a series of designs, you have to select from a choice of figures in order to *complete* it.

Teaser Two
Spot the Odd-One Out

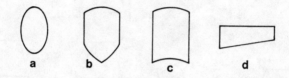

Figure 23

All this demands is to identify which of the designs does not *belong* with the rest.

Teaser Three
Spotting the One that Belongs

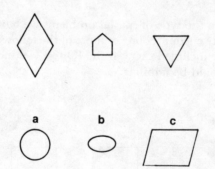

Figure 24

Given the series of designs, you have to select the option that *belongs* with the others.

Teaser Four
Matching the Design

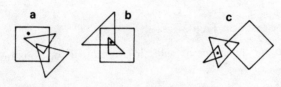

Figure 25

You are given a sample design together with a choice of four or five others and asked to choose the one that has a feature in common with the example.

How to Handle These Teasers

Almost any problem involving shapes can be tackled using the same three-step program that proved so effective for the earlier items we considered.

Step One—Note the number of key parts in the first figure provided.

Step Two—Decide how they change from one figure to the next. See if there are any key parts in common.

Step Three—Apply the same rule to the options open to you. This should make the correct choice immediately apparent.

In the example below, for instance, your first step is to notice that there are three key parts:

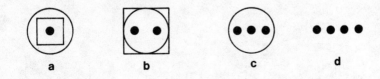

Figure 26

The key parts are . . . .
  (circle; square; dot pattern)

The square first undergoes a *size change,* followed immediately by the *magic act.* In the final design the circle has also done a *magic act.* The dot pattern, as you probably noticed, increases by one moving to the right.

To gain experience with these teasers we suggest you work through the practice problems below.

Practice Session Five

(1) Complete the series by selecting one of the options below.

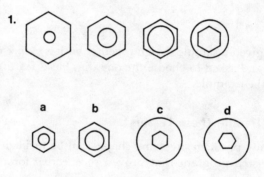

(2) Complete the series by selecting one of the options below.

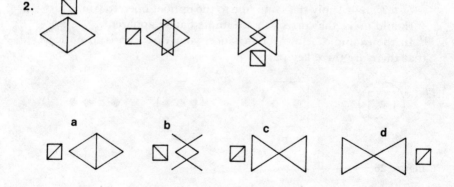

(3) Complete the series by selecting one of the options below.

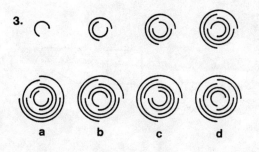

(4) Pick the shape which does not belong to the series.

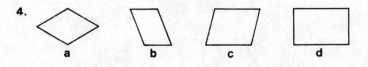

(5) Pick the shape which does not belong to the series.

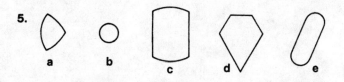

(6) Pick the shape which does not belong to the series.

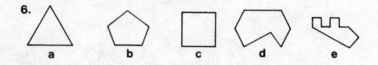

6.   a   b   c   d   e

(7) Select the option which belongs with the four uppermost designs.

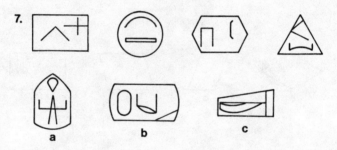

(8) Select the option which belongs with the four uppermost designs.

(9) Select the option which has a feature in common with the uppermost design.

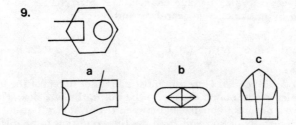

(10) Select the option which has a feature in common with the uppermost design.

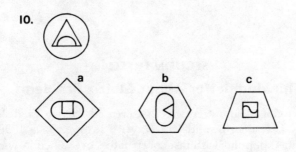

Figure 27

Answers to Spatial Problems

Practice Session One
(1) 1 (2) 2 (3) 2 (4) 2 (5) 4 (6) 4 (7) 4 (8) 2 (9) 3 (10) 2
(11) 3 (12) 4 (13) 6 (14) 4 (15) 4 (16) 3.

Practice Session Two
(1) 1   (2) 2   (3) 3   (4) 2   (5) 2   (6) 3   (7) 3   (8) 2   (9) 2   (10) 3.

Practice Session Three
(1) Shape change.   (2) Spin and size change.   (3) Spin and leap-frog.   (4) Bust-up and flip-flop.   (5) Flip-flop and shading change.   (6) Spin and Magic Act.   (7) Flip-flop, size change and leap-frog.   (8) Leap-frog and shape change.   (9) Size change and Magic Act.   (10) Spin, size change, leap-frog and bust-up.

Practice Session Four
(1) c   (2) d   (3) a   (4) c   (5) a   (6) c   (7) a   (8) a   (9) b   (10) d.

Four Teasers
(1) b   (2) d   (3) c   (4) Here you must add a dot to one of the four alternative designs to match the use of the dot in the first box. The rule here is that a dot has to be placed between two triangles, but not inside a square. The only option which allows this condition to be met is design (c).

Practice Session Five
(1) c   (2) d   (3) b   (4) d   (5) d   (6) c (only figure with an even number of sides)   (7) a (only figure with concave downward key-part)   (8) b (the only letter)   (9) a   (10) c (innermost key-part is curved).

SECTION THREE:

Thinking Better About Matrix Problems

This type of IQ question was first created by two English psychologists, L. S. Penrose and J. C. Raven[19] as long ago as 1938, and has remained popular with test constructors ever since. A wide variety of pattern problems are used in order to explore your ability to spot relationships between different parts of a design. A flexible test item, it can be used to make assessments of people in groups or individually, and the apparent difficulty of the task can be varied considerably. We say *apparent difficulty* because once you understand how to defeat these problems even those carefully created to baffle and confuse become straightforward and fairly trivial mental exercises.

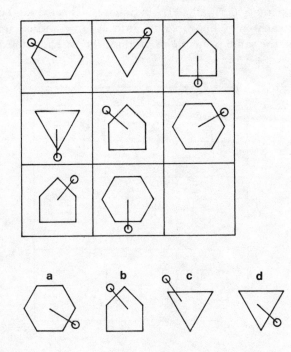

Figure 28

The correct choice of design to complete the matrix is
. . . . ?

(c)

Your task is to complete the blank portion by selecting the appropriate design from the selection offered.

Once you know how to think your way to success with spatial problems, the matrix presents few additional difficulties. Although it may seem that the test designer has a very wide choice in deciding how to make changes between drawings, careful research has shown this is not the case.

To enable you to program your brain for solving this type of problem we are going to provide a powerful technique, developed from our own research, called the Double-Diagonal. Once you have mastered this straightforward procedure it becomes possible to tackle matrix items with little difficulty.

Many psychologists structure matrix problems in the form of

what mathematicians call a "Latin Square." This is a kind of table in which each entry appears once in every row and column. We have used the same principle to produce the design below:

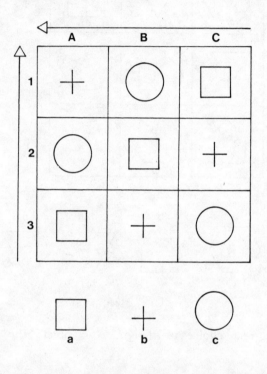

Figure 29

To make this method clear we have completed the matrix, rather than leaving the lower right-hand box empty awaiting your answer. The correct choice from the three possible designs (a, b, c) below the matrix is (c), but it is important to understand exactly why this should be so.

If you study the pattern you will see that each symbol, the cross, the circle, and the square, appears three times in a 3 x 3 matrix. You should also notice that each of them appears *once* per column and *once* per row. If this had been a genuine matrix problem, it is the circle that would be required for the solution. Constructors of these items generally leave the bottom right square empty, although you may occasionally come across a problem where the bottom left square requires completion.

To construct a Latin Square a certain system must be followed when filling in the spaces and it is this system that gives you your first clue when attempting to solve the problem.

Since each design appears once per row, a sensible strategy is simply to scan the upper row, remember which three designs were included there, and then examine the lowest row (where the blank square is usually placed) to determine which design is missing. Finally you should check the answer options and select the one that satisfies the requirements of the missing design. In the problem above it is almost immediately apparent that the missing design in the lower right-hand box is a circle, which gives us (c) as the correct solution.

To investigate how people actually do solve matrix problems we tested a large group of volunteer subjects, one at a time, on a series. We asked the subjects to speak their thoughts aloud while completing this task and, when the recorded strategies were later analyzed, it was found that a large proportion of the group did in fact use the above method. However, although this strategy would prove perfectly adequate for the problem shown above, it would *not* be efficient where the boxes of the matrix contain several key elements, each of which undergoes a different change. What happens then is that it becomes necessary to hold in one's working memory a cumbersome amount of visual information. Since the matrix problems found on adult IQ tests are almost inevitably of this level of complexity, we realized that the discovery of an "easier way" would increase the chances of success on advanced problems.

We carried out a simple mathematical analysis of a large number of matrix problems, which revealed that a simpler strategy does indeed exist. This consists of a brain program that enables you to process complex matrix problems automatically by taking most of the load off your working memory.

Perhaps you saw that one diagonal of the completed matrix above consists only of squares? Both diagonals provide us with immediate insight into the finished design as long as we know what features to look for.

The Double-Diagonal Tactic

As we already mentioned, the blank space that awaits your answer is usually found in the bottom right corner of the matrix, that is, at the lower end of the diagonal row of designs running from the upper left to the lower right of the square. This gives you a valuable shortcut to the correct answer. If the two designs in the diagonal are the *same,* then select an identical design from the options available. In the example below (Figure 30), this would have allowed you to identify instantly (d) as the correct choice.

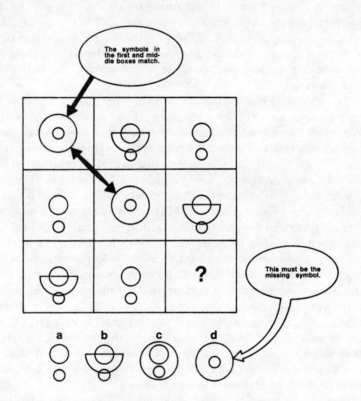

Figure 30

If the two designs in the diagonal are *different,* then notice which symbol occupies the box *directly above the middle one.* This is the answer! The illustration below, Figure 31, shows the double-diagonal method in action where *different* symbols occupy the diagonal in which the answer is found. Here the diagonal contains a large circle and an ellipse. Since these designs are different from one another, the answer is to be found in the design directly above the middle box, that is, (c).

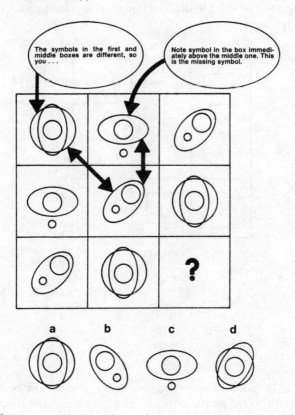

Figure 31

These strategies are infallible for solving any type of Latin Square matrix, since they are based on the inherent mathematical properties of the structure. For this reason you have only to ask one question in order to arrive at the correct solution: Are the symbols on the diagonal with the blank space the same?

If the answer is *yes*, the middle symbol fits the empty box.

If the answer is *no*, the symbol directly above the middle box is the answer.

So far we have considered very simple matrix problems which involved only one key part. In adult IQ tests, however, you rarely find anything this easy. What usually happens is that several key parts and changes are used to create a more challenging mental task. Even so, the double-diagonal method will lead you directly to the correct answer.

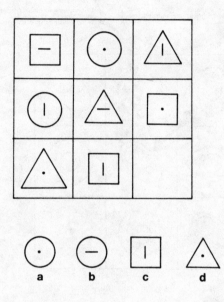

Figure 32

Here is how the double-diagonal technique would be used to tackle the problem above. Start by glancing along the diagonal in which the blank space is located. You will immediately see that the dash, which forms the *inner* key part of the designs, is repeated in the diagonal. This tells you right away that the dash forms part of the correct design. Now observe that the outer key part in these two designs is different, so you should look at the box directly above the one in the center. This contains a circle as its outer key part, so the answer must consist of an outer circle enclosing a dash. From these two simple observations it becomes clear that the choice will be (b).

We suggest that you complete this part of the training by working through the ten problems below. Remember to use the double-diagonal method in each case.

Practice Session Six

1.

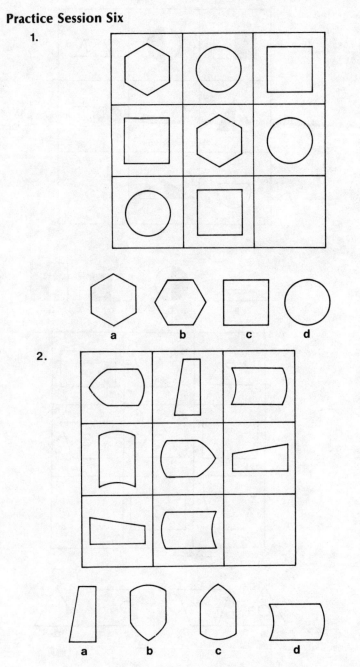

2.

3.

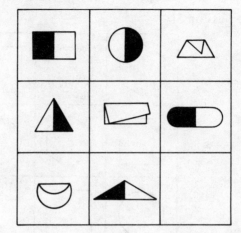

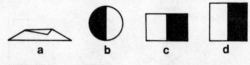

a   b   c   d

4.

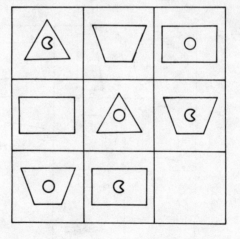

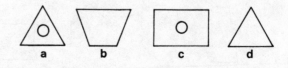

a   b   c   d

5.

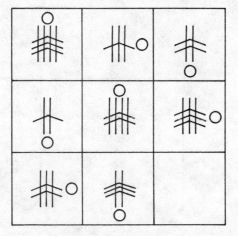

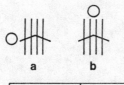 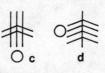

a   b   c   d

6.

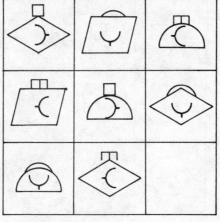

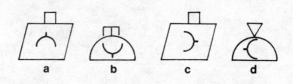

a   b   c   d

7.

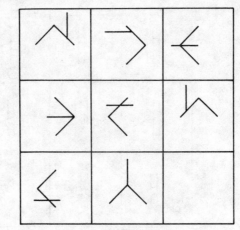

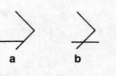

a b c d

8.

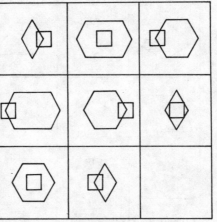

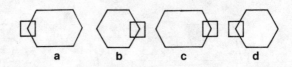

a b c d

9.

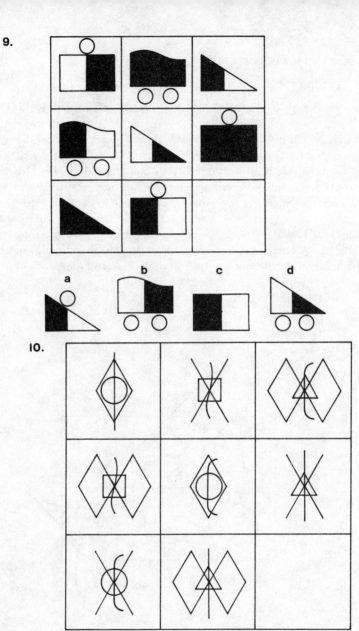

10.

Figure 33

Testing for the Latin Square

All the problems you have just solved were based on the Latin Square, but not all matrices are constructed in this manner, so it is necessary to know how to test whether or not a Latin Square principle has been used.

This can be done very readily by using the *Stripe Test*. In the illustration below you will notice that, running parallel with the diagonal in which the repetition occurs are two other shorter diagonals consisting of two boxes each, which also contain repeated designs. If you see these three parallel stripes, you can be certain that the problem can be solved using the double-diagonal method. If not, you should not attempt to use the double-diagonal method. Instead you should use the information below to guide you to a correct choice.

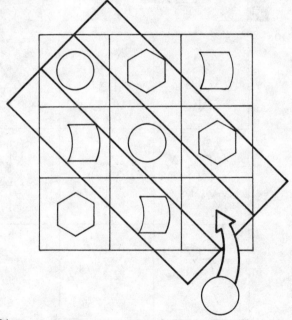

Figure 34

Constant-Change Matrices

In this type of matrix the contents of each box are different and the missing design may also be completely dissimilar to every other design in the problem. Such a matrix is shown below:

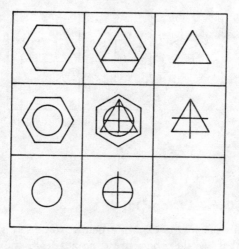

Figure 35

Thanks to the work of Jacobs and Vandeventer,[20] whose studies we looked at earlier, it is now known that there are three main ways in which design variations are produced in constant-change matrices. Once these rules of change are understood, this type of matrix problem can easily be solved.

We have already discussed ten key-part change rules when considering spatial problems. All of these may turn up in a constant-change matrix. However, the three rules outlined below are used to generate the large majority of such problems.

The Add-On

Certain key parts of the first two boxes are added together to produce the design in the third.

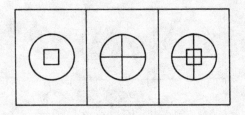

Figure 36

The Add-On and Drop-Out

As you can see in the example below, some key parts may be added together, while others are dropped from the final design. Here the small square and the cross combine, while the large circle disappears.

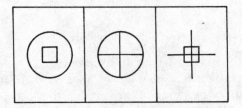

Figure 37

The Count-Up

When this change is brought into play, objects increase from one box to the next according to some counting rule.

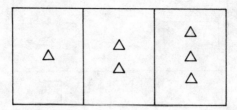

Figure 38

Here are some constant-change matrices on which to practice your new skills. Remember to look for the three new formation rules given above.

Practice Session Seven

1.

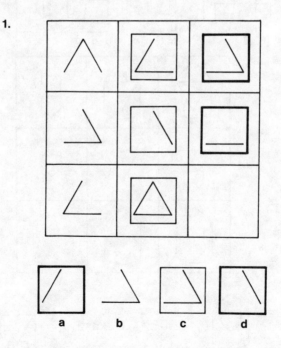

2.

3.

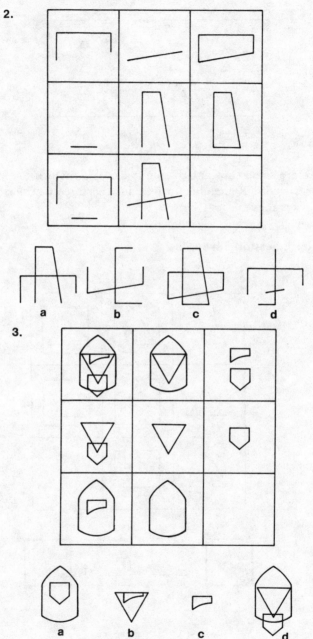

4.

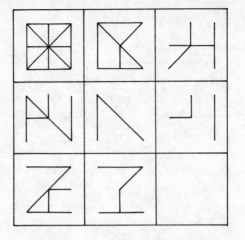

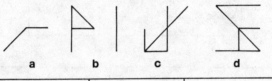

a   b   c   d

5.

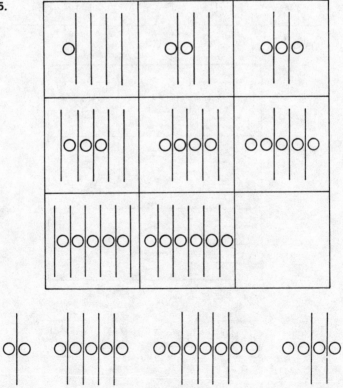

a   b   c   d

6.

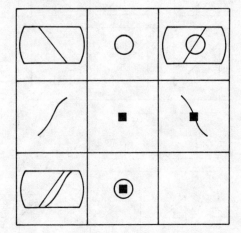

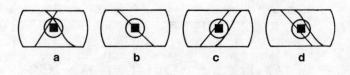

a   b   c   d

7.

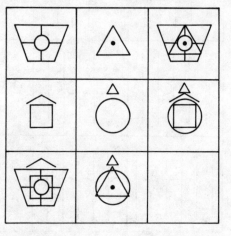

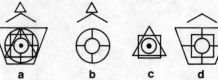

a   b   c   d

Figure 39

Answers to Practice Sessions
Practice Session Six
(1) a   (2) c   (3) c   (4) d   (5) b   (6) c   (7) a   (8) c   (9) b   (10) c.

Practice Session Seven
(1) a   (2) c   (3) c   (4) a   (5) c   (6) d   (7) a.

SECTION FOUR
Thinking Better About Word Problems

As in the IQ test you have just taken, many such tests include a number of word problems. Mostly these do not demand a wide vocabulary or any erudite knowledge about the language because their main purpose is to test your skill in identifying *relationships* between different words. For instance:

HAT is to HEAD as GLOVE is to (a) TIE (b) NOSE (c) HAND (d) JACKET
Here the right answer is obviously (c) since the relationship between a head and a hat is the same as that between a hand and a glove.

Although such problems may not at first appear capable of being analyzed in the way we did with spatial items, they can in fact be approached in a very systematic manner which allows the brain to think about them in the most efficient way.

Dr. S. W. Whitely and Dr. Rene Dawis, of the University of Minnesota,[21] have subjected word problems to the same kind of rigorous study that other investigators employed when examining spatial items, and established that the vast majority of relationships between the words used in such problems can be placed in only eight categories. They also discovered that simply by understanding what those categories are, there is an immediate and significant increase in correct responses. Our own research and the practical experience of performance by people at our workshops confirm the potency of this strategy. We are going to show you how to think better about word problems by telling you what the eight categories of relationship are and explaining how to bring them together in a brain program that will enable you to defeat any such items you encounter.

The Eight Categories and How to Handle Them

Word problems should be approached in the same way as you would now think about spatial items, via three logical stages.

Stage One

Find the relationship between the first two words using the categories given below.

Stage Two

Search among the answer options until you identify a word that has the same relationship to the third word as exists between the first two. In the example above, we would start by recognizing that the HAT and HEAD relationship is one in which the first word performs a function for the second (see category 6 below). Now we look for a word on the list of possible answers that has the same relationship to GLOVE, and this is obviously HAND.

Stage Three

Having selected the word, carry out a final check that you have identified the correct relationship by making certain you have avoided possible traps set by the test constructor. What these pitfalls are, and how they may be avoided, will be explained later.

In the example we gave, you almost certainly identified the right choice at once because it was a very simple problem, far easier indeed than most you will come across in intelligence tests. These generally employ relationships that are much more subtle, which is why a haphazard search method usually generates confusion and wastes precious time. The structured program described here immediately eliminates all confusion and gives you the answer by the most direct and reliable route.

We suggest that at first you work through the categories in the order given here, testing each word in turn against the relationship involved to see if it is appropriate.

The Eight Categories

Start by asking yourself:

1. *Are they similar?*

The answer is yes only when the words have an identical or near identical meaning. For example, in the problem:

SWIM is to FLOAT as SHOUT is to   ?
(a) WHISPER   (b) ARGUE   (c) SCREAM
the first two words, SWIM and FLOAT, have a similar meaning. So
Step One in your program (establishing a relationship) has been
completed.

The second step is to search among the choices offered to find
the word *similar* in meaning to SHOUT.

The first word WHISPER must be wrong since it is the opposite.
By the same reasoning (b) ARGUE must also be incorrect for, while
people may well SHOUT when arguing, the words are not similar.
This leaves us with (c) SCREAM as the correct solution.

The final step is to check our reasoning quickly to ensure we
have not fallen into a trap. With this check completed, (c) can be
given with absolute confidence it is the right choice.

If the answer to your first question is No, then proceed to ask . . .

2. *Are they opposites?*

Does the relationship between the first two words stem from
their being opposite in meaning?

For example:
THESE is to THOSE as GO is to   ?
(a) PROCEED   (b) RUN   (c) COME

THESE and THOSE may look alike and even sound rather similar,
but all we are concerned with here is their meaning. So the answer
to the second question is yes, they are opposites.

The relationship having been established, proceed to search
among the words offered for one which is *opposite* in meaning to GO.

It cannot be (a) since PROCEED is similar in meaning. Nor can it
be (b) since we might well run as we GO, but no opposite meaning
is involved. Again the right solution turns out to be (c) COME.

We may well find that the answers to our first two questions are
both negative. If this happens, then we go on to ask the third question on the list.

3. *Do they share class membership?*

We want to know whether the words belong to the same group
of things or share some feature in common. For instance, birds and
fish have in common the fact that they both belong to the class of
living creatures.

In the problem:

HORSE is to LION as BLUE is to   ?
(a) BIRD   (b) PINK   (c) MOOD

we are looking at a relationship based on class membership since both horses and lions belong to the class of animals.

Having established the relationship, you are ready to pass immediately to the second step and select the word which has the same class membership as BLUE. Since this is a color, there can be little doubt as we are looking for another color. Although both (a) BIRD and (c) MOOD are *associated* in some way with BLUE, only (b) PINK actually belongs to the *class of colors*.

If your answer to the third question is no, then pass on to the fourth possible category of relationship:

4. *Is a class name involved?*

Does one of the first two words name the class or group to which the other belongs?

For example, you might get:

APRIL is to MONTH as BEE is to   ?
(a) FLOWER   (b) SPRING   (c) INSECT

Are they similar in meaning? No.
Are they opposite in meaning? No.
Do they share class membership? No.
Does it involve a class name? Yes. April belongs to the class of months.

So we are looking for a class to which BEE *belongs* in the same way, which makes (c) INSECT the only possible answer.

If you felt that FLOWER or SPRING were likely to be correct, you have been caught by a trap that the designers often employ called "distractors." These are incorrect options which most people would strongly associate with one of the words in the problem. Here FLOWER was chosen because it is an image that comes readily to mind whenever we think of the word BEE. Similarly, APRIL is a month that many automatically associate with the start of SPRING.

They were intended to distract your mind from its task of employing logical reasoning rather than guesswork when seeking an answer. You might have found the association between Bee and Flower, or April and Spring so powerful that the "solution" sprang instantly to mind and appeared so obvious you gave no further thought to the problem. This is especially likely to happen if you are already under pressure from working against the clock during a real test.

The best way of avoiding the siren song of distractors is not to even look at the word options provided by the test constructor until *after* you have worked out the relationship between the first two words. Cover the answers with your hand as you establish step one in the program and only seek out the appropriate option once this is clear.

It is quite possible you will have worked through the first four categories and come up with a negative answer each time. In this case the next question to ask is . . .

5. *Does one turn into the other?*

Here some special process could be involved (i.e., milk into butter) or the transformation might occur with the passage of time, as in the example below.

FLOWER is to BUD as BUTTERFLY is to   ?

(a) POLLEN   (b) WINGS   (c) CATERPILLAR

As in the previous problem, this contains two deliberate distractors, Flower and Pollen, Butterfly and Wings. If a haphazard search method had been used, then either of these might seem correct. But what we are actually looking for is a time transformation since buds become flowers and caterpillars turn into butterflies in due season.

DOUGH is to BREAD as IRON is to   ?

(a) COPPER   (b) STEEL   (c) BUILDING

Here we have another transformation, this time via a man-made process, and the correct choice must be (b) STEEL.

If the relationship still eludes you, pass straight on to the sixth possibility by asking:

6. *Does one perform a function on or for the other?*

The link here is that one of the words is associated with the other by means of some activity which is either carried out on its behalf or actually involves it. For instance:

TEACHER is to STUDENT as DRIVER is to   ?

(a) GOLF   (b) SPEED   (c) CAR

Although both (a) and (b) are associated with DRIVER in different ways, the correct choice is (c) since the driver performs a function on the car, just as the teacher performs a function "on" the students.

There are only two categories left now, but if you have not yet identified the relationship, do not worry. The remainder are just as popular among testers as the others and the next question to ask is:

7. *Is some concept of quantity involved?*

Here we have the straightforward situation of the first two words differing from one another in size or amount. For instance:

MOUNTAIN is to HILL as TIGER is to ?

(a) JUNGLE (b) HOUSECAT (c) LION

Lion may be the first word that comes to mind when someone says tiger, and tigers are thought of as jungle creatures. But be careful because these are distractors and what is really involved is a relationship involving quantity. Since HILL is smaller than MOUN-TAIN we must look for something smaller than a TIGER and the only answer among those offered is (b) HOUSECAT.

Our last category of relationship is not as obvious as the others we have discussed, but psychologists often make use of it when designing IQ tests for adults because a certain amount of creative insight is needed. If you follow routine thinking strategies the answer may not occur to you. The question which overcomes this difficulty is:

8. *Are letter patterns involved?*

GOOD is to HARPOON as ILLUMINATE is to ?

(a) BELLOWS (b) LIGHT (c) ABOLISH

You could waste a great deal of limited test time racking your brain for an answer unless you have first clearly identified the strategy used by the psychologist creating the problem. The most obvious way of being misled here is to try to discover some relationship of meaning between GOOD and HARPOON. Approached in this way the task appears to lack logic. But, once your brain has acquired a systematic program it becomes apparent the *only* relationship that could be involved is that of *word patterns*.

In this problem the *meaning of the words* used is immaterial. The solution is to be found in the *sequence of letters* they contain. Here is another example of the same type of question:

GRILLING is to SIMPLENESS as DELAYED is to ?

(a) CONSIST (b) PERFORMANCE (c) ENSHRINE

As before, any attempt to search for relationships of meaning is doomed to failure. Take a closer look at the words themselves and see if you can come up with a word pattern relationship that would

THE FIVE-STEP PROGRAM / 103

give you the correct solution. The secret of success is to hunt for some structural feature which the three words in the statement have in common with *one* of the possible answer options.

In the first example you will notice that GOOD and HARPOON have the same pair of vowels "OO" in their construction. ILLUMI-NATE has a double consonant "LL." This immediately tells you that the pattern involved is an identical letter pair. You search the op-tions for a word which repeats the "LL" pattern and see that only BELLOWS meets this requirement.

Letter pairs are a popular choice in IQ tests and you should be on the lookout for them whenever a *letter pattern* relationship is sug-gested.

In the second example another commonly encountered letter se-quence has been used. Can you spot it? Perhaps you saw that all three words in the problem statement GRILLING, SIMPLENESS, and DELAYED start and finish with the same letter, a "G" in the first in-stance, an "S" and a "D" in the remaining cases. Clearly you are being asked to find a word which obeys the same rule, and only EN-SHRINE meets this demand.

Occasionally psychologists creating the tests will include some long and perhaps slightly obscure words in the hope of creating confusion. Do not allow yourself to be made anxious by this tactic since once you have established that the relationship category is a *word pattern* rather than any of the other possibilities, the *meanings* of the words become irrelevant to your strategy. You could quite eas-ily come up with a correct choice from the answer option without ever knowing what the words themselves meant, as in the example below:

IDIOSYNCRASY is to SUCCEDENT as PIPING is to   ?

(a) INSULATED   (b) REPENT   (c) STATEMENT

Here not all the meanings of the words may be known to you. The second especially is likely to prove obscure unless you are in-terested in astrology, when you will probably recognize it as a term used to identify the 2nd, 5th, 8th, and 11th houses. A lack of knowledge here might cause you to avoid this problem entirely and pass quickly on to more familiar-looking word questions. Our research shows that 60 percent of subjects give up *within three sec-onds* of starting to consider questions like this.

Using your new brain program, you should have no problem in

first recognizing it as a word pattern relationship and then, by applying the same logical process of analysis, in identifying the construction rules used.

Your best way of starting, at least when you are still gaining experience in word problems, is to note whether each letter is a vowel or a consonant by writing a small "v" or a "c" under each. This is what happens when we do this for the words in the problem above.

IDIOSYNCRASY	SUCCEDENT	PIPING
vcvvcccccvcc	cvccvcvcc	cvcvcc

Now ask yourself these questions:

Am I looking at a letter pattern problem involving:

1. *Identical letter pairs?*
2. *Identical letters start and finish?*
3. *Vowel/consonant patterns?*
4. *Words constructed from two smaller words?*
5. *Words with identical groupings of letters?*

Let us consider each of these possibilities in a little more detail.

1. *Identical Letter Pairs*

In the first example above, the answer to this question would have been in the affirmative since GOOD and HARPOON and ILLUMINATE and BELLOWS do have shared letter pairs in the correct sequence. In the IDIOSYNCRASY : SUCCEDENT pairing, the test constructor has cunningly included a letter pair "CC," but this pattern is not followed by any of the remaining words so cannot be the answer.

2. *Identical Letters Start and Finish*

In the problem: GRILLING is to SIMPLENESS as DELAYED is to (a) CONSIST (b) PERFORMANCE (c) ENSHRINE the answer will be found in just such a pattern and any attempt to relate words in some other way is doomed to failure.

3. *Vowel/Consonant Patterns*

Are there similarities in the arrangement of the consonants and vowels? By identifying each with the "v" or "c" our task of spotting such arrangements is made all the easier.

IDIOSYNCRASY starts with a sequence "vcv." SUCCEDENT also uses a "vcv" sequence placed farther back in the word. Furthermore the *same* consonant is involved in both cases, the letter "D," which gives us a useful clue. We see that PIPING follows the "vcv" rule with the sequence "IPI." We have teased out a pattern from the three words, a vowel-consonant-vowel structure with IDI in ID-IOSYNCRASY, EDE in SUCCEDENT and IPI in PIPING. If that is the pattern involved, then we may expect the correct option word to involve the letters EPE placed toward the end. This is the only way the construction rule laid down by the problem statement can be obeyed, so our final step is to seek out such a word among the options. If none existed, then we would have to think again and search for a different pattern. However this is such a clear structure it becomes extremely improbable we are in error since, if we were wrong, it would mean that the problem had been ambiguously designed, and people devising IQ tests usually go to great lengths to make them as straightforward as possible.

An examination of the option words provided reveals that only REPENT, with its EPE letter sequence, fits the pattern we have identified and must, therefore, be the correct answer.

This was a more than usually difficult problem and you are most unlikely to come across anything harder, even in high-level adult intelligence tests. Word pattern questions, in general, are also among the trickiest to answer because most people find it difficult not to think of the *meaning* rather than the letter sequences involved. The systematic program of elimination and analysis presented here, however, should make it far easier for you to identify the relationship employed and then uncover the internal structure of the words.

4. *Words Constructed from Two Smaller Words*

If we had not, in fact, solved the problem at this point the next question to consider would have been whether the relationship might not lie in the fact that each word was made up of two smaller words. For instance:

BROWBEAT is to MANEATER as CRANKSHAFT is to   ?

(a) ANGER   (b) BOOKSHELF   (c) LIONESS

Finally, we would inquire, all other questions having failed to identify the relationship, whether what was involved might not be:

5. *Words with Identical Groupings of Letters*

The first example we gave consisted of just such a problem with Good and Harpoon, Illuminate and Bellows. Here is another problem which uses the same pattern.

BATTER is to SLATTERN as FIDDLE is to   ?
(a) TUNE   (b) BEAT   (c) RIDDLED

Because IQ tests are not designed to measure general knowledge they usually avoid using very obscure words except when letter patterns are involved. This can *sometimes* provide a clue as to the type of relationship involved, but be warned that there are certain very tough intelligence tests, used at graduate level, which anticipate subjects having a wider than average vocabulary, and their word problems often reflect this expectation.

Beware False Friends

Finally a word of caution about a word trap involving what we call *false friends.* These are words with more than one meaning which may appear to be beckoning the problem solver in the right direction while actually leading him or her astray. For instance:

INVALID is to WRONG as UNFETTERED is to   ?
(a) PATIENT   (b) FREE   (c) CORRECT   (d) SICK

Here the first word clearly has two meanings, either a *person disabled by sickness* or *incorrect.* When used in the sense of a *patient* it is unrelated to WRONG and, by considering only this meaning you would find it impossible to identify the category of relationship. If you appreciate it also means *incorrect,* however, a relationship of similarity is immediately apparent which leads one to see that (b) FREE must be the required answer.

While you are gaining expertise in dealing with word problems, we strongly advise you to work through the step-by-step strategy of eliminating categories. Although this is a slightly more time-consuming procedure than taking a guess at the relationship, it offers two major advantages to the less experienced word problem solver. By making use of a methodical procedure you always have a tactic for starting to tackle the question and this knowledge will reduce anxiety about such items. Secondly, our research has shown that when this approach is used initially, the brain very quickly establishes the technique as its normal method for handling word problems, and, having done so, swiftly works down the list of relationships until it identifies the correct category involved. The speed and certainty of the operation allows you to arrive at the right choice very rapidly and with virtually 100 percent certainty of success.

To make certain you understand these relationships and can quickly identify them we suggest you work through the following examples and note down the category involved. You will find the answers at the end of this section:

Practice Session Eight

(1) Here–There   (2) Stingy–Tight   (3) Seed–Plant
(4) Itch–Scratch   (5) Irrelevant–Useless   (6) Sport–Billiards
(7) Bushel–Dozen   (8) Breeze–Stool   (9) Slight–Comple-
ment   (10) Continue–Persevere   (11) Where–Downstairs
(12) Lenient–Strict   (13) Ascend–Climb   (14) Bearing–Manner   (15) Breeze–Gale   (16) Scientists–Experiment   (17)
Iron–Rust   (18) Trunk–Wheel   (19) Head–Neck   (20) Out-
line–Shape   (21) Herd–Pair   (22) Bush–Plant   (23) Tem-
per–Heat   (24) Earth–Trowel   (25) Thinker–Slink
(26) Scale–Reduce   (27) Rarity–Slalom   (28) Svelte–Corpu-
lent   (29) Lean-to–Skinflint   (30) Rocket–Metallic

We would now like you to use your new skill with complete word problems of the type used in intelligence tests. When answering, try to identify not only the correct choice but also the relationship involved and be on your guard against distractors or words with a double meaning. The answers can be found at the end of this section.

Practice Session Nine

1. GO is to COME as ABOVE is to (a) UPSIDE-DOWN   (b) UP
   (c) TRAVEL   (d) BELOW   (e) OVER
2. FIND is to LOCATE as HOLD is to (a) DISCOVER
   (b) RELEASE   (c) CONTAIN   (d) SAMPLE   (e) CLEAR
3. SMILE is to CHASM as STILTED is to (a) DISCOVER
   (b) GULF   (c) REALIST   (d) GRIN   (e) UNSETTLED
4. MANY is to MAXIMUM as SOFTLY is to (a) MOVE
   (b) SILENCE   (c) GENTLY   (d) SMOOTHLY   (e) GROUP
5. CLUSTER is to PAIR as CROWD is to (a) PEOPLE   (b) PANIC
   (c) HURRY   (d) WALK   (e) GROUP
6. MOUSE is to MAMMAL as ANT is to (a) FLY   (b) INSECT
   (c) LION   (d) CRAWL   (e) DIFFERENCE

7. SEE is to HEAR as SAIL is to (a) TRAVEL (b) SWING
   (c) DRIVE (d) RECEIVE (e) WIND
8. THINK is to PONDER as CHANGE is to (a) TRANSFORM
   (b) REMAIN (c) STORE (d) PERFORM (e) POSITION
9. HOUSE is to FOUNDATION as AUTOMOBILE is to (a) DRIVE
   (b) ACCIDENT (c) TIRE (d) SWIM (e) TRAFFIC
10. CRASS is to MISSING as FILL is to (a) YELLOW (b) EMPTY
    (c) INSTILL (d) SENSE (e) GLASS
11. STEW is to MEAT as LUMBER is to (a) BRANCH
    (b) FORESTER (c) MODEL (d) TREES (e) ARRIVE
12. FLOWER is to BEE as BUILDING is to (a) OFFICE
    (b) CARPENTER (c) DESTROYING (d) GROUND (e) RESULT
13. CARELESSNESS is to ACCIDENT as GLUTTONY is to (a) OVEREAT-
    ING (b) FOOD (c) IMPROVEMENT (d) DINNER (e) HEART-
    BURN
14. ACCEPT is to DECLINE as CONSENT is to (a) ALLOW
    (b) REFUSE (c) REVEAL (d) FALTER (e) SPEND
15. FIRE is to HEAT as FLOWER is to (a) GROW (b) LEAF
    (c) SCENT (d) PETAL (e) GROUND

If you found any difficulty with these problems we suggest you go through those that proved especially tricky and make certain you have worked methodically down the list of possible relationships. Here are the key questions which should be asked as you read each problem:

Question One
Are the first two words similar in meaning? If the answer is No, then go on to . . .
Question Two
Are the first two words opposite in meaning? If the answer is No again then go on to . . .
Question Three
Do the first two words belong to the same class of things? If No, go on to . . .
Question Four
Does one of the first two words name a class to which the other belongs? If No, then . . .
Question Five
Does one of the things named in the first two words change into the other? No again . . .
Question Six
Then ask whether one of the things named in the first two words performs a function on or for the other. If you are still answering No, then ask . . .

Question Seven
Is some notion of quantity involved between the first two words?

If you are still obliged to answer No, it is probable that the relationship involved is based on the sequence of the letters and the pattern of the words themselves rather than on their meaning.

Since IQ test word problems vary considerably in their level of difficulty, you will occasionally come across one in which the precise nature of the relationship between the words is hard to determine. It just does not seem to fit neatly into one of the eight categories we have listed. When this happens, we suggest you use a procedure, developed by American psychologist Dr. A. Willner,[22] who advises that by *transposing* the words in the problem, difficulties in identifying the relationship are often easily resolved.

In the question: PEACE is to HAPPINESS as WAR is to (a) GRIEF (b) FIGHT (c) BLOOD (d) BATTLE, one might work through the eight categories without finding a clear-cut relationship. So try switching the word order by pairing the first and third words, for example. This gives us:
PEACE is to WAR as HAPPINESS is to (a) GRIEF (b) FIGHT (c) BLOOD (d) BATTLE

Now we are obviously looking at a relationship of opposites and can immediately see that the correct choice must be (a) GRIEF.

This tactic is not going to work on every occasion, but it is well worth trying whenever the relationship seems obscure.

Problems of Like and Unlike

A problem popular with psychologists is to ask test subjects to identify a word which shares some kind of attribute with a group of words. For instance, you might be asked to pick one of the four words which fits into the space here:
CURVED ZIGZAG STRAIGHT ?
(a) ALONG (b) CIRCULAR (c) FAR (d) STRETCH

The correct answer would be CIRCULAR because it is like the top three in describing direction.

There are two possible categories of relationships usually involved in this type of question which makes them relatively easy to deal with. You should look for either *class membership* or *word patterns*.

In the example above, the relationship was that of class membership.

A few further examples will help to make matters clear:

SAIL SWIM ROW   ?
(a) WALK   (b) FLOAT   (d) TRAVEL   (d) APPROACH

The correct choice here is FLOAT because all the words in the top line relate to ways of moving on water.

MAN WOMAN TEENAGER   ?
(a) APE   (b) INFANT   (c) FAMILY   (d) RELATIONS

The correct choice here is INFANT because the first three belong to the class of human beings. Only infant also has membership of this class.

ARK ALL ANT   ?
(a) BAT   (b) CAT   (c) AND   (d) ALE

Here the relationship sought is one of . . . . and the correct choice is . . . . (word pattern; and)

The pattern involves the vowel "A" followed by two consonants. Only AND fits this requirement.

By the way, did you spot the use of ALE as a distractor?

Now we would like you to try your hand at similar examples. The answers can be found at the end of this section.

Practice Session Ten

(1) Here   Yonder   Away   ?
   (a) These   (b) Far   (c) There
(2) Eye   Kidney   Lung   ?
   (a) Brain   (b) Ear   (c) Heart
(3) Niece   Granddaughter   Mother   ?
   (a) Father   (b) Cousin   (c) Wife
(4) Period   Comma   Colon   ?
   (a) Word   (b) Hyphen   (c) Letter
(5) Slalom   None   Total   ?
   (a) Rare   (b) Stick   (c) Upper
(6) Skill   Capacity   Talent   ?
   (a) Motivation   (b) Ability   (c) Potential
(7) Dog   Cow   Chicken   ?
   (a) Wolf   (b) Pig   (c) Lion
(8) Note   Bass   Flat   ?
   (a) Show   (b) Score   (c) Quiet

Odd-Man-Out Problems

The final sort of word question you might come across is the exact opposite of similarities. In these problems you have to identify which of a group of words does *not* belong there. For instance:

SUN   CANDLE   ELECTRIC LIGHT   MIRROR

Here the answer required is MIRROR, on the basis that the first three produce light directly, but a mirror only reflects it. This is a fairly obvious example and the difference you have to spot is likely to be less obvious, especially in the higher level intelligence tests.

As with similarity questions the words are usually associated by the relationships of either class membership or word pattern. In the problem above, the first three objects are all members of the class of things which give out light, but a mirror is not.

If the problem had been presented as:

MERCURY   MIRROR   SILVERPLATE   CANDLE   the odd man out would have been CANDLE, as the only direct source of light.

When presented with such a problem, ask yourself if class membership is involved; if not, then seek out word patterns. You will find a selection of each sort in the practice questions below, with the answers at the end of this section.

Practice Session Eleven

(1) Wonder   Think   Muse   Wave
(2) Sale   Smile   Rule   Move
(3) Walk   Swim   Wear   Drive
(4) Best   Worse   Fewer   More
(5) Golf   Tennis   Soccer   Squash
(6) Elevate   Agape   Provision   Indicate
(7) Banking   Publishing   Insurance   Investing
(8) Triangle   Circle   Square   Rectangle
(9) Confess   Duress   Suppress   Surpass
(10) Indicate   Abdicate   Irate   Berate

Answers
Practice Session Eight
(1) Opposites   (2) Similarity   (3) Change   (4) Function   (5) Similarity   (6) Class Name   (7) Quantity   (8) Word Pattern   (9) Opposites   (10) Similarity   (11) Class Name   (12) Opposites   (13) Similarity   (14) Similarity   (15) Quantity (i.e., both measures of

wind force) (16) Function (17) Change (18) Class Membership (19) Function (20) Function (21) Quantity (22) Class Membership (23) Function (note this is an example of the "false friend" with two meanings) (24) Function (25) Word Pattern (26) Similarity (27) Word Pattern (vcv form) (28) Opposites (29) Word Pattern (both words comprised of two smaller words) (30) Class Membership.

Practice Session Nine
(1) d (2) c (3) c (4) b (5) e (6) b (7) c (8) a (9) c (10) a (11) d (12) b (13) e (14) b (15) c

Practice Session Ten
(1) c (2) b (You have two pairs of everything in the problem statement. Only ears fit this pattern) (3) c (4) b (5) a (6) b (7) b (8) b

Practice Session Eleven
(1) Wave (2) Move (3) Wear (4) Best (all the others are relative terms—best is an absolute because nothing can beat it) (5) Soccer (6) Provision (7) Publishing (8) Circle (only one with no corners) (9) Surpass (ends in "ass" rather than "ess" (10) Berate (lack of "i" in word)

SECTION FIVE

Thinking Better About Number Problems

If you are one of those many people who dislike solving number problems, do not let the fact that most IQ tests contain a selection of them cause any concern. We are going to give you fast, effective brain programs for handling all such items so that, even if your math ability is very limited, you can still be certain of coming up with the correct answer on every occasion. Our ways of thinking better about number tasks can transform anyone into an expert and allow you to tackle even apparently complex questions with assurance.

Missing Number Problems

We will start by considering a type of problem much favored by psychologists designing IQ tests. You have already encountered several of them in the test we asked you to take in Step One, so they should be fairly familiar. In this sort of question you are asked to discover a missing number in the sequence provided. For example:

| 3 | 7 | 12 | ? | 25 |

What is clearly required is for you to discover the underlying construction principle used to create the series. Once that has been correctly identified, it becomes quite easy to provide the missing number.

Whether or not you found the answer to the problem above, we would like you to think about the mental strategy used to search for it. In our research we asked large numbers of people to do just that and, as they hunted for the answer, to speak their thoughts aloud so we could tape-record them. When this was done, it was possible to identify the reasoning processes involved and discover which approach most appeared to use: "If I subtract 3 from 7, I am left with 4. Now 7 from 12 is 5, a larger difference than before. I wonder if the principle here is that the difference increases by one each time we move to the right? If that is correct, I would expect the difference between 12 and the missing number to be 6, which would make the number I am looking for 18. I can check that idea by adding 7 to 18. It comes to 25, so my reasoning is correct. The answer lies in adding one to the difference between the numbers in the series moving from left to right."

Such thoughts seem to be fairly typical of the reasoning process that lies behind attempts to discover the missing numbers. It is likely that your own approach was rather similar, although you may not have spotted the construction principle quite so quickly. Such a strategy is inefficient for two important reasons. First of all, it is a haphazard search method, a hit-or-miss technique that could waste a considerable amount of time chasing down blind alleys. Secondly, it forces you to hold too much information in your working memory, overloads its capacity and so causes confusion. Remember that our sample problem above is a good deal easier than most you will encounter in IQ tests and that the more complex the problem, the greater the chances for error when using an unsystematic strategy.

We have developed a program for dealing with number problems that is fast, because it leads you to the right answer by the shortest possible route, and is consistently reliable since it keeps the information to be held in working memory down to an absolute minimum. Called the Galloping V, for reasons that will become clear in a moment, it enables even the seemingly most complicated number problems to be solved with speed and ease. We are going to demonstrate the way it works on a fairly simple number problem and then show you how to apply the same techniques to more complex ones.

Find the missing number in the series:

5   9   13   ?   21

The first step when using the Galloping V is to connect each of the numbers with a series of "V"s.

Now, where possible, subtract each number from the one in front of it, moving from left to right, and place the answer below the "V" connecting the numbers

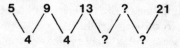

(i.e., 9 − 5 = 4; 13 − 9 = 4; which is as far as we can go with the blank there). We see that this leaves us with a 4 beneath each of the first two "V"s. Because of the position of the missing number we cannot tell what will go beneath the last two "V"s. If you want to check this simple piece of math all you have to do is *add* the number in the series to the number beneath it at the tip of the V.

This gives us 5 + 4 = 9 and 9 + 4 = 13. It also points us toward the missing numbers. Since the first two "V"s were completed with differences each equal to 4 it seems a fair bet that the last two "V"s can also be completed using a 4. So let's try replacing the question marks with this number.

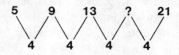

Remember, however, that for the moment it is only a tentative conclusion which will have to be checked.

What happens if we continue to add the numbers in the series to the number at the tip of the Galloping V? Clearly, 13 + 4 becomes 17. Similarly 17 + 4 is equal to 21.

This tells us the answer is 17 and allows us to check it by making certain that when 4 is added to the answer, it produces the final number in the series.

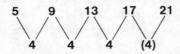

Incidentally you will find that IQ test constructors seldom make it this easy for you. The missing number can be located almost anywhere in the series. For instance, the above example might have been given to you as:

5 9 13 17 ?

or

5 9 ? 17 21

The Galloping V method is completely unaffected by such changes. You simply join the numbers with a series of "V"s in the usual way and put in the differences.
For example:

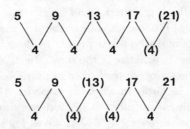

The only time you will have to make a minor adjustment to the method is if the number to be found comes at the start of a series.

For example:

	?	9	13	17	21
or	5	?	13	17	21

Start, as usual, by drawing in the "V"s and working out the differences between each number in the series.

This time, however, you *subtract* the tentative difference from the number located diagonally to its right.

A couple of worked problems should make this modification clear.

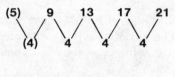

or

In the first example $9 - 4 = 5$. So 5 is the missing number.

In the second example $13 - 4 = 9$. So 9 is the missing number. We can check in this case by subtracting the remaining 4 from 9. This gives 5, which is the first number in the series, so our answer must be correct.

We have deliberately started with a simple problem so as to make the method easy to understand. Because it is easy, the chances are that you worked out the right answer without having to go through the steps described. At first, however, it is important to practice the Galloping V method on fairly straightforward number problems so that it becomes your automatic mental response to such questions. As with the other programs described in this part of the training course, practice is the most effective method for establishing these new procedures firmly in mind and we would like you to complete the problems below, applying the Galloping V even when the missing number is immediately apparent to you. Carry out the procedure exactly as described above by putting in the "V"s, making the subtractions, arriving at a tentative answer based on this subtraction, and drawing in lines around the numbers to be added together.

In some of the problems you will find that the numbers get smaller rather than larger as you progress from left to right. Since this is a variation of the series which is likely to occur in IQ tests, it will be useful to gain practice in solving such problems. You should tackle them by first reorganizing the numbers so that they increase from left to right in the normal way, i.e., 11 9 7 ? 3 should be transformed into 3 ? 7 9 11, before you start using the Galloping V. (Answers to the problems will be found at the end of this section.)

Practice Session Twelve

(a) 5   7   ?   11   13
(b) 4   ?   12   16   20
(c) 2   7   12   ?   22
(d) 0   ?   12   18   24
(e) 42   37   ?   27   22
(f) 7   16   25   34   ?
(g) 120   99   ?   57   36
(h) 0   ?   34   51   68
(i) 3   ?   19   27   35
(j) 51   74   97   ?   143

The problems we have looked at so far are among the easiest you will ever encounter in an adult intelligence test. Only a single row of "V"s is needed to produce the solution and, because of this, they may be termed one-level problems. When designing their questions the test constructors are seldom willing to allow you to escape so lightly and will make number items harder by introducing two-level and sometimes even three-level tasks. The Galloping V method will enable you to deal with even these more complicated problems just as easily, merely by adding further rows of "V"s.

Two-Level Problems

3   5   9   15   ?   33

Before looking at our solution to this problem, try and work out the missing number for yourself. You will find that the relationships involved here are more intricate and interesting than those in the earlier series.

Start as usual by drawing in the first row of "V"s and carrying out the subtractions in the normal manner:

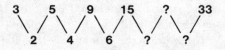

The numbers beneath the "V"s look like those you might find in a one-level problem, so treat them as such and apply the Galloping V:

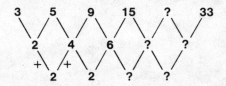

Since $2 + 2 = 4$ and $4 + 2 = 6$, it seems very probable that the numbers in the bottom line are all going to be twos. If this assumption proves correct, then the remaining missing numbers are found by addition in the usual way.

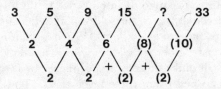

Notice that, as before, we use brackets to show that certain numbers are the result of guesswork rather than some direct mathematical process.

Now we use the Galloping V method to find the missing number:

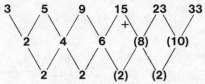

Finally we check our result with the next number following the blank:

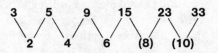

We see that the answer checks out and 23 must be correct.

We would like you to try some practice problems. You should find that after completing a few two-level problems, there is no longer any need to write in the lower line of "V"s. At first, however, we suggest you write out all your calculations in full so that you understand exactly how the Galloping V works on a more complicated series.

Practice Session Thirteen

(a)	1	5	10	16	?	31
(b)	2	4	7	11	?	22
(c)	1	4	9	16	?	36
(d)	3	6	12	21	?	
(e)	2	7	14	23	?	47
(f)	1	5	13	25	?	
(g)	0	5	15	?	50	
(h)	2	6	12	?	30	42
(i)	0	2	7	?	26	40
(j)	23	17	12	?	5	

(*Hint:* Remember to rearrange the series so that the lowest number is on the left and the highest on the right. Also remember to work from right to left when using the double-V because the missing number will now be at the start of the series. Check back to the start of this section if you are uncertain of the method.)

Three-Level Problems

In our intensive studies of all kinds of IQ problems we have come across many tests which went further than the two-level number series and required yet another row of "V"s to be added before an answer could be found. But once that step is taken, the solution becomes obvious and you can handle them exactly as you would the two-level series, except that there is an additional row of numbers to work on.

We have never found a test which included a series problem that went beyond the three-level stage. So here's an important rule for drawing in the "V"s. Stop drawing them in when the bottom row contains *only the same number.* You will notice that in the last two-level example we worked through, our second row of "V"s gave us two 2's; as they were identical, we stopped drawing any more "V"s.

If you remember this simple rule, you will never try to turn a two-level problem into a three-level task. Also *if you arrive at the third row and no repetition occurs in the last set of numbers, you can safely assume that some method other than simple addition has been used to construct the problem.* We will explain how to tackle this type of series in a moment. But first, since three-level problems do show up in IQ tests it would be good to have some fun getting the upper hand on them.

Here is an example of what a three-level number series looks like:

$$1 \qquad 3 \qquad 6 \qquad 11 \qquad 19 \qquad ?$$

Before reading on, try and come up with the answer using the information you have gathered so far.

Here is the full diagram. If your own Galloping V result looks like this, then congratulations. If you made a few errors, notice why they occurred but do not become discouraged since like any unfamiliar skill, using this method takes a little practice to perfect. Learn from your mistakes and check back over the procedures we have described to make certain you have grasped the key steps involved:

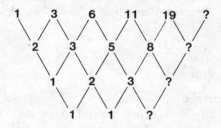

As you can see, the three-level problem simply requires you to add another row of "V"s, but its solution, once this is done, works just as before and should cause you no more trouble than the two- and one-level series.

Make an inspired guess that the missing figure on the last row is another 1, and write this in as a tentative difference.

If you are correct in your assumption, then the missing number in the second row becomes a 4. Remember, you always add the number in the series to the number to its right along the diagonal, so write in 4 as the second tentative difference.

Now add (4) to 8 to fill in the next blank. It gives us a tentative difference of (12).

Finally add 19 to (12)—the number to its right along the diagonal—to produce 31 as the required answer.

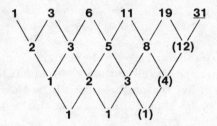

Here are a few three-level problems for you to brush up your Galloping V skill. You will find the answers at the end of this section.

Practice Session Fourteen

(a) 3 5 8 13 21 ?
(b) 2 5 9 15 24 ?
(c) 0 1 5 13 26 ?
(d) 1 2 4 10 23 ?
(e) 2 4 7 12 ? 32

When the Numbers Don't Add Up

So far, we have looked at number series formed by addition, but what happens if they fail to add up because the psychologist creating the question has used some process other than addition from one number in the series to the next? Just to keep people taking IQ tests on their toes, test constructors occasionally use multiplication to produce a series. For example:

3   6   12   24   ?

If you look at these numbers carefully, it is apparent they *double up*, moving from left to right, so to find the missing number all we have to do is multiply 24 by 2, which gives 48 as the answer.

Writing the problem out using the Galloping V system, we get:

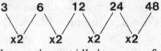

Any time a number series *rapidly* increases from one number to the next, you may reasonably suspect that a multiplication series is involved. For example:

1   3   9   ?   81

Here the jump is so large between the third and final number it is clear that multiplication rather than addition has to be involved.

In the series below the multiplication is by three, and written out in the Galloping V format it looks like this.

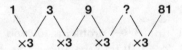

This gives $3 \times 9 = 27$. Since $3 \times 27 = 81$, we know that the answer is correct.

It is usually easy to tell whether multiplication or addition has been used to construct the problem because of the way the numbers increase in value.

The rule to follow, therefore, is this:

1   3   5   <u>7</u>   9

1   3   9   <u>27</u>   81

1. If numbers increase in value slowly, then it is probably a series based on addition.

2. If numbers incease in value rapidly, then multiplication was likely to have been used.

You can instantly recognize that addition rather than multiplication has been used when the series starts with a zero, as in questions (d) and (h) of Practice Session Twelve. Since any number multiplied by zero equals zero, you can at once see that the series cannot have been formed by multiplying each term it contains by a constant.

When performing calculations on problems in which multiplication has been used, you *divide* rather than *subtract* each number from its neighbor, going from left to right. We will work through an example together so that these simple modifications to the familiar Galloping V become clear. In this problem we are going to provide most but not all of the information necessary to complete the series.

Find the missing number:

1   4   16   ?   256

Noticing that the numbers increase sharply in value, we realize at once it is a series based on multiplication and that division rather than subtraction will be needed. After drawing in the "V"s, we get the following second level of numbers by dividing:

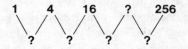

(Answer)

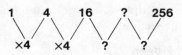

Next we make an inspired guess that all the numbers in the second row will be a 4.
This gives us:

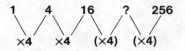

Now we find the missing number by . . . . each number in the series by the "V" number on the diagonal to its . . . . (multiplying; right)
This gives us:

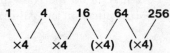

Finally we check the answer by . . . . the number we have come up with by . . . . If it is correct, we should get . . . . This will confirm the solution.
(multiplying; 4; 256)

In the problem above, the same number was used for each of the multiplications, but there is no reason why the test constructor should not use two alternating multipliers, as in the following series:

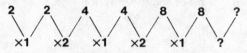

Here the answer is clearly 16.

Once you are aware that this variation can be employed, it becomes easy to identify those occasions when multiplying by the same number is not going to produce the series. As this is a fairly rare type of problem, you are unlikely to encounter it in most IQ tests, but if you do, a little thought enables the Galloping V to be used as effectively as for any other series.

If any lingering doubts about multiplication series remain, we suggest you go through the worked problem a few times until the method for applying the Galloping V to these items becomes completely familiar. When you are confident of your ability, try your new skills on the practice problems below. We have included one series which was not multiplied, so watch out for our trap. Answers are at the end of this section.

Practice Session Fifteen

(a) 2   4   ?   16   32
(b) 2   6   ?   54   162
(c) 1   2   6   12   36   ?
(d) 15   21   24   30   33   ?
(e) 256   64   16   ?
(f) 7   ?   63   189   567
(g) 1   1   4   4   16   16   ?
(h) 2   4   16   ?   128   256

Big MAC Problems

There is one last type of number series problem on which the Galloping V provides a fast route to the right answer. We call it Big MAC, which means: Multiplication and Addition Calculations.

Here is such a problem together with the completed Galloping V structure. As you can see, the first and second levels involve addition, but the second and third are related by multiplication. Study this example carefully and make sure you understand how the two processes have been brought together in this series.

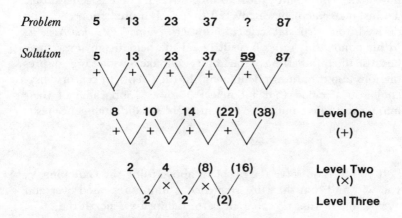

As a matter of interest you might like to work through the same example, this time using *only* addition to see how Big MAC can mislead you.

The Galloping V technique allows you readily to identify Big MAC since it soon becomes clear, as you work through the levels, that addition alone will not give you the correct answer. When this happens, try multiplication, as in the worked example above, and the solution will then emerge.

Try your skill on the problems below if you want to gain some practical experience with this combination series. But, as we have explained, it is most unlikely you will be expected to tackle anything this hard in the average IQ test. This time you can find the answers at the bottom of page 126.

(a) 3 4 7 16 ? 124
(b) 3 6 10 16 ? 44
(c) 0 2 10 42 ? 512

(*Note:* Remember what we said about series which start with zero. Here you can see that this only rules out the use of multiplication in the first line of the problem.)

Fibonacci Numbers

During the Middle Ages an eminent Italian mathematician, Leonardo Fibonacci, turned his attention to rabbit breeding. Perhaps he had heard the story about starting with a pair and ending up with thousands of them, because he decided to find out exactly how many you might expect to breed over numerous generations. To his amazement he discovered that such a prediction could be derived from a special series of numbers. Named *Fibonacci Numbers* in his honor, this series has intrigued mathematicians ever since because the numbers have the ability to make a wide range of predictions about natural phenomena. In the twentieth century, psychologists decided that Fibonacci Numbers and some of their many variations would be excellent problems for intelligence tests.

1   1   2   3   5   8   ?

If you try and solve the problem above using the Galloping V, you will find that the same sequence is simply repeated over and over again, or that no coherent pattern appears beneath the "V"s.

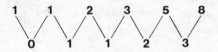

It is immediately apparent that some special technique of construction has been employed and that a different approach must be adopted. But this need give no cause for concern since such sequences actually have a very basic hidden structure.

This structure can be discovered by inspecting the arrangement and applying a little thought:

1   1   2   3   5   8   ?

Answers
a. 43. Each number under the first row of "V"s is three times larger than the number before it.
b. 26. Each number under the second row of "V"s is twice as large as the number before it.
c. 170. The first row of "V"s is an addition series, the second involves a multiplication by 4.

Here each number in the series, after the first, has clearly been derived by adding the two numbers which came before it:

$$(1 + 1) = 2 \; (1 + 2) = 3 \; (2 + 3) = 5, \text{ etc.}$$

This tells us the missing number must be 13. In putting together IQ tests, psychologists occasionally employ this principle, or one similar to it, to produce number series.

For your final practice session in this section, therefore, we would like you to solve some problems based on the Fibonacci Numbers idea. If you attempt to use the Galloping V, it quickly becomes clear that it will not produce a sensible answer. (You might like to try it on some of the problems below and see what happens.)

Instead, you need to search for some relationship where each number in the series is determined by directly combining some of the numbers which come before it.

Practice Session Sixteen

(a) 1   3   4   7   11   ?
(b) 0   4   4   8   12   ?
(c) 1   2   2   4   8   ?
(d) 1   3   4   8   15   ?
(e) 2   3   6   9   54   ?

Most of the number problems you will encounter in IQ tests can therefore be seen to fall into just four basic categories:

1. *Number Series Based on Addition*
You can identify them by the way in which number values increase and tackle them using the Galloping V. Variations on this theme include two- and three-level problems, but all can be resolved quickly using this technique.

In some series the numbers will be arranged so that they decrease in value from left to right. Rearrange these before applying the Galloping V so that they now increase from left to right, then deal with them in the usual way.

2. Number Series Based on Multiplication

These can be identified by the fact that the number values increase sharply. They may consist of two or three levels and, again, numbers are sometimes arranged in reverse order to make them appear more complicated. Rearrange, where necessary, and apply the Galloping V in the normal manner. Remember there is no rule which obliges the test constructor to multiply by the same amount each time in the series. He may alternate the multiplication.

3. Big MAC (Multiplication and Addition Calculations)

The hardest of all number series, these are likely to be found in only the toughest intelligence tests. They can still be tackled using the powerful Galloping V technique, which also allows you to identify them by making explicit the point at which addition cannot lead to the correct answer.

4. Fibonacci-type Numbers

Galloping V produces only a repetition of the original series or an apparently random string of numbers. The answer must be found through inspecting the sequence and identifying how each number is generated by those which come before it. Once they are identified as such, Fibonacci Numbers pose few difficulties and the missing value can usually be determined quite rapidly.

Remember that in any series which starts with a zero, *every* other number would be zero if multiplication were used, so it must be based on addition.

Finally, a good rule of thumb for these—and indeed, for all other kinds of problems—is that the simplest solution is always the best. As you arrive at each level of the Galloping V ask yourself the question: *Is there a single number which used either as an adder or a multiplier will complete that level and, hence lead to a problem solution?*

Now you are fully prepared to tackle any number series with ease and complete confidence. Your brain has been provided with a series of simple but direct and consistently reliable programs that lead to the right solution by the shortest route. If you are still uncertain about anything we have discussed in this section, then read through our explanations again and work on any problems you got wrong the first time. You can gain further practice by inventing your own number series, since, even though you *know* what the right answer must be, the experience gained by using the Galloping V is still helpful.

Answers
Practice Session Twelve
(a) 9 (b) 8 (c) 17 (d) 6 (e) 32 (f) 43 (g) 78 (h) 17 (i) 11
(j) 120

Practice Session Thirteen
(a) 23 (b) 16 (c) 25 (d) 33 (e) 34 (f) 41 (g) 30 (h) 20
(i) 15 (j) 8

Practice Session Fourteen
(a) 33 (b) 37 (c) 45 (d) 46 (e) 20

Practice Session Fifteen
(a) 8 (b) 18 (c) 72 [the pattern here is: one number is multiplied by 2, the next by 3, the next by 2, then 3, and so on] (d) 39 [here 6 and 3 are alternately added to the series numbers, following a similar principle to that used in (c)] (e) 4 (f) 21 (g) 64 [another alternating problem; multiplying here by 1, 4, 1, 4, 1 and so on] (h) 32

Practice Session Sixteen
(a) 18
(b) 20
(c) 32 (Each number is formed by *multiplying* the two numbers which come before it.)
(d) 27 (After the first two numbers, all the rest are formed by adding the *three* numbers which precede them.)
(e) 63 (After the first two numbers, the rest are formed by alternately adding and multiplying the preceding two numbers.)

SECTION SIX

How to Handle Face-to-Face Problems

It is, of course, impossible to list and describe every type of problem you may encounter in an intelligence test. Everything you have learned so far, however, will stand you in good stead for the majority of questions likely to be asked.

These sorts of IQ items are found in pencil-and-paper assessments which you might take as a member of a group. In some circumstances you will be tested individually in a one-on-one relationship with the tester. He or she is likely to be a psychologist, probably one specializing in educational, industrial, or clinical matters. Under these conditions it is possible for the test to include items that would not be practical where numbers of people were being tested at the same time. They are sufficiently interesting and unlike those already discussed to deserve some attention.

Number Memory

In the mid-fifties American psychologist George Miller wrote a fascinating paper for a professional journal with the title: "The Magical Number Seven, Plus or Minus Two."[23] He published the results of his research into the limitations of the *working memory*. Dr. Miller found that seven, a number which the ancients associated with magical properties, seemed also to mark the average capacity of this memory. A few of his subjects could recall nine items of information, but others could only remember five—hence his choice of title for the article.

Interestingly this upper limit seemed to relate to chunks of information, not necessarily single items. Covering a row of letters to learn very quickly, a person might only remember seven of them when they were presented in a random order, such as *s c k l u o w r c,* and so on. But if those letters were combined into groups of words (for instance, See Can Kill Love Under Out Wine Run Cat), up to seven or more *words* could be recalled with the same amount of practice. This means that from remembering only seven letters a subject might jump to a memory for twenty or more letters, provided they could be taken into the working memory in groups.

In IQ tests where the psychologist can ask you questions directly, the performance of your working memory will often be tested by your being asked to listen to a group of numbers and then repeat them back. You may be asked to say them in their original form, or, to make the task harder, in reverse order.

What happens is that the tester will start with three or four numbers, giving them at a rate of about one per second, and then tell you to repeat them. The series will increase by one until your memory is overloaded and you become confused or are unable to reply at all. As we have said, this normally occurs at between five and nine digits, with seven as the average.

Thanks to the work of Calvin Thorpe and George Rowland of the Bell Telephone Laboratories,[24] there now exists an effective strategy for greatly increasing your memory span for numbers. It is a method which relates closely to Dr. Miller's finding that you help yourself recall information by learning things in chunks.

They found that if you group sequences of digits in *threes*, the capacity of the working memory is greatly increased, so during an IQ test you would use the strategy like this. Let us suppose the tester is reading off the following numbers: 2, 3, 9, 5, 7, 4, 8, 3. As these are being given to you, say each group of three numbers very rapidly to yourself. Pause, then say the next group of three, and so on. The sequence above would be organized like this: 2-3-9 (Pause) 5-7-4 (Pause) 8-3.

This rehearsal technique allows you to repeat the sequence at least twice before you have to recall the numbers, and grouping them in threes seems to produce an arrangement that fits in extremely well with memory function.

Our own research into this technique showed that if the subjects tapped the foot in a quick rhythm of three beats: Tap-tap-tap (Pause) Tap-Tap-Tap (Pause) Tap-Tap-Tap, while repeating the numbers, this improved the working memory even more.

Rehearse this method by asking a friend to read out rows of numbers which you have not seen at a delivery rate of around one per second. After only a small amount of practice you will amaze yourself at how powerful your recall will become. Do not forget to try some of the series backward as well as forward so as to be ready if the IQ tester requires you to do this.

Block Problems

In some individual IQ tests you will be given a collection of colored blocks shaded in different ways and asked to use them to produce a design that matches either one the tester creates with his or her own blocks or an illustration on a card.

The purpose of this test is to assess your skill in breaking down a whole into its component parts. Since this is exactly what you have been doing throughout this section, you will find the block test just another variation on a familiar theme.

A typical block design is shown below:

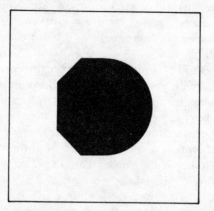

Figure 40

The secret is to split the square visually into four quarters as shown below. This can be done most easily by carrying in your mind's eye the cross pattern found in a telescopic sight. Impose this pattern over the design in order to quarter it and, using the blocks, place each of the four quarters in turn. The order in which this is done is unimportant. What matters is that by focusing on portions of the design, rather than trying to pay attention to the whole pattern, a potentially confusing task is made extremely simple.

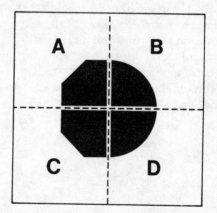

Figure 41

If you are going to take a one-on-one IQ test and want to practice this skill, we suggest you cut and shade some squares of cardboard to the design shown below and then attempt to make up the patterns in Figure 43.

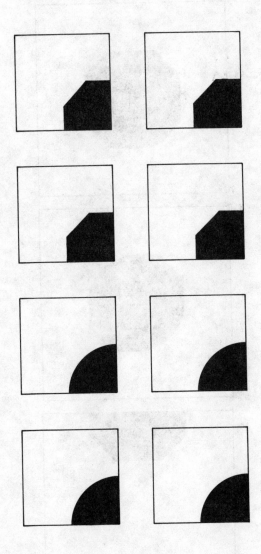

Figure 42

Make up these squares from cardboard. Now use them to assemble
the patterns below:

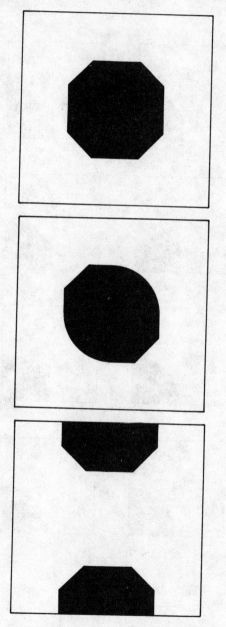

Figure 43

SECTION SEVEN

Six Tips for Succeeding with IQ Tests

If you are going to take an actual intelligence test in the next week or so, you will be particularly interested in this section. When you are faced with such an assessment, success can be made far more likely by applying all the brain programs discussed in Step Two of the course and by following this general advice on the day itself.

1. Give yourself an immediate advantage over less well-prepared candidates by arriving for the test *at least fifteen minutes early.* It is only natural to feel slightly anxious if the test is being used to assess your suitability for a job, a place on an educational program, promotion within your company, or for any other type of selection important to your future. By planning to arrive early, you avoid the additional worries of being caught up in traffic, delayed by stalled public transportation, or confused when looking for the room where the test will take place. Rushing and becoming nervous about being late is going to decrease your performance immediately. Research clearly shows that a short period of relaxation prior to a problem-solving session significantly enhances your mental ability.

When it is time to take the test, you will probably find a form containing the problems and an answer sheet lying face down on the desk before you. The administrator will read out the test instructions and tell you how much time is allowed. This is a crucial element in achieving a good score and you should immediately make a note of it.

Take off your watch and place it on the desk beside the test form so that it can be consulted easily and frequently because, to maximize your test-taking strategy, it is essential to keep track of the time remaining. If possible, use a stopwatch or one with a stop function, so that you know exactly how long you have left. In a moment we will tell you how to take maximum advantage of this knowledge.

2. Work down the list of problems methodically, but don't spend too much time on any particular problem. If you become confused because one of the questions seems especially difficult, move on, having first made a mark on the answer sheet to remind you to come back to it later. Research by Arthur Frankel and Melvin

Snyder of Dartmouth College,[25] has shown that when someone is given a problem that cannot be solved, their failure to find an answer decreases performance on subsequent problems which might otherwise have been answered quite easily. So do not wrestle in vain with anything that strikes you as too tough, as it will damage your capacity to cope with the next few problems. We'll be telling you how to deal with the really difficult questions a little later.

3. As you solve the problems, talk to yourself silently, since this helps your brain operate more efficiently as studies by Dr. M. Schadler and Dr. James Pellegrino of the University of Pittsburgh[26] have demonstrated. They found that getting people to talk to themselves about the goals of a problem and how they were attempting to solve it greatly improved performance. Our research has shown that such silent self-talk enhances concentration and leads to a more organized approach to problems.

4. When dealing with a problem which offers a set of answer options, be especially careful of choices in the fifth and third position.

Merle Ace and Rene Dawis of the University of Minnesota,[27] have discovered that where the correct choice in an IQ item is in the *fifth* position, more errors are made irrespective of the difficulty of the problem. The second most error-prone position is the third in line.

For example, in the question:

FINE is to ROUGH as GOOD is to   ?

(a)   SMOOTH   (b)   SLIM   (c)   WONDERFUL   (d)   BARK
(e)   POOR

more mistakes will be made by subjects when the right choice is in position (e) or (c). Why this should be is not certain, but one possibility is that the subject suffers a loss of concentration after making a number of careful comparisons.

To avoid the same mistake, switch around the order in which you examine options. Rather than work from (a) through to the last choice, vary your starting point. On the first problem begin with the last option, then consider the *third* one on the following question and so on.

5. We have mentioned the need to keep a careful watch on time as you work through the test. Do not be too upset if you find yourself unable to complete all the problems, as most tests are designed so that they *cannot* be completed within the period allowed.

Make the maximum use of test time by changing your tactics *five minutes* before the end. When this is all the time you have left, go back to the start of the answer sheet and begin to tackle those problems you skipped the first time. By now you will have a feel for the type of question which comes most easily and can devote your attention to any unanswered questions that fall into this category. You may well find that practice on the other, possibly easier problems has increased your skill and confidence to the point where you can readily see the solution.

6. Finally, we advise you to practice with a friend or someone else taking an IQ test, if possible. Both solving problems which the other has invented and inventing them yourself powerfully schools your mind in carrying out its problem-solving programs smoothly and successfully.

The Second IQ Test

This brings us to the end of Step Two of the training. Now is the moment to put all that you have learned into practice by tackling an IQ test of similar difficulty to the one which you took at the start of this training course.

Resist the temptation to try the second IQ test until you have carried out all the exercises in this part of the training. Make sure you really understand the programs to be followed when dealing with word, number, and various kinds of spatial problems.

As before, set aside a time when you can work without interruption for thirty minutes.

Do not turn over this page until you are ready to take IQ Test Number Two.

THE SECOND IQ TEST—NOTE THE TIME NOW
AND STOP AFTER EXACTLY THIRTY MINUTES

1.

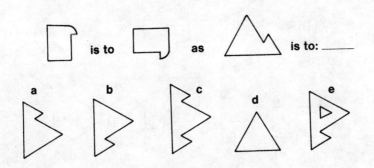

2. TRUTH is to LIE as LARGE is to: ——
   a. grow   b. small   c. falsehood   d. see   e. biggest

3. 6, 11, 16, ——, 26

4.

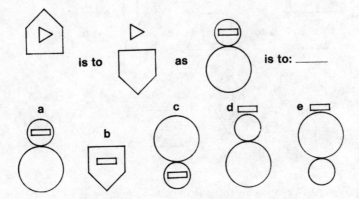

5. ALLOW is to PERMIT as CREATE is to: ——
   a. invent   b. destroy   c. license   d. undo   e. reprieve

6. 8, ——, 20, 26, 32

7.

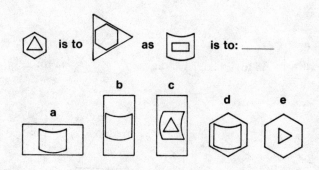

8. INK is to PRINTING as TELEPHONE is to: ——
   a. wire   b. communication   c. receiver   d. deliver   e. black

9. 3, 6, ——, 24, 48

10.

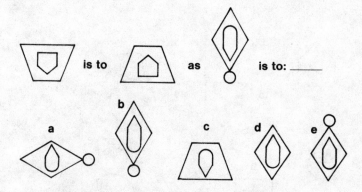

11. PREPARATION is to GROUNDWORK as ESCAPE is to: ——
    a. confinement   b. deliverance   c. intention   d. rehearsal
    e. fugitive

12. ——, 6, 18, 54, 162

13.

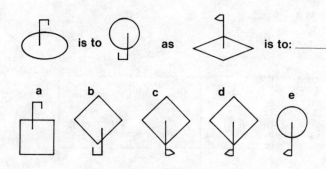

14. GIANT is to DWARF as LAKE is to: ——
    a. boat   b. puddle   c. rain   d. liquid   e. grow

15. 5, 6, 8, 11, ——, 20

16.

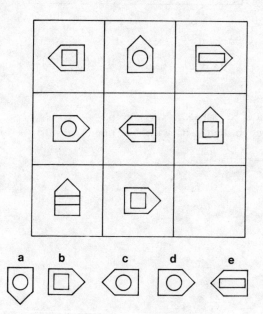

17. PAPER is to APPLAUSE as OBOE is to: ——
   a. boor   b. flute   c. reed   d. telescope   e. clever

18. 1, 3, 7, 13, ——, 31

19.

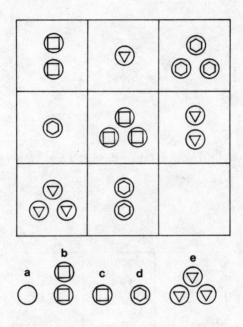

20. HARBOR is to OCEAN as GATE is to: ——
   a. hinge   b. field   c. swing   d. open   e. ship

21. 2, 5, 11, ——, 32, 47

22. Complete the series.

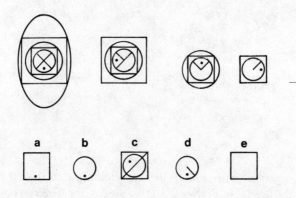

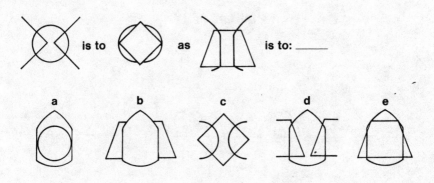

23. COMPLETE is to UNFINISHED as CERTAIN is to: ———
    a. sure   b. incomplete   c. true   d. possible   e. foreseen

24. 5, 7, 10, 15, ———, 35

25.

26. STOCK is to INVESTMENT as ANGER is to: ———
    a. emotion   b. calm   c. sincere   d. pity   e. continue

27. 0, 4, 10, 20, ———, 50′

28.

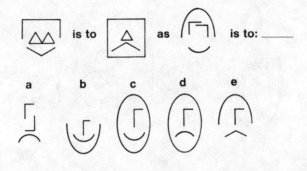

29. Choose the word which does not belong with the others.
    a. matured b. digested c. ripened d. labored e. wrought

30. 0, 1, 4, 11, 26, ——

31.

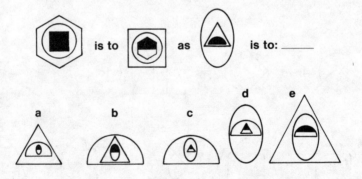

32. Choose the word which does not belong with the others.
    a. tray b. envelope c. frame d. basket e. pail

33. 1, 4, 5, 9, 14, ——

34.

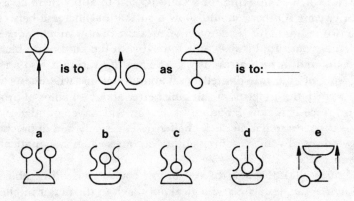

35. SELDOM is to TINSEL as NOTARY is to: ———
   a. ought   b. imbibe   c. lawyer   d. scribe   e. cannot

36. ———, 7, 9, 16, 25, 41

Answers

Problem Number	Answer	Problem Number	Answer	Problem Number	Answer
1	b	13	c	25	b
2	b	14	b	26	a
3	21	15	15	27	36
4	e	16	c	28	d
5	a	17	a	29	d
6	14	18	21	30	57
7	b	19	c	31	b
8	b	20	b	32	c
9	12	21	20	33	23
10	e	22	b	34	d
11	b	23	d	35	e
12	2	24	23	36	2

To determine your new IQ as measured by this test, check your total score against the IQ chart given earlier. Then subtract your score on the test in that chapter from the score on the test you have just taken. This will tell you exactly how much your IQ performance has improved.

If you have followed the brain programs we described and been careful when completing the second IQ test to apply them consistently, your IQ score should show a substantial increase between the two results. This is an objective measure of how much more efficiently your mind is now able to deal with the kind of problems encountered in such assessments. The new IQ rating is also a fair measure of your raised intellectual ability, not just where tests are concerned, but in terms of thinking better about all kinds of problems, since it is now far more likely you will have confidence in your capacity to handle such challenges effectively and appreciate how powerful your reasoning ability becomes when systematically organized.

As you work through the rest of this course you will be able to apply the same precise and logical approach to the major intellectual tasks of learning, problem solving, and decision making.

Most psychologists, including ourselves, regard these as the key components of intelligence. The more efficiently you are able to learn, solve problems, and make decisions, the higher your IQ. Therefore, you become more intelligent by acquiring more brain programs for thinking better when dealing with such mental activities. It is important to understand that your improved performance in all these areas, the natural outcome of following this training course, is not based on a series of tricks or cunning strategies that somehow enable you to sidestep thinking. You are actually mastering the skills needed to do such thinking in the most effective manner possible.

STEP THREE
Thinking Better About Learning

In this part of the course we are going to show you how to give your brain the programs necessary to make learning as accurate and effortless as possible, no matter what subject you are studying. This can be achieved through an understanding of two key factors on which better thinking depends. The first is your personal learning style, the way your mind likes to work best when trying to learn anything new. This will be assessed by means of a special questionnaire and you will then be provided with the techniques necessary to use this style to greatest advantage. The second key to success, the organization of material prior to any learning taking place, has been identified as the single most important difference between good and bad learners.

There is no need to try and *remember* any of the techniques described in this part of the course; indeed any attempt to do so could well lead to confusions when you began to put the procedures into practice. We have found that the surest method for assimilating the information is to read through it in a relaxed way, identifying your personal learning style and then noting how this dictates the overall arrangement of material to be mastered. The next time you have anything to learn, refer back to this step of the course and follow the techniques described carefully. By doing so you will find that the time needed to remember new knowledge is greatly reduced (by up to 50 percent in some cases, our studies have shown) and the accuracy of recall enormously enhanced. In many cases it will be possible to attain 100 percent accuracy of information retrieval over extended periods with far less effort than you might now believe possible.

The Secrets of Successful Learning

When the great nineteenth-century French novelist Gustave Flaubert commented that: "Everything from talking to dying must be learned,"[28] he was expressing a profound yet seldom recognized truth about human behavior. With the exception of a relatively small number of inborn responses, *we are what we learn*. That is to say, all we think and feel, attempt and accomplish, strive for or avoid, comes about as a result of learning.

When considering learning, however, most people think in terms of the more formal studying carried out at school or in college and from practical experience when performing our everyday work. In this sense, especially, it has long been assumed that the ability to learn reflected an individual's general level of intelligence. The seemingly common-sense belief, largely shared by psychologists, was that the brighter you were, the more rapidly you acquired new knowledge and the more accurately you were able to recall it. It was not until fairly recently, when researchers made a careful analysis of the way in which learning occurs in educational settings, that the falsity of this apparently plausible explanation was revealed.

Learning, it is now clear, is not an innate and largely fixed mental ability related to levels of intelligence, but a series of skills that have to be mastered and perfected if effective learning is to take place. In other words, *we have to learn how to learn,* and if previously poor students are provided with these missing lessons their performance immediately, substantially, and permanently improves.

That so many people learn poorly when confronted by formal studying is really not at all surprising if you consider the haphazard manner in which the skills have to be acquired. We are never taught in any systematic way how to learn, but have to pick up the necessary techniques as a result of experience, from watching others performing certain tasks, by following rules for rote memorizing, and out of the mistakes we make. Such methods are not merely inefficient; they are frequently extremely damaging to performance. The child who, simply because learning skills have been poorly developed, consistently makes mistakes and receives reprimands is very likely to become anxious about all learning activities and develop negative attitudes to all intellectual activities. Some people do manage to develop learning strategies sufficiently effective for them to achieve their academic and professional ambitions, but they are still probably not using their brains as efficiently as they might. Many more fail to devise sufficiently reliable study techniques and so fail to gain the grades and pass examinations necessary to fulfill their ambitions. If you feel that your learning skills are not as good as they might be, then do not fall into the trap of attributing past failures to any lack of natural ability. We will teach you the simple but potent procedures needed to master any new knowledge rapidly and reliably. Each of the techniques you are about to learn has been found to double or even treble learning performance when used *on its own*. In this training program we have brought them together for the first time to produce one of the most powerful systems for learning how to learn ever devised.

Assessing Your Personal Learning Style

The starting point on the road to successful learning is to discover how your brain likes to learn. Each of us has a personal style which has to be taken into account when organizing our study methods and you can discover yours by completing the assessment below. Simply select the statement that corresponds most closely to your own approach to learning:

1. When studying an unfamiliar subject do you:
   a. Prefer to gather information from many topic areas?
   b. Prefer to stay fairly close to the central topic?

2. Would you sooner:
   a. Know a little about a great many subjects?
   b. Become an expert on just one subject?

3. When studying from a textbook do you:
   a. Skip ahead and read chapters of special interest out of sequence?
   b. Work systematically from one chapter to the next, not moving on until you have understood earlier material?

4. When asking other people for information about some subject of interest do you:
   a. Tend to ask broad questions which call for rather general answers?

    b. Tend to ask narrow questions which demand specific answers?

5. When browsing in a library or bookstore do you:
    a. Roam around looking at books on many different subjects?
    b. Stay more or less in one place, looking at books on just a couple of subjects?

6. Are you best at remembering:
    a. General principles?
    b. Specific facts?

7. When performing some task do you:
    a. Like to have background information not strictly related to the work?
    b. Prefer to concentrate only on strictly relevant information?

8. Do you think that educators should:
    a. Give students exposure to a wide range of subjects in college?
    b. Ensure that students mainly acquire extensive knowledge related to their specialties?

9. When on vacation would you sooner:
    a. Spend a short amount of time in several different places?
    b. Stay in just one place the whole time and really get to know it?

10. When learning something would you rather:
    a. Follow general guidelines?
    b. Work to a detailed plan of action?

11. Do you agree that, in addition to his/her specialized knowledge, an engineer should know something about some or all of the following: math; art; physics; literature; psychology; politics; languages; biology; history; medicine? If you agree and select *four or more* of the subjects, then score an "a" on this question.

    Now total up all the "a"s and "b"s.

What the Test Tells You

    The eleven questions above have been adapted from the researches of Gordon Pask,[29] one of Britain's foremost educational researchers and computer scientists, who set out to find ways of matching teaching techniques to individual learning needs. Volunteers were given a series of specially designed tasks and their performances were carefully monitored. When the results were analyzed, Professor Pask found that the majority of his subjects used one of two very different approaches.

These are the styles of learning assessed by the test you have just taken. Your score will place you in one of two categories of learners we call *Stringers* and *Groupers*.

If you scored six or more "a"s on the test, you are a Grouper; six or more "b"s and you are a Stringer. The higher your total of either "a"s or "b"s, the stronger your Grouping or Stringing tendencies are, and the more closely the descriptions below illustrate your learning methods.

Groupers

This style of learning involves taking a broad view of any subject under study. Groupers prefer to search out general principles rather than meticulous details and relate one topic to as many other areas of knowledge as possible. They are quick to find relationships and to draw parallels among different areas of study.

Groupers learn most easily and effectively in unstructured situations and do less well if everything is presented according to some rigid plan. Because they are able to bring together a wide range of information, they are likely to prove more successful than Stringers when an all-around approach is required.

As Professor Pask points out, however, much current teaching—at all levels—is not presented in this way. Lesson plans, textbooks, and training schemes, whether in the factory, the university, or the classroom, are usually designed in a systematic, step-by-step manner that favors Stringers. This approach works to the disadvantage of Groupers, who prefer to come to grips with overall principles before getting down to the finer details of a topic.

Stringers

As we have suggested in the comments about Groupers, a systematic, methodical approach best suits the learning style of Stringers. The exact opposite of Groupers in many ways, they learn most successfully by mastering specific details before moving to more general concepts.

Their best approach is to establish a series of clearly defined goals that allow knowledge to be accumulated gradually. Only facts directly related to the topic under study should be considered, while less relevant information, no matter how interesting in itself, must temporarily be ignored. Stringers tend to achieve good grades in college because the highly structured nature of most academic work favors their particular style of learning.

The higher your "a" or "b" score the greater your need to follow a Grouper or a Stringer method of learning. If your style is primarily that of Grouping, then read the section below before turning to page 154; if you are a Stringer, then turn to page 156 and read through Section Two.

SECTION ONE

How Groupers Learn Most Successfully

The work of Professor Pask has revealed that, as a Grouper, you should start out by studying general concepts and gain a good understanding of the broader issues before getting down to finer details.

The best advice is to dive right in at the deep end without spending very much time on preparation. All you need to do before embarking on a course of study is create a fairly simple plan that ensures that the wider issues are fully explored.

To illustrate how this approach might work with a specific topic we are going to look at how a Grouper could best approach the study of photography, a subject chosen because it is of equal interest to men and women and combines both technical and creative concepts.

Your starting point would be to read books and magazine articles, not only on such technical matters as camera function and how a film produces its image, but also on practical applications of photography in news work, fashion, and industry.

Far from proving confusing, this approach will match your learning style and make progress more rapid as links are created in the brain between different aspects of the subject. This approach is known as *Top Down Learning* and a plan of action might look like this:

Figure 44

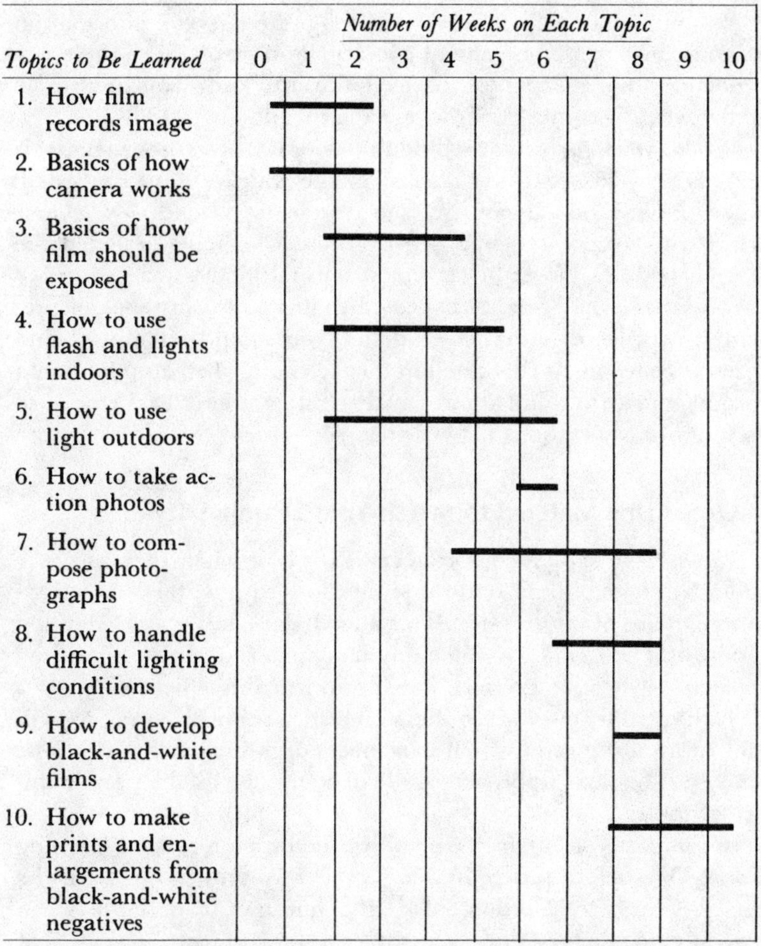

Topics to Be Learned	Number of Weeks on Each Topic										
	0	1	2	3	4	5	6	7	8	9	10
1. How film records image	━	━									
2. Basics of how camera works	━	━									
3. Basics of how film should be exposed		━	━	━							
4. How to use flash and lights indoors		━	━	━	━						
5. How to use light outdoors		━	━	━	━	━					
6. How to take action photos						━					
7. How to compose photographs					━	━	━	━			
8. How to handle difficult lighting conditions							━	━			
9. How to develop black-and-white films								━			
10. How to make prints and enlargements from black-and-white negatives								━	━	━	

If you are interested in finding out how a Stringer would approach the same learning task, you should compare this program with that on page 158.

As you can see, Top-Down Learning involves a considerable overlap between the topics, with several aspects of photography being studied at the same time. Since your natural learning style causes you automatically to form myriad mental associations among different items of information, this will prove the fastest and most effective way of acquiring the necessary knowledge.

You must take care, however, not to ignore essential information as you concentrate on general concepts and ideas, since there is a tendency among Groupers to excel at overall knowledge, but to be shaky when it comes down to specific details.

When working on a self-administered study program, it is usually easy to organize material in the way we have suggested. But this may not always be true if you are attending a course where the structure is imposed by those who have designed the study schedules. Nevertheless, you can usually exert a fair degree of control over what you are expected to learn. For instance, if presented with lectures that stress detail, you should attempt to find general concepts to tie these into. Take time, when studying on a formal course, to think about how each item relates to the next, so as to build associations betwen them.

Organizing Material to Match Your Learning Style

As we have explained, Groupers learn best when they can take full advantage of their natural ability to form mental connections among items of information. This knowledge enables us to develop a powerful program by which any new material can be organized in such a way as to produce maximum learning efficiency.

To illustrate how you set about creating such a program, we will look at an instance in which four pieces of information have to be learned. The same approach could, of course, be used for any number of topics.

In the past you might have approached such a task by learning Topic One before proceeding to Topic Two and so on down the list. Research by Gordon Pask, and our own experience when teaching people how they can best learn how to learn, reveals that this seemingly straightforward approach actually impedes retention and recall. To obtain the best results, Groupers should organize the material as follows:

Learn the first two items separately and then rehearse them *together*. Now do the same with the third and fourth topics, repeating the previous rehearsal procedure. Return to the first two topics, go through them in your mind and carry out the same recall technique on topics three and four. Finally rehearse all four items to-

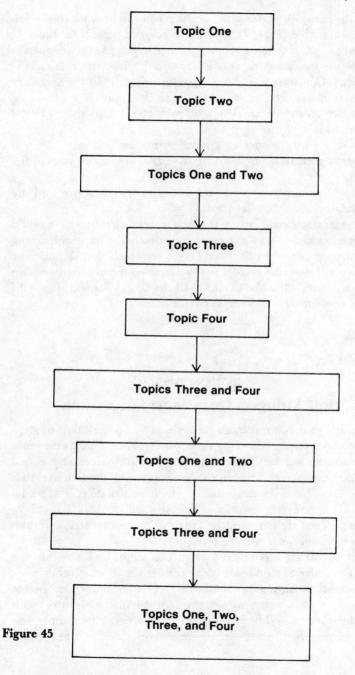

Figure 45

gether. If learning about photography you might work to the following timetable (Fig. 47) in order to acquire basic techniques.

You can go on to learn as many other topics as you like merely
by selecting four more areas of study and dealing with them in the
same way. Continue to expand the schedule until all the necessary
information has been acquired or the session is at the end.

As a Grouper there are two basic rules you should always follow
in order to learn successfully:

One—Start by considering general principles and get a grasp of
the overall picture before starting to master specific aspects of the
subject.

Two—Organize your study schedules as shown above and use
the rehearsal sequence specified.

These strategies will ensure that the information being studied is
organized in such a way as to match perfectly the natural learning
style of your brain. In Section Three, to which you should now
turn, we will describe further easily acquired techniques to ensure
that, no matter what the demands of the task, your learning skills
will be consistently rapid and reliable.

SECTION TWO

How Stringers Learn Most Successfully

Because your natural learning style favors a methodical, step-
by-step approach to gathering facts, you will learn most efficiently
by constructing a very careful plan of action before any actual
studying takes place. This imposes a structure on the material that
gives you control over the order in which information is to be acquired. Our research has shown that it is uncertainty about how
best to proceed that creates the greatest anxiety in Stringers, and
this strategy eliminates all uncertainty.

Start by taking a detailed look at the major topics within the
subject in order to gain some idea of the order in which they must
be mastered. In most areas of knowledge, material to be learned at
a later date is in some way dependent on information or skills
gained earlier on. While learning to drive a car, for example, one
has to know how to start the engine and operate the brake, gears,

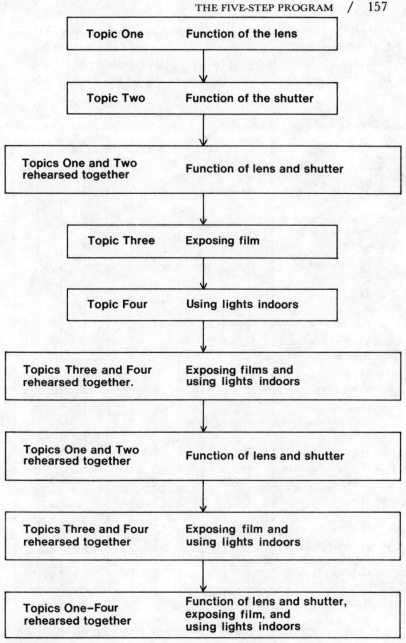

Figure 46

and clutch before attempting to gain practical experience of driving in heavy traffic.

When studying photography, an initial learning plan designed to give you a general understanding of the subject could look like this:

Figure 47

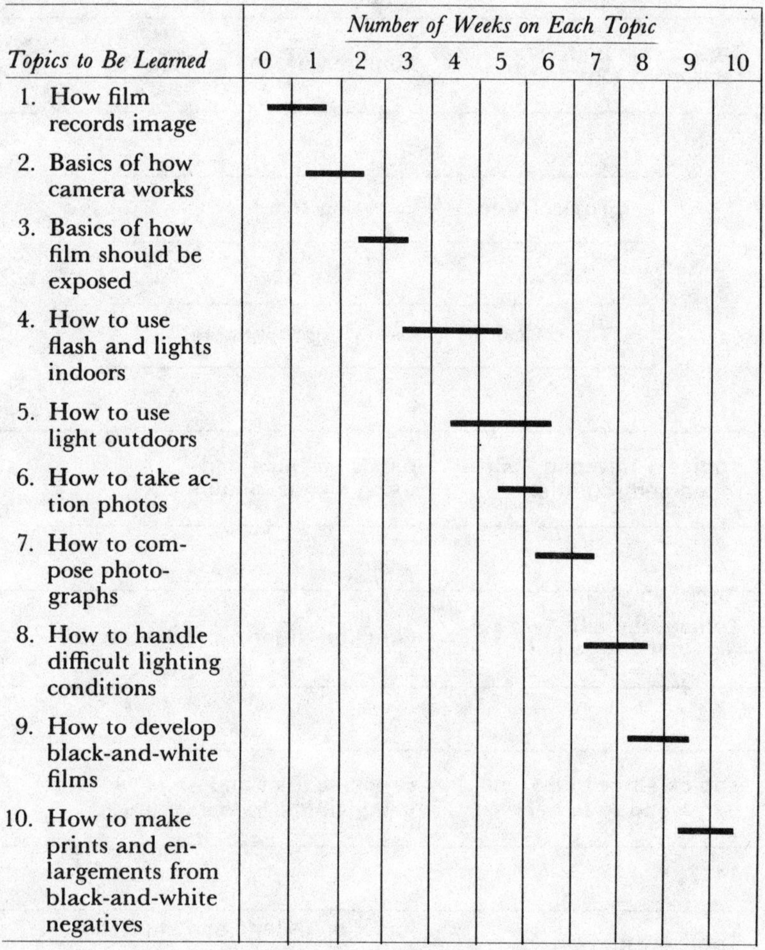

Topics to Be Learned	Number of Weeks on Each Topic
	0 1 2 3 4 5 6 7 8 9 10
1. How film records image	▬ (0–1)
2. Basics of how camera works	▬ (1–2)
3. Basics of how film should be exposed	▬ (2–3)
4. How to use flash and lights indoors	▬ (3–5)
5. How to use light outdoors	▬ (4–6)
6. How to take action photos	▬ (5–6)
7. How to compose photographs	▬ (6–7)
8. How to handle difficult lighting conditions	▬ (7–8)
9. How to develop black-and-white films	▬ (8–9)
10. How to make prints and enlargements from black-and-white negatives	▬ (9–10)

If you compare the above schedule to the learning plan for Groupers on page 153, you will see that there is little overlap between items and the information is acquired one step at a time. You should adopt the same approach no matter what subject is being studied because this is the way you can best match your natural style to the material being learned.

This way of organizing material matches your brain's need to proceed methodically from one topic to the next, only moving on when earlier information has been fully understood. Because this approach builds knowledge progressively, it is known as *Basement-Up Learning* and contrasts markedly with the overlap of information needed by Groupers in their Top Down system of learning (see page 152).

Start by mastering specific facts and only then move on to learn more general concepts. When studying photography, for instance, this would mean acquiring a clear understanding of technical matters such as how each part of the camera works and the way in which exposure to light produces an image on the film. Once basic technique has been grasped, it is possible to consider photography in its wider applications, by looking at the work of sports, magazine, fashion, and portrait photographers, for example. Prepare a study plan that lists the key topics to be covered and indicates the period of time over which learning has to take place. If you are attending a formal course of study, then be sure to get hold of a detailed schedule so that you know in advance the areas included and can develop this information into a Basement-Up Learning timetable. In this you will almost certainly be assisted by the fact that most well-planned courses build up a student's knowledge in the systematic manner most favored by Stringers. As we have already mentioned, this gives you a big advantage over Groupers, who generally find academic programs less suited to their natural learning styles.

After a few weeks, review your plan to ensure that you are still on target and make any modifications that may be necessary in the light of experience. You should find that learning the material presents few difficulties if you adopt the study procedures described below. But keep in mind the important caution that your learning style, although beneficial in many ways, also contains one potential weakness that could reduce overall success. Because your mind is especially good at grasping specific details and forming associations between groups of facts, there is sometimes a tendency to overlook equally essential broad concepts. A perpetual hazard to the Stringer is that he or she will fail to see the woods for the trees. You can easily avoid this danger by making notes on your learning schedule to remind you of general principles and overall concepts to be studied toward the end of the study program once a large body of basic information has been accumulated.

While nobody likes to make mistakes when learning, research by ourselves and Gordon Pask has shown that such errors are likely to prove more damaging to Stringers than to Groupers, undermining motivation, reducing confidence, and increasing anxiety. For this reason, it is important for you to minimize the likelihood of your making study errors by adopting a procedure known as Profragging. We will be describing this invaluable technique more fully in the next section of the training program, but essentially it is a means of breaking down information to be learned into component parts sufficiently small to be easily understood and readily remembered. By ensuring that every step you take when acquiring knowledge matches your intellectual stride, you avoid taking a mental tumble and perhaps damaging your ability to learn. Profragging produces stepping-stones toward gaining knowledge that are close enough to safeguard against mistakes yet still spaced in such a way that rapid progress can be achieved.

Organizing Material to Match Your Learning Style

Our studies have shown that Stringers can double or treble their learning efficiency by steadily building up knowledge in the way we have described. This could mean, for example, that a subject which previously required one hundred hours work to attain a reasonable level of expertise might be mastered to the same extent in little over thirty hours studying. No matter what is being learned, you should proceed according to this type of schedule:
As the learning plan shows, you should first study the initial two topics separately before going over them together. Next learn Topic Three and then rehearse all three topics mentally. Finally, study Topic Four and go over this, together with the three earlier topics, in your mind. If, as will usually happen, there are more than four items to be learned, simply treat the fifth topic on the list as if it were Topic One and repeat the same study sequence.

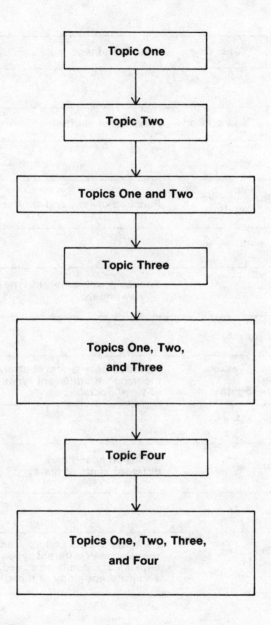

Figure 48

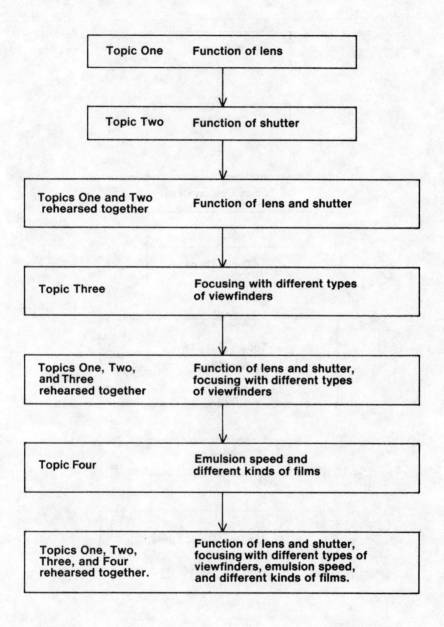

Figure 49

Using our sample subject of photography to provide a practical illustration of such a schedule, we might learn four basic techniques of camerawork according to the following plan:

As a Stringer there are two basic rules you should always follow in order to learn successfully:

One: Build your knowledge in a systematic way, starting with specific details and only going on to consider more general aspects of the subject once you have gained a sound and detailed understanding of essentials.

Two: Organize your study schedule as shown above and use the rehearsal sequence specified.

These strategies will ensure that the information being studied is organized in such a way as to match perfectly the natural learning style of your brain. In Section Three we will describe further easily acquired techniques to ensure that, no matter what the demands of the task, your learning skills will consistently be rapid and reliable.

SECTION THREE

How to Learn Like a Computer

Have you ever found an answer by forgetting about the question? Most people do occasionally. You have struggled in vain to solve a problem, remember a name, recall a phone number, or untangle a crossword clue. After all attempts end in failure, you abandon the task as hopeless. Then, unexpectedly and possibly some time later, the answer comes unbidden. You succeed by no longer trying so hard.

When this happens you have just experienced the remarkable power of your brain's *knowledge network*. This is the vast, incredibly complex mental system which links together every single item of information retained in the human memory.

While you were preoccupied with other mental activities, your mind continued to search for the elusive answer by relentlessly tracking along the pathways of that network. It was able to do this even when your brain was busy meeting new intellectual challenges, but it worked faster during sleep when the other pressures eased off. Which is why sleeping on a problem often means waking up with a solution.

If you think about how the answer finally came to mind, you may recall that, immediately prior to its arrival, the ideas in your head somehow related to the unresolved problem. This is because, as the brain neared the end of its search through the knowledge network, it began to produce information associated with the required solution.

Psychologists make use of the knowledge network to help patients recover previously lost memories through a procedure called free association. This can be helpful to learning as well, and in the next section we will explain when and how to make use of it.

If you would like to use free association in a simple experiment designed to help you explore your knowledge network, here's what to do. Start by thinking of some everyday object, an automobile, desk, table, or TV set, for instance. Now allow your mind to run free and form whatever associations it likes. Move from one idea to another without attempting to direct your thinking, and stop after about fifteen associations have been made. You will almost certainly be thinking about something very different from the starting idea. There may appear to be little or no connection between the first and last thoughts, yet your brain has established that there is a relationship by following its unique pathway.

In a series of experiments designed to investigate these mysterious pathways of the mind, Dr. Allen Collins and Dr. Ross Quillian of the University of California[30] noted how long it took people to decide whether statements made to them were true or false. They discovered that the speed of answering depended on the degree of association between the concepts involved. Where they were very close, the replies came almost instantly, but a less direct relationship produced a bigger time lag. For instance, when asked to confirm the truth of the statement: "A canary is yellow," people replied at once. But confirmation that "A canary is an animal" took longer.

If we think of these different concepts being positioned along the knowledge network, as in the diagram below, an explanation of the time differences is easy to see. Just like any other journey, the trip along the pathways of memory is faster and more certain when distances are short. As they increase, not only is more time required, but the risk of making a mistake, taking a wrong turn and losing one's way increases.

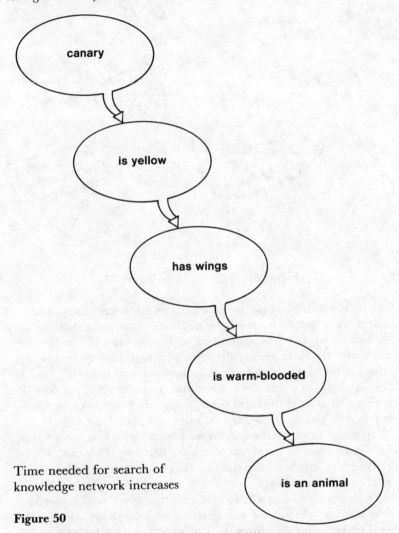

Time needed for search of knowledge network increases

Figure 50

At the start of this chapter, we explained that disorganized, haphazard learning produces ineffective storage, recall, and understanding of information, a failure illustrated in the drawings below (Figures 51 and 52).

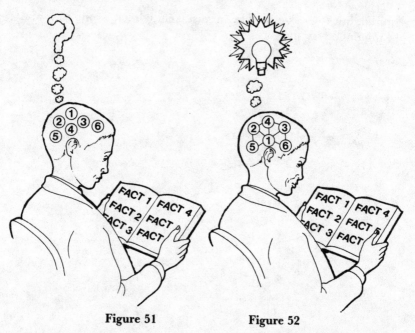

Figure 51   **Figure 52**

This is a simplified picture of what actually takes place, since no matter how poor the learning methods, some relationships *are* formed between the new material and everything else in the network. But the links are usually unhelpful and inadequate because they are indirect. Instead of producing a clearly defined pathway between related items, the connections meander off in random directions. It is as if to travel from New York City to Washington, one had to go via Dallas, Los Angeles, and Salt Lake City.

To recall information quickly and accurately, your brain must follow the shortest pathways along the network. This can only be achieved by imposing the right kind of relationship on the knowledge *as it is being learned.*

From our own research, and that of other psychologists, we have developed a method for constructing and using knowledge networks based on procedures used to structure data for computers. This enables you to combine rapid input and retrieval of information with the mind's unique ability to reason intuitively.

By learning to learn like a computer, you need not worry that acquiring knowledge must become a mechanical chore drained of all spontaneity and pleasure. In fact, quite the opposite will happen since you are going to *remove* most of the tedium from routine learning. At present you probably find certain necessary learning tasks rather monotonous, even when the subject itself is extremely interesting. Most people would like to speak another language, for instance, and know that they could gain great personal satisfaction and pleasure by doing so. The trouble is that mastering lists of words and acquiring the necessary rules of grammar is such a boring activity that many lose motivation and give up early.

If you have abandoned some study program for similar reasons, you should not regard this as a negative reflection on your basic desire to learn, or a comment on your natoral ability to do so. It is merely, the almost inevitable outcome of trying to remember and recall information wothout paying attention to the requirements of your brain's knowledge networks. Learning like a computer removes most of the effort and almost all the drudgery from study by liberating the mental processes from the restrictions and pressures which inefficient use of the network generates.

Creating a Perfect Knowledge Network

As before, we are going to use photography to illustrate effective learning procedures. Here we will be looking at just one aspect of the subject—the important topic of exposure technique. To learn the essential details of this area of study you would start by writing a short description of the key facts involved. Enclose this information in an oval, as shown in Figure 53 below, to create what computer scientists call a *node*. Continue to write down items of information and separate them from one another with ovals until you have exhausted all the important aspects of the subject.

The next step is to select any particular node that appears to be a logical starting point for creating the network. Choose that item of information you would need to know right off if you were to make sense of the technique, then pick a second node containing some facts which are logically related to the first, and join the two with a line. Continue to create the network by linking the second node to a third whose information, as in the first instance, bears a logical relationship to what has been said before. You go on doing this until all the nodes have been joined together and finish off the

network by linking the first and last nodes. The only difference between our example and the knowledge networks you will be constructing lies in the number of nodes involved. For the sake of
keeping the illustration straightforward, we have confined ourselves to creating just four of them, but in practice there should
normally be a minimum of at least fifteen.

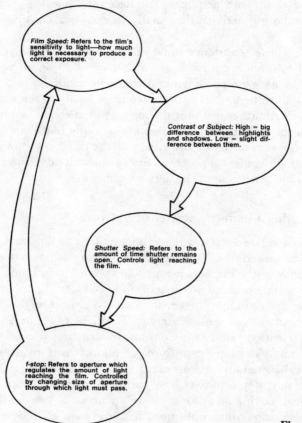

Figure 53

An important point to bear in mind when joining up the nodes
is that *there is no such thing as an incorrect knowledge network.* Connect
the nodes in any way that seems meaningful to you, because the
logical association you see between items will be the order in which
they are *best represented in your brain.* Since the perception of relation-

ships varies from one person to the next, no two knowledge networks will necessarily look alike.

To Understand It—Profrag It!

Perhaps at school you were forced to learn by rote, something which seemed totally meaningless and maybe in adult life you have sometimes done the same. You may not have fully understood what you were trying to learn but trusted to luck and your memory to somehow make sense of it in the end. Such an approach makes learning one of the most painful tasks the human brain ever has to contemplate. If it happens too often, the likely result is that you will not only despair of your ability to learn successfully but be discouraged from studying.

In order to acquire knowledge effectively, *it is essential to understand it first.* This may sound like something of a paradox because many people assume that understanding is a result of learning, but they are seriously mistaken. You can and must know what you are storing in your memory in order to do the job properly.

The key to such understanding is to break concepts into smaller and smaller parts until every confusion is resolved and all uncertainty vanishes. There is, in our view, no such thing as a difficult problem. But there are problems which can *appear* extremely difficult, just as there are subjects which *look* very complex. When this happens it is because you are trying to travel too far too fast.

If in doubt, break the topic into simpler components, and, if you are still baffled, split the concept even further. Go on doing this until you reach a point where the meaning suddenly becomes clear. When this stage is reached your understanding of the simplest element in the learning task automatically works its way back up the sequence of ideas to the original source of confusion, which is immediately resolved.

Computer scientists use this process to enable their computers to "understand" extremely complicated ideas, but our research has shown that exactly the same method can be employed to great advantage by the human brain. When subjects who had learned the procedure applied it to learning fairly complex material, their speed increased by 30 percent and the accuracy of recall by 75 percent when compared to earlier results using their haphazardly acquired strategies of study.

We call the technique Progressive Fragmentation—Profragging for short—and it may be used with any type of learning task to produce complete understanding of the subject. In the fourth step of this program, when we discuss ways of increasing problem-solving ability, you will come across a similar procedure, called Creative Carving, which allows you to come to grips with involved problems more easily by breaking them into more manageable proportions.

Profragging involves taking any aspect of the subject that remains unclear and fragmenting it by stages into information which you fully understand. In the knowledge network below, we will suppose that the notion of an "f-stop" (detailed in the last node) was causing problems. Instead of simply learning this concept in a purely mechanical way, without properly appreciating just what an f-stop is or realizing exactly how it controls exposure, you would gather sufficient further knowledge to develop a second network which looked exclusively at the topic. The result might look something like this:

As you can see, this method clarifies ideas about f-stops and ensures that the concepts are linked in a logical manner, making recall easier. This example is only intended to illustrate the general approach to creating a knowledge network and does not set out to represent all the major aspects of f-stops. It would, of course, be possible to expand the network, or to create new networks dealing with specific topics contained within the overall concept, if this aided understanding. For instance, one might want to take the idea of the camera's *diaphragm* (mentioned in the second node) and investigate aspects of this important piece of equipment still further by considering its effect on depth of field focus, automatic and manual methods of control, and so on.

The rule for Profragging is to continue to analyze the information by chopping it into smaller and smaller items, until every topic contained in each node is fully understood. Enclose the items in ovals and join them by connecting lines, as shown, so that you can move easily from one idea to the next. This not only makes association between separate pieces of information easier, aiding recall, but allows you to use the knowledge network with a simple, but powerful, learning device which we have designed. Called a Teaching Machine, it can be constructed from nothing more elab-

A Knowledge Network for the Concept of f-Stops

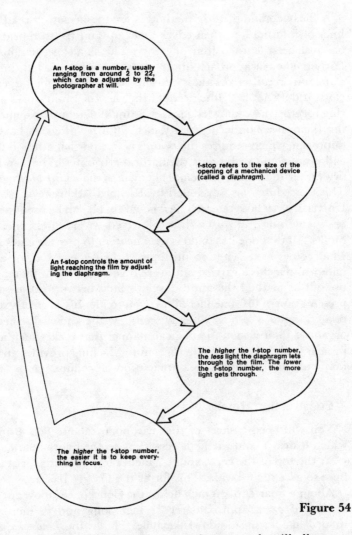

An f-stop is a number, usually ranging from around 2 to 22, which can be adjusted by the photographer at will.

f-stop refers to the size of the opening of a mechanical device (called a *diaphragm*).

An f-stop controls the amount of light reaching the film by adjusting the diaphragm.

The *higher* the f-stop number, the *less* light the diaphragm lets through to the film. The *lower* the f-stop number, the more light gets through.

The *higher* the f-stop number, the easier it is to keep everything in focus.

Figure 54

orate than a sheet of stiff cardboard and once made will allow you to absorb any new information, from lines in a play to complex technical data, swiftly, reliably, and with a minimum amount of effort.

How the Teaching Machine Works

A fairly common study method is for the person to read a few lines of information, then cover them up and try to repeat what has just been learned from memory. This is a slow, tedious, and fairly inefficient approach, more likely to lead to wasted time and numerous recall errors than efficient learning. It fails largely because it does not take into account the way the brain works in putting together new knowledge, associating different items, and storing them away under a variety of mental headings. A far better approach, which requires the brain's active participation in the recall process and works *with* the natural attributes of human memory rather than against them, is known as the *anticipation* method. This procedure was developed by Richard Atkinson of Stanford University,[31] whose research has shown that it can be used to memorize anything from lists of unconnected words to chemical formulas. All that one has to do is use one item to provide clues about what comes next. The second topic is then guessed at, or anticipated, and a check carried out to see if you were right. By repeated use of this method the mind develops links between ideas so that presentation of just one fact allows you to identify correctly all the related topics. We have already seen how the knowledge network organizes information in a logical manner that makes such an approach straightforward. The Teaching Machine provides an automatic method for using the anticipation procedure.

Construction Details

You will need a sheet of thin cardboard about 12 x 8 inches, which is drawn and then cut according to the figure below.

At the top of the card, about 2 inches from the edge, cut an ellipse some 4 inches wide. This forms the *Concept Window*.

About a quarter of an inch below the Concept Window cut out a section of card, approximately 1 inch long and ½ inch wide, shaped like an upside down keyhole. This is the *Leads To* guide.

The final parts to cut out are the three sides of a rectangle some 4 inches long by an inch wide, which should be located about ½ inch below the Leads To guide. By cutting along the dotted lines shown, you will produce a flap still attached to the card by the right side.

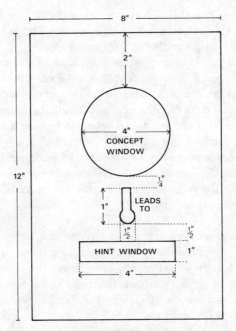

Figure 55

Draw in a *Direction Arrow* just beneath the *Leads To* guide, pointing toward the center of the opening.

The Teaching Machine is used as follows in conjunction with your knowledge network.

1. Place the Concept Window over the first node, read the information it contains, and try to recall which topic comes next on the network. If you have any difficulty in remembering, then take a guess.

2. Rotate the card, keeping the node view through the window, until the connecting line appears in the Leads To guide. If you were able to remember all, or most, of the material in the adjoining node, then slide the card along the line—using the Direction Arrow to help guide you—until the second node appears in the Concept Window and you can check to see if your recollections were correct. Now attempt to recall the material contained in the third node and, having done so, move the Teaching Machine along the network as before. You should continue to do this until every node has been recalled. If you get completely stuck and are unable even to guess at what the next node might contain, slide the card along the line until you are just able to see the top of the next

node's outer line through the opening of the Leads To guide. Lift the Hint Window, which will expose part of what has been written in the node, and use this to jog your memory.

If you are unable to recall it, even with this hint, then move the Concept Window into place and simply read the notes.

You can assume that you have mastered the topic once it is possible to recall correctly the contents of all the nodes in that knowledge network. It is usual to achieve this level of learning after only a couple of trips around the network, which is why a minimum of fifteen nodes is necessary to make the exercise worthwhile. If there are any less the learning tasks become far too easy!

To make the most effective use of this procedure bear in mind these important points:

• When preparing the nodes, write your notes using abbreviations and try to confine yourself to major items of information. A useful clue as to whether you are getting the amount of material per node correct is to ensure that all the notes can be contained within the 4-inch wide Concept Window. If there is too much information to be included, then your node is overlong and should be Profragged down to more manageable proportions.

• Make quite certain you fully understand everything that is being learned. Do not allow any ambiguity or confusion to get through because it will not only make it harder to retain, recall, and use that particular item, but will also introduce a flaw into the network that could impede the formation of clear associations. Once again, the answer is to Profrag the item and to develop further networks—or additional nodes—as needed.

• Remember that, because the network reflects the way your brain prefers to learn, you can start and finish anywhere, provided all the nodes are recalled correctly.

• When first creating your networks you may find it useful to draw outlines for the nodes—using the Concept Window as a guide—*before* writing any notes. This method ensures that all the information is contained within the right area. Work on large sketch pads or sheets of white shelf-lining paper.

The knowledge network you create externally will be duplicated within the brain, ensuring that all the topics are associated with one another in the same clear, logical manner. When you recall one topic and search for related ideas, the mind will travel along the shortest and most efficient pathways so that recollection of what has been learned will always be fast and accurate.

In our studies, previously inefficient learners have proved capable of improving their performance, both in terms of the reduction of time needed to acquire new knowledge and in the accuracy with which the material was recalled, by up to 300 percent. Even previously effective learners reported gains of more than 100 percent on many learning tasks and generally found that much tedious memorizing had been eliminated from their study practice.

There is one further learning procedure which we would like to describe, a memory enhancement technique that actually enables you to remember things better with the passage of time.

SECTION FOUR

How to Learn Twice as Much in Half the Time

Time may be a great healer, as many claim, but it is usually fatal where memory is concerned! Most people experience its damaging effect every time they try to learn something new. No matter how diligently one studies, no matter how well the material seems to have been learned a few moments after completing the task, it is not long before time begins to erode remembering. An hour after finishing the learning it may be possible to recall little more than a half or even a quarter of what was so painstakingly committed to memory. A day later, almost everything seems to have evaporated from the mind and it is almost as if the learning had never taken place.

How and why people forget things has long intrigued psychologists. A century ago they started to investigate remembering and ever since a steady body of knowledge has built up about the rate of loss and the conditions under which it is likely to occur most rapidly.

These studies have shown that people forget what they have tried so hard to remember in a way which, when drawn out on a graph, looks like this:

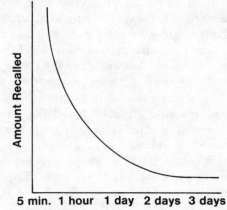

Figure 56

5 min. 1 hour 1 day 2 days 3 days
Time Since Learning Took Place

The curve that represents the rate of forgetting sweeps swiftly downward, showing that only five minutes after something has been learned a significant amount of the new knowledge is already being lost. Memory continues to suffer a rapid decline and an hour later about two thirds of all we tried so hard to remember has been forgotten. A day later, forgetting levels off at around 90 percent of loss and stays there, which means we end up retaining only some 10 percent of the information we hoped to commit to memory.

But suppose that graph could be turned upside down so that the amount recalled *rose with the passing of time.* Then we would get a situation which looks like this:

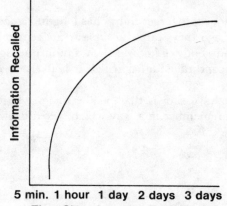

5 min. 1 hour 1 day 2 days 3 days
Time Since Learning Took Place

Figure 57

Here the passage of time is actually producing an improvement in recall, with the peak being reached two days after the studying took place. In other words, we are looking at an enrichment of memory of around the same proportions as the earlier memory loss.

Dr. Matthew Erdelyi of the City University of New York[32] is the psychologist who first showed that such a dramatic reversal of normal memory function can be achieved without too much difficulty. In his studies, volunteers found themselves remembering *twice as much* information the day after learning had taken place than they could five minutes after studying the material.

From Matthew Erdelyi's research, practical techniques have emerged that enable anyone to reverse the usual forgetting curve and remember things better as time goes by.

Suppose you have to attend a conference or lecture where it is not possible to take careful written notes, at the same time you need to remember accurately what is said for future reference. To ensure effective recall, you can easily give yourself a program that stores the information in the most efficient manner possible by adopting the following procedure.

As the session progresses make a mental note of any key points by repeating them silently to yourself. Keep a running total of the points you want to recall so that at the end you know how many separate items should be held in your memory.

Exactly *five minutes* after the session ends, find a quiet place where you can sit down, relax, and go through those key topics in your mind. Do not worry if, even in that short space of time, quite a lot seems to have been forgotten. Spend only a couple of minutes on this initial session and never strain to recall elusive items. You can, however, make an educated guess about anything you cannot bring readily to mind. Repeat each of the topics to yourself *just once*. If you are able to make a written note of the key points, this is all to the good because it enhances your memory program still further. Immediately after the recall session, however, throw these notes away, since it is the action of writing them down rather than keeping them for future reference that is important. If there is no time to make notes, do not worry; the effect of this program is so powerful that simply silently repeating and remembering each point *once* will be sufficient.

About *one hour* afterward have a second recall session. Proceed exactly as before, going through the topics without undue strain. Relax, allow your mind to focus on the items to be recalled, and repeat each one silently to yourself once only.

The third recall session should take place some *three hours later,* the next after *six hours* with, if possible, a final one just prior to going to sleep. Repeat the recall procedure three or four times on the second and third days, spacing the sessions evenly throughout the day. From then on, you can keep the material fresh in your mind by having a recall session every three or four days. There is no need to try and repeat each item in its entirety as a few key words that remind you of each topic will be quite sufficient.

Matthew Erdelyi found that most of his subjects recalled information most easily if they had been able to conjure up mental images associated with a particular key topic. It seems that the mind handles images, especially vivid or unusual ones, far more effectively than it deals with words, numbers, or abstract concepts. You can make use of this fact by forming briefly a picture of each major topic as you think about it. Try to make these images as unusual as you can and to imagine them as clearly as possible, since both these tactics further enhance retention and recall.

If you get stuck at any point, use the method of free association to jog your memory. Remain relaxed and think about the *first thing* that the *last item* you were able to remember reminds you of. This will produce an association of some kind that can be used as the trigger for another association and so on until, after eight or ten such links, one of the missing topics will usually reappear.

Because there are individual differences in the way memory functions best, you should experiment for yourself with the techniques we have described. Compare the effectiveness of using or not using vivid mental images as an aid to recall; try changing the times between retrieval sessions; use free associations on some occasions, but not on others. In this way you will be able to develop memory enhancement strategies best suited to your personal needs and so find it possible to learn twice as much in half the time.

Dangers to Avoid

There are two common mistakes frequently made by people with inefficient learning skills, which not only turn studying into a painfully tedious chore but also lead to confusion more often than comprehension.

Never attempt to carry out any learning task until you have organized the material according to the needs of your personal style and along the lines we have described. The act of structuring information in itself aids understanding and learning. People who have never learned how to learn waste an enormous amount of time striving, usually in vain, to memorize information that has been left in its original, generally unstructured form.

Finally, never fall into the trap of attempting to learn information by reading through a list of facts and then trying to recall them. Many use this tactic in the belief that it aids memory; in fact, research has shown that just the opposite is true. Unless topics are related one to the other in a clear and meaningful manner, it is an extraordinarily difficult task to retain and recall them, however much effort you put in and no matter how much midnight oil gets burned. It is, in fact, a tribute to the brain's truly remarkable learning ability that anything at all is retained through such ineffective strategies.

If you are contemplating or in the process of learning a foreign language, the information provided in the last part of this training program should prove of special interest.

SECTION FIVE

How to Become a Super Linguist

The final aspect of learning we want to consider is learning languages, one of the hardest and yet simplest tasks we ever accomplish! During infancy we can master any number of languages with ease, as children raised in multilingual households demonstrate. In adult life, however, the challenge often defeats us and we have to rely on others when traveling abroad for work or pleasure. Many people would very much like to learn another language but find themselves daunted by the enormous amount of studying necessary before even modest fluency can be achieved. When one realizes that merely to talk at the level of a six-year-old native-born speaker, a vocabulary of around 2,500 words is required, the amount of solid learning involved becomes apparent.

Our techniques can help you to become a super linguist by offering a program which allows words to be remembered with far greater ease. In a remarkably short space of time it is possible to build a large vocabulary and, with this solid foundation of knowledge, to acquire confidence and fluency far more readily than might otherwise prove possible.

One of the world's most remarkable linguists was Cardinal Giuseppe Mezzofanti, keeper of the Vatican Library during the nineteenth century, who had fluent command of fifty languages and could converse in a dozen more. It was, by any standards, a staggering accomplishment, but recent research by Richard Atkinson of Stanford University[33] suggests that, behind his prodigious ability, lay an easily acquired memory skill.

It is called the key-word method and Richard Atkinson's studies have shown that this approach can make learning any language three times faster than usual. It does so by tripling the speed with which new words are remembered, a chore normally occupying 85 percent of the time needed to acquire another language. So if, in the past it required an investment of 150 hours to remember 2,500 words, Richard Atkinson's method will enable you to reduce this to around 60 hours, or allow you to acquire an 8,000-word vocabulary in the same amount of time!

By quickly acquiring the ability to regard and use language as a living system of communication, rather than collections of words and grammar rules in a textbook, you develop a feeling for the subject that makes learning even easier and more rewarding. As you are able to order meals, reserve hotel rooms, negotiate deals, understand the literature and cinema of another country, motivation to perfect your knowledge still further is greatly increased.

This is the way you learned to speak your native tongue as a child, *by using words to make yourself understood.* At times during infancy your pronunciation and sentence construction were far from perfect, but adults generally knew what you were trying to say, and the minor errors could easily be corrected, either through direct instruction or simply by listening to the language being spoken around you.

So the secret of learning languages is to build a comprehensive vocabulary as rapidly as possible, and it is here that Richard Atkinson's key-word method comes to your aid. In the past you may have attempted to memorize new words by reading lists of them, repeating each over and over again, and hoping that a few would come to mind when needed. This, as you will realize from what we have already explained about memory function, is an extremely ineffective way of trying to retain information. The key-word method, by comparison, requires no rote learning at all and makes use of the mind's powerful ability to think in images. Numerous studies have shown that, by forming a mental picture of something to be remembered, an impression is so firmly created in the brain that forgetting becomes virtually impossible. This is a technique that can be used for many types of intellectual activity and, a little later on in the course, we will be explaining how you can exploit it for creative problem solving. Here we will give you the procedures by which mental images can raise your speed and accuracy in remembering foreign words by up to 300 percent.

How the Key-Word Method Works

To use the key-word method you need only follow two simple steps.

Step One

Start by finding an English word that sounds like part or all of the foreign word to be learned. In order to illustrate the method we are going to take two words from Spanish, two from German, and two from French, but exactly the same system could be used for words from any language.

Spanish	English	French	English	German	English
Perro	Dog	Bureau	Office	Bahn	Road
Charco	Puddle	Ville	Town	Speisekarte	Menu

We'll look at the Spanish words to start with and see how *perro* (pronounced pear-o) might be matched to an English word. A good "sound-alike" is clearly *pear* which gives us a satisfactory pronunciation. As far as *charco* is concerned, we might use *charcoal*, with the final "l" removed as a suitable match.

Bureau requires two English words to match the sounds, and we have chosen *beer row*, which, while leaving something to be desired as far as pronunciation is concerned, is a reasonable sound-alike. It will bring the word immediately to mind and the pronunciation can easily be corrected through usage. For *ville* we have selected *veal* as a sound-alike.

Barn is our chosen match for the German *bahn* while *speisekarte* requires two words, *spies* and *cart,* to produce a suitable sound-alike.

Once you have found words to match those being learned—and you should search for English *nouns* as the sound-alikes since they are easier to use as the basis for image creation—you move to the second stage of the procedure.

Step Two

Now relate the English key words to the *real* meaning of the foreign word. Use mental imagery to conjure up a scene that is as vivid and as bizarre as possible. The more unusual the picture you create in your mind's eye, the more successful the learning will prove. For instance *pear* (*perro*) might be pictured as a huge, slavering dog guarding a giant pear, or you could conjure up an image of a dog, complete with napkin and knife and fork, seated at a table eating a pear.

Charco (*charcoal*) might be envisaged as a deep puddle of charcoal through which someone is having to wade, stumbling in the depths of the puddle and getting it smeared over his clothes.

Bureau (*beer row*) could be imagined as an office stacked from floor to ceiling with cans of beer. They should be seen lined up in rows along the desks, the filing cabinets, the window ledges, and so on.

Ville (*veal*) conjures up a picture of a town whose buildings are entirely made out of slabs of pale white meat.

Bahn (*barn*) causes few imagery problems. We could picture a large barn, filled with bales of straw and constructed across a busy road so that cars hurtle in through one side and out of the other, scattering straw and frantic farmyard animals as they go.

Finally, *speisekarte* (*spies; cart*) brings to mind the curious spectacle of a group of sinister-looking men being transported in a large open cart while busily taking secret photographs of a pile of menus!

Those images may strike you as absurd, improbable, and fantastic, and they were intended to. The mental pictures not only *must* be conjured up extremely vividly—try to hear, smell, touch, and even taste the scenes as well as see them—but must be as uncommon as possible. The more extraordinary the images, the more firmly they will be remembered and the more exactly they can be recalled.

At first this may seem like a very odd way to set about learning languages. In practice you will find it is the best method for building a wide-ranging vocabulary. Professor Atkinson found that people who used his method remembered 88 percent of the words they learned, while subjects who tried to memorize them in the conventional manner could recall only about 28 percent.

Think of the six foreign language words you have just read. If they were unfamiliar to you, try to conjure up the images we described. Now match the English to the Spanish, French, and German translations in the list below:

English	Spanish	English	French	English	German
Dog	?	Office	?	Road	?
Puddle	?	Town	?	Menu	?

How many did you get right? We believe that most if not all of them came to mind as soon as you flicked up the appropriate image. If you had evolved those pictures for yourself, the learning effect would have been even more powerful. And fading of memory will not take place as quickly as by the conventional learning methods.

By devoting ten minutes a day to learning vocabulary in this manner it is easily possible to acquire between fifteen and twenty new words. As you get more practiced with the system, key words and mental images start flowing very readily. This would mean that, in just six months of regular practice, in coffee breaks, while traveling to work, or at any other spare, otherwise wasted moment, you might build a vocabulary of around 3,300 words. This is more than enough to give you good comprehension of the language and make conversation a pleasure.

If you intend to study a language more seriously, then take into account all the other essential points we have discussed. Organize the material correctly before starting. Apply the learning rules determined by your personal style. If you are a Grouper, study general concepts about the language in addition to words and rules of grammar; if a Stringer, then build your knowledge slowly but surely.

Apply the key-word method to ensure that powerful visual links are created between each word. Employ images of *things* when painting pictures in the mind, since psychological research has shown that concrete nouns are more readily remembered than abstract concepts. Create a knowledge network and use the teaching machine to develop word order, syntax, and grammar skills.

Pronunciation is best acquired from records or, even better, by talking to native speakers. There is no substitute for regular, real-life practice to perfect fluency and create self-confidence. By building your vocabulary as fast as possible, you soon reach the stage where such conversations can be both meaningful and interesting.

If you have tried without great success to learn a language in night class or from a home study course, you may have the impression that it is an extremely difficult skill to acquire. You may well have experienced a failure of learning. But, as we have stressed throughout this book, a poor performance does not necessarily reflect any lack of mental ability. Mastering a language, just like any other learning experience, involves presenting information to the mind in the most suitable form. Start working with these methods and you will find that it takes less effort, less time, and creates less risk of error than the seemingly straightforward approach you use today. Once you have found just how fast and simple learning can be when the correct mental programs are employed, you will never want to use any other system again.

Learning is one of the three main ways in which intelligence is assessed. No less important, of course, is being able to transform what has been learned into practical actions by solving problems and making decisions. In Step Four we will tell you how all kinds of problems—from the most straightforward to the most complicated—can be solved with a minimum of effort and the maximum of success by realizing your hidden intellectual potential.

Thinking Better About Solving Problems

"If you think your problems are bad," remarked a cynical government employee, "just wait until you've tried our solutions!" It's a comment that reflects a widely held and frequently well-justified belief that mankind is generally better at creating problems than finding solutions! When mistakes are made they can prove costly, time-consuming, and wasteful, yet surprisingly little consideration is given to thinking about ways in which we can think better about solving problems.

In this part of the course we are going to provide some powerful mental programs to help you eliminate errors and smooth out confusions when seeking answers to complex questions. You will be shown how to assess your personal problem-solving style—for, as with learning, there are important individual differences in the way our brains prefer to tackle problems—and then discover how to apply this knowledge to the organization of information from which a solution can be found.

The Secret of Successful Problem Solving

The real problem about problems is that we never learn any systematic procedures for finding answers to them. It is true that we are taught methods for dealing with specific problems—for example, we are given fairly precise sets of operations by which to solve math questions—but the area of general problem-solving strategies is almost always neglected. As with learning, we are expected to acquire these vital procedures as best we can from everyday experience and inevitably this results in haphazard techniques, confusion, and error. The brain is forced to work with programs that are frequently ineffective and nearly always inefficient. Instead of the mental processes leading from the problem statement to the required solution by the most direct and therefore the fastest and most consistently reliable route, the processes are usually indirect and imprecise. When handling familiar problems they are often slower and less certain than they should be and, confronted by an especially difficult or unfamiliar task, they may fail completely.

If, in the past, you have found yourself becoming confused and making mistakes when dealing with certain types of problems, the tendency may well have been to blame your brain for such setbacks. But, as we have stressed throughout the training course, this is both unreasonable and unhelpful. Your mind is quite capable of solving any sort of problem with which you may care to present it, once the correct programs for dealing with the task have been acquired.

The starting point for mastering these essential procedures is to assess your preferred problem-solving approach since, as in the case of learning, we each have one of two fundamentally different styles of solution seeking. Just as material for study must be organized in a way that best suits your personal learning style, so too is it essential to identify the way your mind likes to work when handling problems. The secret of success here, however, lies in developing *both* styles to a high level of expertise so that you can cope with the full range of problems likely to confront you. In this part of the course we will show you how to identify your personal problem-solving style and then explain how it should be used to best effect. But you will also be taught how to master the alternative approach to finding answers, a style with which you are currently less confident and familiar, and use this skill, too, with maximum effect. To make the assessment, simply note the letter beside the response below which most accurately reflects your approach to the situation described.

Assessing Your Problem-Solving Style

1. I prefer to solve most problems:
   (a) By relying on a logical approach.
   (b) By relying on hunches and inspiration.

2. If told I must follow one of the two professions, I would sooner be:
   (a) A mathematician.
   (b) An advertising copywriter.

3. I think people should solve problems by:
   (a) Careful analysis—you cannot afford to overlook details.
   (b) Thinking up a large number of possible solutions—one might work.

4. If searching for an address in a strange city I would sooner:
   (a) Look it up on a street guide.
   (b) Ask a local resident how to get there.

5. Most problems can be solved by:
   (a) A step-by-step process of elimination.
   (b) Trying out all the possible solutions which come to mind.

6. If I have mislaid something, I usually:
   (a) Search methodically through every possible hiding place until it comes to light.
   (b) First think of the places it might be and then check them out.

7. If asked for advice I usually:
   (a) Offer a few carefully considered suggestions which are almost certain to work.
   (b) Come up with a large number of suggestions which may or may not work.

8. When seeking the answer to a problem, I am most successful:
   (a) Working toward a solution on my own.
   (b) Exchanging ideas as part of a team.

9. When a piece of equipment breaks down, the best way of fixing it is to:
   (a) Take it apart, component by component, until the fault is found.
   (b) Get a general idea of what might have gone wrong before trying out suitable repairs.

Now total up the (a) and (b) responses to score your assessment. Before we explain what this reveals about your personal problem-solving style, we want to consider a situation in which finding the solution fast may literally be a matter of life and death.

Two children get lost in a remote part of the country and a search is mounted to find them. Depending on weather conditions and the type of terrain, the authorities could decide to use either or both of two methods. Groups of rescuers may be sent out on foot to cover the area where the youngsters were last seen. They will probe the undergrowth, hunt diligently through woods, explore mountain tracks and forest trails, go into caves and climb down ravines as they carry out a detailed and methodical search. At the same time that those foot searchers are scouring the countryside, rescue helicopters might be called in to survey wide areas of the terrain from several hundred feet above.

Both methods have advantages and limitations. The people on foot, using what we can call a *pathfinder strategy,* will cover the ground extremely thoroughly and are unlikely to miss the children, provided, of course, they are looking in the right places. The disadvantage is that the method is time-consuming and may bring help too late.

The *helicopter strategy* enables a great deal of ground to be covered very rapidly and, if the crews are observant and lucky, the children may be found within minutes rather than after several hours or days. But there is always a risk the crews will fail to see their quarry and falsely conclude that they have left that area.

There are, as we have said, situations in which both helicopters and foot patrols may be used to advantage. At other times only one method will be possible; for instance, searchers on foot would be needed in densely wooded countryside, but an air search is clearly essential over the ocean.

When it comes to solving everyday problems, people generally adopt one of these two approaches as their preferred problem-solving style. There are the Pathfinders, who work their way systematically through the task until they arrive at an answer, and there are Helicopter Pilots, who prefer to take a far more general view of the task and are less concerned with being methodical.

If you scored five or more (a)s on the assessment, then you favor the Pathfinder approach. This means you are likely to be careful, patient, and logical, generally intolerant of uncertainty with a dislike for hunches, ambiguity, and guesswork while seeking solutions. When faced with a problem of any type you tend to analyze the information provided in meticulous detail and proceed systematically from one conclusion to the next as you seek the answer.

If you scored five or more (b)s then you are more likely to be a Helicopter Pilot, a style which is more intuitive and less systematic in approach than the Pathfinder's. You prefer to concern yourself with a broad view of the task and proceed by intuition more than analysis. You scan the available information rapidly and come up with a number of possible solutions which can then be put to the test. By taking the wider view, you may reach a solution more rapidly than the methodical Pathfinder, but run the risk of missing an important point or overlooking essential details.

The key difference between these styles, and one which dictates the type of problem on which each is liable to prove most effective, is that while the Pathfinder sets out to discover a single, correct solution, the Helicopter Pilot prefers to search for as many answers as possible. Depending on the circumstances, either of these styles may provide the best approach. There are some problems in which the methodical tactics of the Pathfinder will enjoy the greatest success while, with others, the broader visions of the Helicopter Pilot may be essential. This is because there are not only two fundamentally different styles of problem-solving, but also two essentially dissimilar kinds of problem.

After devoting a lifetime to the study of intelligence and human reasoning, the eminent American psychologist J. P. Guilford[34] has concluded that the problems we have to deal with can, in the main, be classified as either "convergent" or "divergent." The demands they make on our intellect are quite different and so is the approach required in order to produce the best possible results. To explain the ways in which such problems differ, let us consider how such tasks might appear to that master problem solver, the great Sherlock Holmes.

The detective and his faithful Dr. Watson have been invited to New York at the urgent request of the dirty tricks division of the espionage service to advise them on a matter of grave national importance. After resting briefly in his hotel room, the sleuth is about to set off by cab for the agency headquarters, but, before leaving, he has one vital task to complete—his expense account. Since the United States Government has agreed to cover all his costs, Mr. Holmes is making sure that even the smallest item of expenditure is included in the long list which he and Watson are preparing. When each is satisfied their costs have been adequately covered, Holmes totals the amount and then converts it from pounds sterling into dollars. After checking that the calculation is correct, he slips the account into his pocket, pulls on his deer stalker, and sets off for work.

The problem Holmes so easily and pleasurably solved was a *convergent* one. All the information available, that is the expenses incurred and the rate of the pound against the dollar, were brought together to produce one, single, correct answer. There was no room for error in the solution-finding strategy because any mistake would have rendered the answer useless. All convergent problems share this key feature, and you are expected to bring the related facts together in order to achieve the required goal. The questions used in our IQ test, those included in school examination papers, and quite a number of problems faced in everyday life are convergent in nature. Many more, however, are divergent, in that the facts provided may lead to a number of possible answers, several of which could prove equally satisfactory.

As he was being briefed by the head of the agency, Holmes quickly realized he was facing just such a divergent problem, and a ticklish one at that. The facts provided for his consideration were as follows: A key agent in the organization had defected and was currently under close security in the prison of a hostile power. In a few days he was expected to give evidence in a show trial which would not only do great harm to the security of the United States but would also cause considerable political embarrassment. They wanted to silence the traitor permanently but could think of no method for doing so. Prior to the hearing, which was to be in a closely guarded courtroom from which all members of the public would be excluded, the man was being held in an antechamber on the thirtieth floor of the courthouse building. The only entrance to this room was via a steel door which was watched night and day by armed soldiers. There was no way in by the ceiling or floor and the unglazed window was protected by steel bars.

It might be possible to plant a sniper in the building across the street, but if the man was shot, the hostile power would be able to make political capital out of the assassination. The only answer seemed to be to kill him in such a way that his death remained a profound mystery to his guardians. A rare poison had been suggested, but all his food and drink were prepared under guard and tasted by officials before he ate or drank. A nerve gas had also been proposed, but there seemed no way of introducing it into the chamber, since the outside wall had no ledge along which an agent could crawl and was a hundred feet from the rooftop. After considering the facts for some minutes, the time it required to smoke two pipefuls of tobacco, Holmes offered his solution, which was immediately and gratefully acted upon. The following day the agent was found dead in the antechamber with his skull crushed, but no sign of any break-in or weapon was ever discovered. What had Holmes suggested? We will be providing our answer later on after you have had a chance to apply our techniques for solving divergent problems to this difficult case.

Divergent problems are often given to people in order to assess the flexibility of their thinking strategies when such an ability could prove essential to success in a particular career. During officer selection in the armed services, for instance, practical tests of divergent thinking form an important part of the assessment procedure. A small group of candidates might, for example, be required to construct a bridge across a ravine using some planks, rope, and oil drums. There could be any number of ways of completing this task successfully, although a few of the methods are likely to be more effective than the remainder. What the selection teams are looking for, of course, is the ability to think under pressure in an imaginative way and to lead the rest of the group toward a satisfactory outcome.

Pathfinders work most successfully on convergent tasks, where their methodical approach ensures that no details are overlooked and they are able to proceed systematically to the required solution. Helicopter Pilots, on the other hand, find divergent tasks far more to their taste because they do not have to get bogged down with small details and they can use imagination and originality in dreaming up answers. To the Pathfinder their approach is likely to seem slipshod and sometimes irrational, but they are equally inclined to consider methodical strategies tedious and needlessly restrictive. To add up his expenses correctly, Holmes needed to adopt a Pathfinder tactic, but to eliminate the traitor required the thinking of a Helicopter Pilot.

Because most people favor one method over the other, they are unlikely to feel equally confident when tackling both types of problem. As a result there is a tendency for Pathfinders to go into jobs where most problems are of the convergent variety, for example, in the physical sciences, computer technology, or engineering, while Helicopter Pilots favor the social sciences and art subjects.

In order to be completely effective as a problem solver, however, it is essential to be capable of dealing with both convergent and divergent tasks. In real life we may be forced to cope with problems that cannot be handled successfully using our preferred style, and the failure to do so correctly might one day cost us dearly. Furthermore, there is always the possibility of a problem starting out by demanding one skill, but changing halfway along and requiring a completely different approach. This was a situation that frequently confronted Martin, a young electronics engineer who attended one of our early training workshops. Although an excellent technical man, Martin felt he lacked any real creativity and could only solve problems that required knowledge and logic to produce the correct solution. This was fine while he worked as a technician, but promotion to an executive directorship within his company meant that he was expected to contribute ideas for new products and come up with original marketing concepts. He frequently encountered problems that started out by requiring a convergent approach—with which he was familiar and felt complete confidence—but developed into divergent questions as he was required to propose practical uses for the products whose design problems he had so successfully solved. Martin needed no real help in improving his convergent skills, although he found that our procedures dramatically reduced the amount of time taken to come up with the right solution to some highly complex problems, but he did need guidance in developing divergent thinking abilities.

You have already seen how, by *matching* material to be learned to your preferred style of learning, it becomes possible to master new knowledge more effectively. Where problem solving is concerned, exactly the opposite holds true, since you must now acquire the skill of *switching* your favored problem-solving style as the task demands. This can be achieved quite easily by applying a few basic principles of solution finding, and we will explain exactly how it is done in the next section of this training schedule. We will also tell you how to make the best possible use of your preferred approach so that the type of problems with which you already feel at home can be solved more quickly and effectively than ever before.

SECTION ONE

How Problems Are Put Together

All problems, whether convergent or divergent, simple or complex, are constructed from three basic components. These have been identified by Wayne Wickelgren, Professor of Psychology at the University of Oregon[35] and one of America's most eminent problem-solving experts, as the *Givens,* the *Operations,* and the *Goals.*

In order to understand a problem correctly, the essential first step toward finding the right answer by a fast, consistently reliable route, one must identify these components and appreciate their full implications. A frequent cause of wrong answers and confused thinking is an initial failure to realize fully how problems are put together.

Here is an example of how mistakes can occur as the result of an initial misunderstanding of the true nature of any one of these elements. During our research we put the following question to large numbers of people: A candle is 15 inches long and its shadow is 45 inches longer. How many times is the shadow longer than the candle? Think about this for a moment and try to come up with an answer. If you said it was *three times longer,* then your answer corresponds to that given by 87 percent of those we asked—and you are wrong. Reread the problem and, this time, notice that the statement informs us the candle's shadow is 45 inches *longer* than the candle. In other words, the shadow is 60 inches in length and therefore *four times* as long as the candle.

If you got the correct answer, congratulations, but if—like the vast majority—you made a mistake, do not feel too bad about it. Once you understand the three components of that, and every other problem, you are most unlikely to make such an error again.

Examining that problem you will see that information is provided or implied under three headings. First of all, we have the Givens, that is, the facts concerning the length of the candle (15 inches) and the length of the shadow (45 inches *longer* than the candle). In order to solve the problem we have to manipulate the Givens in a particular way. This information is not provided but *implied* by the nature of the task, since anyone with an elementary grasp of mathematics will realize that simple division is required.

Finally there is the Goal, or solution, which we are required to find. Here it is clearly stated because we are asked to say how much longer the shadow is than the candle. As we will explain in a moment, the Goal is not always so clearly specified and, in certain kinds of problems, it is discovering the true Goal that makes up the major part of the task.

If you came up with the wrong answer to that problem, the source of your error almost certainly lay in a misinterpretation of the Givens. You read 15 inches for the candle length and took the second Given, the shadow length, as 45 inches without realizing that the true Given was the information that the shadow was 45 inches *longer* than the candle or 60 inches in length. The whole trick in this problem is, in fact, to disguise the real nature of the second Given. Before embarking on any problem, therefore, you must be certain of the answer to three questions:

Do you understand the Givens—all of them?

Do you understand the Operations—all of them?

Do you understand the Goal(s)—all of them?

Only once you are certain on all these points can you be sure of embarking on your quest for a solution in a manner likely to lead to a successful outcome. Because these three building blocks of problems are so important, we want to look at each one in a little more detail before telling you how to use further procedures to take problems apart.

The Givens

A failure to understand the Givens is a common source of mistakes. It may occur because some aspect of the information provided is overlooked, as in the problem above, or because an essential Given is not stated or even indirectly implied but *assumed* from a general knowledge of the subject. Here is an example of how this may be used to turn an extremely simple problem into a seemingly complex one.

Two men on bicycles face each other down a long, straight track, twenty miles apart. At exactly the same moment they begin to cycle toward one another, each maintaining a speed of precisely 10 miles per hour. As they move off, a fly on the handlebars of one bicycle takes off and flies to the second bike, then immediately returns to the first. He continues in this way, flying to and fro along an ever decreasing distance at 45 mph. Assuming that no time is lost in turning around at the bikes, how far will he have flown when the cyclists meet?

Here the Givens are the distance apart at which the cyclists start, their speed, and that of the fly. Can you work out the answer? If not, then think very carefully about a crucial additional Given which is nowhere stated as such in the problem, but which you actually know. Still stuck? Then turn to the end of this section where we will provide an answer and an explanation.

A similar problem, which frequently places rather more emphasis on general knowledge than the one above, is the kind of classic challenge that a good detective writer uses when seeking to deepen the mystery by obscuring the nature of important Givens in a story. For example, one might be told the following:

The butler explained to the detective that he had been suspicious when his master, millionaire banker Charles Foot, failed to come out of his darkroom at lunch time. An enthusiastic amateur photographer, the banker had gone into the well-equipped darkroom soon after breakfast with the intention of making some black-and-white prints. In his statement the butler said: "I went inside and found my master slumped over the workbench beneath the glow of the red safety light. At first I thought he must be asleep, then I saw that his shirt was deeply stained with blood. I did not touch anything, but went out and called the police."

The detective's problem, and that confronting the reader, is to spot whether the butler is lying and, if so, where he has made his fatal mistake. The story provides a number of Givens, but the key one is never stated. The writer assumes a certain knowledge—on the part of his hero as well as his audience—which will lead to the solution. Once again, we will be providing an answer and an explanation at the end of this section.

Givens can also be made ambiguous through the use of statements or words with more than one meaning. We saw, in the word problem section of the IQ training, how this tactic can be used to introduce a trap for the unwary. By including words like invalid, model, conduct, patient, and so on, the true meaning of the Given, as it relates to that particular type of problem, can often effectively be disguised.

So never take anything for granted where Givens are concerned.

Before making any assumptions about the nature of the problem, answer these three questions carefully:

Have I identified all the Givens in that problem—including those which are implied by the other Givens or might be assumed from a general knowledge of those Givens?

Have I identified and taken into account any ambiguity in the Givens which could be putting me on a false trail?

Have I correctly understood the information provided by the Givens, both those directly stated in the problem and those which I have added to the list from my knowledge of the subject?

Only when you are able to answer all those questions in the affirmative is it safe to proceed to the next stage and begin to identify the Operations which must be performed on those Givens. Now try your skill at the following problem, in which the secret of success lies at the level of *fully* understanding the Givens. Once those have been grasped, you cannot make a mistake, but any failure at this point will inevitably lead to an incorrect answer.

Four volumes of a dictionary stand side by side on a shelf. The books, which are the right way up and in sequence with Volume I on the left and Volume IV on the right, are each 4 inches thick and have covers ⅟₁₆th inch thick.

A bookworm starts to eat through the books starting at page one of Volume I and stopping only when it reaches the final page of Volume IV. How many inches has it traveled?

The Operations

These are the methods by which information provided in the Givens may be moved around. Our candle problem contained a single operation, that of dividing the length of the candle (15 inches) into the *total* length of the shadow. If you assumed the shadow was 45 inches long, then your answer was 45 divided by 15 = 3, which was incorrect even though the operation had been performed perfectly properly. If you identified the Givens correctly, then your operation was 60 divided by 15 = 4, which produced the right solution.

In many problems the Operations, like the Givens, are disguised, implied, assumed, or rendered ambiguous in order to make the task harder. In a number of IQ problems you are actually being tested on your ability to spot the operation needed in order to arrive at an answer. The brain problems provided during our intelligence test training were, in fact, highly efficient *operations* which you could perform on the Givens of the problems in order to find the right solution quickly and effortlessly.

As a general rule it pays to be flexible in your thinking when coming up with suitable operations, as a major stumbling block to success is a form of tunnel vision that sets the mind in an intellectual rut and causes it to try and solve the problem by familiar but, on occasion, inappropriate tactics. For example, if you were given *six* matches and told to form *four* equal-sided triangles from them, you would need to identify a special type of Operation in order to produce an answer.

Try your hand at the task—you may find it easier to use real matches—and see what happens. The answer, and an explanation of why people fail to find it in the majority of cases, is provided at the end of this section.

With our next problem, think hard about the Operations and make certain you understand *exactly* what is happening before deciding on your answer.

Eight diplomats greet one another at a conference. Each shakes hands with all the others just once. How many handshakes are there?

The answer, as usual, is at the end of this section.

Where certain problems are concerned, both Givens and Operations may be overlooked due to a form of mental blindness which psychologists call a *set*.

PARIS IN THE

THE SPRING

The phrase above illustrates a set in action. What does it say? If your answer was *Paris in the spring,* then you fell into the trap. Read the words again, more carefully this time, and you will see that an additional "the" has been included. This is frequently overlooked, even by diligent readers, because their minds identify a familiar phrase and fail to detect the unexpected and unnecessary extra word.

Related to the problem of *set* is a form of mental blindness which Dr. Karl Duncker,[36] an early pioneer of problem-solving studies whose work we will look at later when considering divergent tasks, termed *functional fixedness*. In a typical experiment, Karl Duncker gave subjects a candle, matches, tacks, and a box, then asked them to find some method of fixing the candle to the surface of a wooden door. In one version of the task the items were placed separately on a table; in the other, the box contained the candle, tacks, and matches. When offered the materials in the first condition, few of the subjects found any trouble in solving the problem by fastening the box to the door with some tacks and then, by melting a little wax, securing the candle to the box. When the box was used as a *container* for the other items, however, only a minority were able to appreciate its second possible function as a candle holder. They were made mentally blind to this essential operation by seeing the box *only* in its primary role as a container.

Before you arrive at any solution to a problem, therefore, answer these questions:

Have I identified the operations provided, implied, or assumed correctly?

Have I fully explored *all* the ways in which the objects and information provided might be manipulated and not only the obvious ones?

If you are satisfied on both these points, then turn to the final component of the problem, the Goal.

The Goal

In the problems we have used so far, all the Goals have been clearly stated, as is usually the case where convergent problems, such as those provided in this section, are concerned.

With some kinds of problems, however, a solution can only be found by restating the Goal in different terms. This is especially true about divergent tasks where you may find it impossible to devise satisfactory operations for achieving one sort of Goal, but have no difficulty at all if you can reformulate what needs to be done. Here is a classic problem from Arabia that illustrates this important point.

A wealthy merchant had two sons who prided themselves on their horsemanship and the speed of their stallions. Each boasted that his mount was superior to the other and his skill in the saddle outshone the abilities of his brother. At length the merchant grew so tired of listening to their arguments that he offered a wager to settle matters once and for all. His fortune would be bequeathed to whichever of the young men won a race from his palace to the city, some hundred miles away across the desert. But it was to be a most unusual race for, instead of the prize going to the man whose horse reached the city gates first, it would go to the son whose mount was *last!*

The riders set off, each traveling as slowly as possible, so that after several days they were still only a few hundred yards from their father's home and it seemed likely that the race would last for ever. Indeed, such might have been the case but for the arrival of a wise man who, after being told the nature of the challenge, was able to give the men sound advice. Seconds later they were galloping toward the city as fast as their mounts could carry them. What words of wisdom did the old man offer?

We will tell you at the end of this section.

Before starting to solve any problem, having made sure you understand the Givens and the Operations correctly, be absolutely certain that the Goal is equally clear in your mind. If you cannot see how to use the Givens and Operations to produce the Goal which the problem *seems* to state, then ask if that same Goal could not be viewed in some other way. Think in terms of opposites and you will often spot what needs to be done to reach a solution. If, for instance, the task asks you to *raise* some object, and this looks impossible, consider whether the Goal might not also be achieved by *lowering* something else. If it states that one thing must be *first* and you cannot figure any way this might be done, then ask if, by making something else come *last,* you might not gain the same outcome. The problem above, for example, can be solved by adopting exactly this technique.

In this section we have been looking at the fundamental building blocks of all problems. In Sections Two and Three we will tell you how, from this starting point of knowing how problems are put together, you can use two further procedures in order to take problems apart and, by doing so, make the right answer obvious.

Answers to Problems

Bicycles and Fly

The answer is 45 miles. You reach it most easily by analyzing the problem in terms of the Givens as follows:

Distance of cycles apart	20 miles	(stated in problem)
Speed of cyclists	10 mph	(stated in problem)
Speed of fly	45 mph	(stated in problem)

Number of miles flown by fly in one hour ... 45 miles (implied from the Given provided above).

Amount of time which passes before the cyclists meet . . . (not Given but assumed from a knowledge that cycling at 10 mph they will meet at the center of a track 20 miles long in 60 minutes).

So the solution must be 45 miles. The fact that the fly traveled on a decreasing flight path between the two bikes is a deliberately misleading Given. If its speed was 45 miles an hour, then this is the distance flown in one hour *no matter where it flew!*

The Murdered Banker

In classic detective fiction the butler *always* seems to be the culprit and this short mystery is no exception. But how did the detective come to that conclusion? What was the fatal flaw in the man's story? Consider the Givens:

Dead man found in darkroom

Dead man slumped on workbench

Room illuminated by red safety light

Man's shirt stained with blood

Butler went at once and called police

Clearly not all this information is going to help us unravel the mystery, so here the secret lies in identifying which of the Givens provided actually has any bearing on the solution. A Given which is not provided, but reasonably assumed from general knowledge, is that blood is *red*. If this is added to our list, the relevance of another, stated Given becomes readily apparent.

Man's shirt stained red with blood.

Room illuminated by red safety light.

Since in red light you cannot see red, the butler could not have seen the bloodstain.

Dictionaries on the Shelf

If you got the answer wrong, your most likely solution was 17 inches. This is because you failed to understand the Givens in terms of the problem statement. Your mind probably pictured a book and placed the first page on the left side and the last page on the right, as this is how they are whenever you open a volume in order to read it. But here the dictionaries are standing side by side on the shelf, and this completely changes the Givens.

Page one of a book on a shelf is to the right of the volume, so that all the worm has to do initially is eat through *one* cover (distance traveled $\frac{1}{16}$th inch). Next the worm must bore through another cover, four inches of paper and a second cover to eat its way out of Volume II. This distance is repeated for the third volume, which brings it up against the cover of Volume IV. The last page of this book is not on the right, as it would be in the reading position, but on the left. After eating through one further cover, therefore, the worm arrives at the final page. It has gone through six covers, total distance $\frac{3}{8}$ inch, and two sets of pages, total distance 8 inches, so the *correct solution is $8\frac{3}{8}$ inches.*

In this problem the hazard of set, mentioned in connection with Operations, probably played a part in misleading you. Your mind was so used to thinking about page orders as they appear when a book is being read that it failed to spot the trap and applied the same sequence to books on a shelf.

Three Triangles from Six Matches

This problem can only be solved in one way, by breaking out the mental set which forces you to reason in two dimensions. Instead of moving the matches around on a flat surface, build a pyramid out of them with three forming the base and three the sides. This gives you a total of four equilateral triangles.

Diplomats at the Conference

If you said 56 handshakes, then your source of error lies in the way you manipulated the Givens, that is, the 8 diplomats. The correct answer is 28 for this reason: once A has shaken hands with B, B has also shaken hands with A and need not do so again.

The Merchant and His Sons

Here the boys were given a Goal which, if not totally impossible to attain, was clearly very impractical. But it is possible to reformulate that Goal so that the challenge becomes straightforward. The problem states that the winner will be the son whose *horse* reaches the city's gate last; it says nothing about the *son* who arrives last. The answer the wise man provided, and the one we hope you saw, was for the young men simply to change *mounts*. This done, they would gallop as fast as possible along the course, since by arriving first the winning son would ensure that his *horse* arrived last.

SECTION TWO

How Problems Can Be Taken Apart

A good way of finding out how something works is often to take it to pieces and see how the various parts interact with one another. By doing so it is usually possible to get a clear understanding of functional relationships and to identify the key components. It goes without saying that the dismantling operation must be done very carefully and methodically if you are to avoid being left with a multitude of pieces and no clear idea how they fit back together!

Exactly the same holds true for problems as you start taking them apart to discover not only the Givens, Operations, and Goals but essential structures and relationships lying at a deeper level. Without a logical system of analysis you are likely to produce more questions than answers and end up feeling more confused than when you started. Yet, because people are never taught how to take problems apart in a methodical manner, this is the most likely outcome of their generally haphazard approach.

To dismantle problems effectively you need to make use of two basic techniques of analysis: Creative Carving and Solution Trees. In this section we are going to describe these procedures and provide practical experience in using them to analyze some fairly elementary problems. In Sections Three and Four we will show you how they can be applied to even the most complex convergent and divergent tasks in order to simplify greatly the solution-finding process.

Creative Carving was developed by George Miller, Professor of Psychology at Princeton University,[37] and is based on the eminently sensible, though seldom appreciated proposition that it is easier to solve two small problems than one large one. By using Creative Carving you reduce the information provided to its key elements in a way that preserves the functional relationships between various aspects of the task and so enables the separated elements to be rebuilt into an answer. When we discussed ways of enhancing learning, a somewhat similar procedure, Profragging—Progressive Fragmentation—was described. In some ways Creative Carving is like Profragging, in that both are concerned with reducing complexity and breaking large units of information into smaller, more manageable ones. The essential difference is that while you can Profrag material in any way that suits your personal learning style, Creative Carving is dictated by the structure of the problem and must always yield elements capable of being used in the second of the two procedures, Solution Trees.

Solution Trees are used by scientists when making detailed analyses of problems that have to be solved using computer problems. They enable all the possible pathways to a solution to be explored so that the most direct and reliable route to a correct answer can be found. When the same approach is adopted for dealing with problem solving by humans, mental confusion is eliminated and the speed, consistency, and success of answer finding greatly enhanced.

During our research into ways of increasing intellectual performance, we have carried out many studies on Solution Trees and found them invaluable in solving all types of problems. Once the straightforward procedures have been mastered, both convergent and divergent tasks, even extremely complex ones, can be dealt with in less time and with a far greater probability of discovering the correct solution.

Creative Carving in Action

We are going to illustrate how this approach is used by applying it to two different types of problem. So that you can compare your current strategies with this new procedure, we would like you to think about both problems before reading our explanation of how Creative Carving can be employed. While doing so, note the time it takes to come up with an answer and reflect on the thought processes you use. When you use Creative Carving on the same problems, you should find that the solution becomes obvious almost immediately.

The Problem of the L-Shaped Office Space

We want you to imagine yourself the manager of a rapidly expanding company whose success has led to the hiring of additional staff and more office accommodation. Unfortunately the only remaining space in the building has the awkwardly shaped floor area shown in the illustration below.

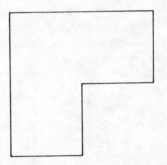

Figure 58

Your task is to divide this space into four offices, identical in size and shape, for junior executives with equal status in the organization. The job is made trickier by the fact that you can only use straight partitions and each office has to accept the same amount of standard furniture, so you must avoid any oddly shaped rooms. You are under pressure to produce a design because the construction crew has arrived to build the offices and, to make life even more difficult, you have forgotten to bring a ruler or any other measuring device to help you make calculations of the floor area.

How can you quickly and easily solve the problem and produce four identical offices in the space available?

The Problem of the School Textbooks

As headmaster of a school with 1000 students you have the task of ordering textbooks for each course. Pupils can elect to study either languages or a science subject and, this semester, you learn from the language department that 400 have asked to take Spanish and 300 will take French. One hundred fifty of the language students want to take both. How many science textbooks must you order to ensure that each student not electing for languages will have one?

Now Use Creative Carving

The L-Shaped Office Space Problem

At first you may feel the room can only be divided into three offices of equal size as shown in Figure 59 below. Perhaps you even sketched in some partitions to produce this result before deciding that approach did not seem to be leading anywhere. You had, in fact, started to carve up the problem, but without having any clear sense of direction. If you had continued with the process the answer would have been obvious. Four identical offices have been constructed and the problem solved.

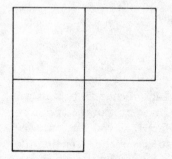

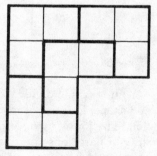

Figure 59

Figure 60

The Science Textbook Problem

The correct answer is that you will have to order 450 science books, and not 300 as you might have assumed. Start by looking at *all* the Givens:

Total number of students	1,000
Number taking Spanish	400
Number taking French	300
Number taking both Spanish and French	150

If the solution you came up with was 300, then your mistake was to look only at the first three Givens. You added up the number of Spanish and French students, arrived at a total of 700, and subtracted this from 1,000. In doing so you ignored the 150 taking both languages by assuming they were included in the larger number.

To creatively carve this problem you should start by considering all the elements and the relationship between them. This becomes far easier to do if the task can be diagrammed.

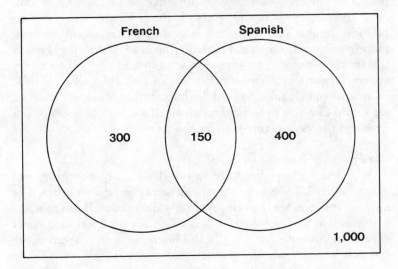

Figure 61

Here the oblong represents the total number of students in the school; the oval on the left, Spanish students, and that on the right, French students. The overlap indicates those 150 pupils taking both languages. Because these students come into *both* groups this figure must be subtracted from the total in order to discover the overall number studying languages.

We start, therefore by adding French and Spanish students 400 + 300 = 700.

Now we have to subtract the number taking both 700 − 150 = 550.

Finally we subtract this total from 1,000 to discover how many students will not be taking languages, and arrive at a figure of 450 who need science textbooks.

Illustrating aspects of a problem in this way very often aids an understanding of the information and prevents you from falling into traps.

Solution Trees in Action

When we consider the use of Solution Trees in the next two sections, the convergent and divergent problems used will be of sufficient complexity to justify this procedure. Clearly there is little point in using a Tree if the task is so simple that an answer is almost immediately obvious. For the purposes of illustrating the way this procedure works, however, we are going to apply it to a very straightforward problem which you can probably solve in little more time than it takes to read the information provided. Even so, we would like you to work through the Tree with us so as to understand the steps involved in its construction.

The Problem of Water in the Desert

At a desert camp you have to transfer exactly two gallons of water from a full five-gallon can to an empty ten-gallon drum. The only other container is an empty three-gallon drum. Because water is so precious you cannot afford to waste any and you should not expend any more effort than is absolutely necessary. What is the quickest way to make the transfer?

As we said, this is such a simple problem that you can manipulate the various Givens in your head to produce an Operation that will achieve the stated Goal. But let us look at the way we would set about turning the information provided into a Solution Tree.

With all Trees the starting point is to state the problem. When this is done here, it becomes apparent that there are only two options. Water can be poured from the five-gallon can into either the three- or ten-gallon drum. This choice represents the first level branches on the Tree, as follows:

Problem Statement

Start

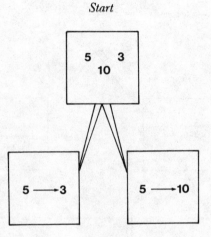

Figure 62A

At this stage of the Tree we have three possible ways of proceeding. Water remaining in the five-gallon container can be poured into the ten-gallon drum; water in the three-gallon container can be transferred to the ten-gallon drum, or water in the ten-gallon container can be poured into the three-gallon drum. Once again these moves may be drawn into the Tree.

Clearly only the first and last moves will produce the required result of leaving exactly two gallons in the ten-gallon container; the middle maneuver fails to do so. We can, if we wish, confirm that this is a false move by writing out the Tree to the final stage of development.

In neither case do we finish up with the required amounts of water in the largest container. The complete Solution Tree for this problem would therefore look like the figure below.

As you will have realized, the problems above were examples of convergent tasks. In each case there was only one *correct* solution which was clearly specified in the original problem statement. This did not mean, however, that there was only one way of arriving at the required answer, as our second example clearly showed.

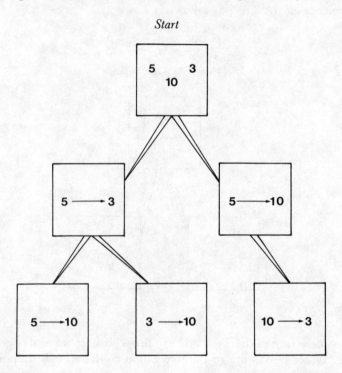

Figure 62B

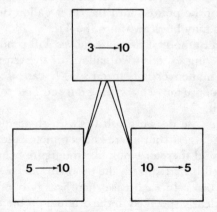

Figure 62C

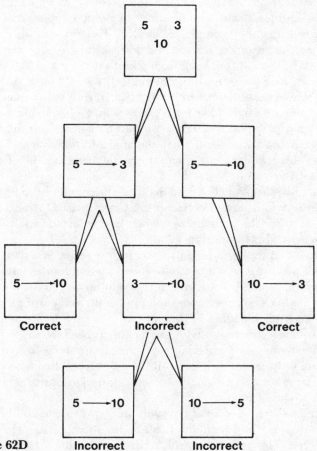

Figure 62D

Whether you started by tipping water from the five-gallon drum into the three- or the ten-gallon container, you still produced a correct result. Of the alternatives, the second (5 into 10) was perhaps slightly better since it clearly led to the final answer, while the first approach introduced the possibility, however remote, of pouring from the three-gallon into the ten-gallon drum and coming up with an incorrect outcome.

With many problems there are a number of alternative ways of arriving at the right solution and your skill lies in selecting the best approach. By best we mean the route from the problem statement to final answer which is the fastest—so as to avoid needless delay—and least confusing, in order to eliminate sources of error. If we consider the example of Sherlock Holmes and his expense account, for instance, we can see that he might have converted each of the expenditure items from pounds sterling into U.S. dollars before adding them up. But, although this would have led to the same answer as adding them and then carrying out the necessary calculation, it would have been a slower and less reliable method. Each multiplication could have produced an error and this might have been harder to detect when the final addition was performed.

The three keys to success problem solving can, therefore, be summarized as follows:

Start by getting a clear and detailed statement of the problem. Make sure you fully understand the Givens, the Operations and the Goals. See the problem as a whole and so avoid pitfalls which can arise at this initial stage.

Break a complex problem down into a series of smaller and smaller problems that are easy to solve. By finding the solution to these you automatically arrive at the right answer to the big problem. Creative Carving means doing just that, and cutting through the apparent difficulties of the task.

Computer scientists advise taking this procedure to its logical extreme by creatively carving away at sub-problems so that these become simpler and simpler until the point is reached where there are a large number of small problems, the solutions to which are either trivial or obvious.

The final step is to relate the sub-problems to one another in a logical manner and then link them by lines to construct the Problem Tree. This technique will become increasingly clear as you work through the examples at the end of this section.

In scientific method there is a constant striving after what is termed *"elegance,"* and academics, especially in the fields of physics and mathematics, speak of Occam's Razor and the need for "elegance" in their theories. Occam's Razor is a term meaning that all unnecessary facts and components of the subject being analyzed have been eliminated; an *elegant* theory is one which offers explanations in the most direct and parsimonious fashion possible. When using Solution Trees to develop pathways through problems, it is well to be guided by the notion of parsimony and to make your strategies as straightforward as possible. Keep them simple and there is less risk of your becoming confused, ensure they are direct and you will find the required answer in the least possible amount of time. The Solution Tree, because it makes it possible to identify and examine possible routes to the required solution, ensures that such an approach is easily adopted. To appreciate how effective the technique proves in practice, we will now use it to solve a fairly complicated convergent problem.

SECTION THREE

How to Handle Convergent Problems

Although convergent problems have only one correct solution, there may be a number of pathways to that answer. Your task is to discover which one will take you there by the fastest, surest, and most direct route, and the Solution Tree makes this simple.

If your problem-solving style is that of the Pathfinder, then this systematic Solution Tree approach for handling convergent problems should seem especially logical and attractive. If you are a Helicopter Pilot, however, you may feel slightly put off by the methodical approach it is essential to adopt when handling convergent problems. You should pay special attention to this section, despite this reaction, as you need to expand your skills so as to be able to cope with this type of task as efficiently as you handle divergent problems. This will greatly increase the flexibility of your problem-solving skills and ensure you approach any kind of problem with confidence.

The best way of explaining how convergent problems are solved using the Tree procedure is to work through an actual example. We will then provide you with some problems, together with solutions, so that you can practice for yourself.

The Problem of the Three Salesmen

You are the owner of an auto parts store and business has been so good that you are expanding by opening a second branch across town. At your present location are three experienced salesmen, Al, Bob, and Chuck, whom you want to transfer to the new premises to help build up trade. You intend to replace them with three novice salesmen who will have to be trained.

Your plan is to bring only one of your experienced men to the new store at a time, work with him for a few weeks until he is used to the routine, and then return to your original premises to train an inexperienced salesman. You will continue to alternate your time between the stores until your old store is staffed by the three new men and you are working with Al, Bob, and Chuck in the second store.

This would be a straightforward process except for a few staff difficulties. You feel you can only train one new man and break in one experienced salesman at a time. There are also human factors to take into account since you know from experience that when Al and Bob work unsupervised they soon start to argue, producing an unpleasant atmosphere in the store which upsets customers. You have also found that it is a bad idea to leave Bob and Chuck working together without supervision because, being good friends, they tend to waste time chatting.

None of this mattered in the past because they all worked well while you were around and had proved themselves very effective employees. Now, because you want to transfer them to the new premises one at a time, a situation could easily arise in which either Al and Bob or Bob and Chuck have to work together without your being around to keep an eye on things. The old store is too small to allow more than five people to work there at any one time, so you cannot hope to resolve your difficulties by increasing the number of staff in those premises.

Your problem is to come up with a way of moving staff around which satisfies these conditions: New salesmen must be trained and experienced staff familiarized with the new premises in such a way that you end up with your original premises staffed by three newly trained assistants while you work with Al, Bob, and Chuck in the new store. At no time during the transitional period, however, can either Al and Bob or Bob and Chuck be allowed to work together unless you are present.

Before reading any further we would like you to try and solve the problem. While doing so, think about the mental processes involved and see how your current strategies cope with the demands of this task.

Like a simpler version of chess or checkers, problems of this kind require you to think out your moves while retaining essential information in working memory. As we have already explained, the capacity of this memory is fairly limited, and attempts to force in more facts than it can cope with lead to confusion and loss. The more complex the problem, the harder it becomes to retain the material you need while working out the moves required. Although this problem is of only moderate complexity, our research has shown that no more than 30 percent of people could work out the correct sequence of moves in their head and half of these were experienced problem solvers who enjoyed this kind of challenge. The majority needed to write down information as they went along, thus off-loading working memory and, even then, many made mistakes. Some 25 percent found it necessary to represent the salesmen in some physical form, by using pieces of paper or matches, for instance, so they could be moved around like pieces on a chess board as various combinations of staff and different sequences of movement were considered. Neither of these tactics is especially effective because they are time-consuming, confusing, and generally unreliable. The best approach, especially if you are unfamiliar with problems of this sort, is to develop a Solution Tree.

At this point you might like to try your hand at constructing such a Tree using the method described in the previous section. Begin with a statement of the situation as it exists at the start of the problem and see how well you can expand the Tree by building branches at different levels from that point.

You will find it simpler, both in this particular task and others of a similar nature, to use some kind of shorthand for the main items of information provided. Here we are going to represent the Givens in the following way: Al, Bob, and Chuck will be A, B, and C; the new salesmen will be X, and you, the owner, will be U. The additional Givens, the old and new stores, will be shown by boxes to be drawn in at each level of Tree construction as the solution unfolds. Incidentally, the name given to such boxes in computer terminology is *nodes* and this is the expression we shall be using from now on.

Once we are satisifed that the Givens have been correctly identified and we are aware of the precise Goal required, it is possible to begin working out the Operations by which it may be achieved.

The root from which your Tree will grow is shown below. From this starting point try to work out the logical development of moves before reading further:

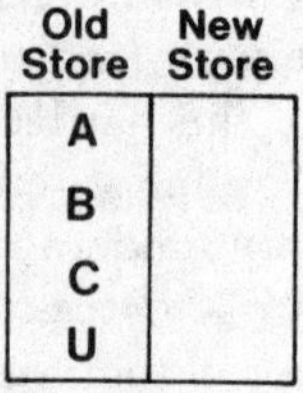

Old Store	New Store
A	
B	
C	
U	

Figure 63A

How did you get on?

If you found it fairly easy to construct a Tree which led directly to the required solution, then congratulations. It seems that this invaluable problem-solving procedure presents few difficulties and can be used with confidence whenever you have to tackle complex convergent tasks. But if the Tree became confused after only a modest growth had occurred, do not be discouraged or feel that the procedure is too complicated for you to cope with. Like any mental skill this one takes time and practice to master, especially if your personal problem-solving style is that of the Helicopter Pilot. Familiarity with the method will quickly dispel initial confusions and leave you equipped to handle the most involved convergent tasks. You can acquire this level of expertise by working through the Tree with us and then trying your hand at the practice problems below.

A Tree for the Store Problem

After ensuring that the starting statement satisifes the conditions set down in the problem, we consider all possible initial moves and write them out in full to create the first level of the Tree:

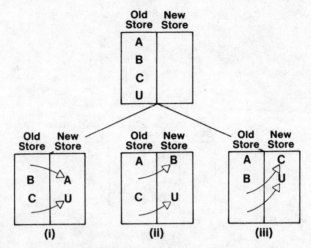

Figure 63B

Two of these moves can be eliminated right away since they violate conditions laid down in the problem. In (i) Bob and Chuck work unsupervised, a situation leading to time wasting, while in (iii) Al and Bob are alone together and this will produce friction and a loss of customers. Only the middle node (ii) need be considered and further developed; the others can be forgotten.

We know from the problem statement that, having taken an experienced salesman to your new premises, you plan to work with him for a few weeks until things are running smoothly, then return to the old store to train a replacement.

To build the next level of nodes, therefore, we assume that Bob has been left alone in the new premises while you have returned and completed training an additional salesman in the old. This staff member is to be represented, we have decided, by an X.

Now you must transfer a further experienced salesman, either Al or Chuck, to work with you and Bob at the new store. Given this condition, you will see that the Tree can only be expanded in two ways:

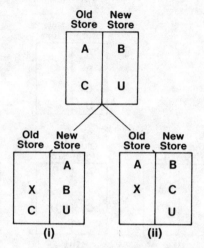

Figure 63C (i) (ii)

Node (i) shows what would happen if you took Al along with you to the new premises, while (ii) depicts the situation if Chuck had been chosen. Note the X in the "old store" position of the node to signify that a replacement salesman has been trained.

Looking at this further development in the Solution Tree, however, we see that both combinations lead to a situation which violates the conditions laid down in the problem.

If you take Al with you, as shown in node (i), then Bob and Al will be left alone together when you return to the old premises to train another novice salesman. Similarly, if you take Chuck with you as indicated in node (ii), then he will be working unsupervised with Bob after your departure, a situation you must also avoid.

Does this also mean the problem cannot be solved?

There are problems in real life for which no solution actually exists, at least not within the conditions specified, and the great advantage of using a Solution Tree is that such intractable tasks can be identified quickly. This saves a great deal of wasted time in searching for answers which cannot be found and enables you to reconsider either the Givens or the Goal(s) so as to formulate, if possible, a problem that is capable of being solved.

In a problem of this type, however, it is most unlikely that there is no solution and when you come up against an apparent obstacle such as this, you should suspect that you have encountered a trap. As with many real-life problems, the answer lies in reconsidering the information provided, by taking a long, hard look at the

Givens and the Goal. Here the Goal is clearly stated and does not offer any room for compromise or reformulation, so we must examine the Givens more closely. Our difficulty would be resolved if we took one of the experienced salesmen back to the old store with us, leaving the other man to work alone. Many people fail to solve this problem because they *assume* that once an experienced salesman has been transferred to the new store, he must remain there. But the Givens lay down no such conditions, so there is nothing to prevent you from moving men backward and forward at will, provided there are never more than five people at the old premises and the unacceptable staff combinations are avoided.

The Solution Tree makes apparent what might otherwise easily have been missed. A new initiative is required if any further progress toward a solution is to be achieved. Once this crucial insight has been attained, two further nodes may easily be added to the Tree.

Only the left side of the Tree has been developed, as we will deal

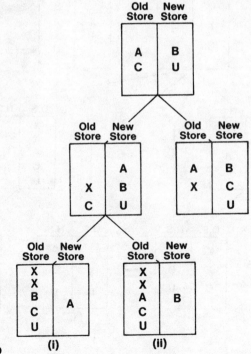

Figure 63D

with what would happen if the right node was expanded later in this section.

Do the new nodes meet all the conditions laid down in the problem?

A quick check assures us that no prohibited combinations of unsupervised staff have been created and there are no more than five people at the old store.

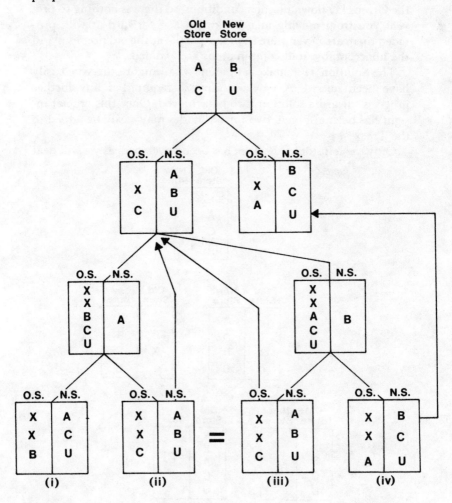

Figure 63E

The next step is to see what happens when you return to the new store, taking one of the experienced salesmen with you, which means that the two nodes can each be further carved to produce a total of four more.

At this point the Tree can conveniently be pruned and simplified. The first thing to notice is that nodes (ii) and (iii) are identical, which could mean that *only one of them* should be considered further. But as they are also equivalent to the node two levels farther up the tree (arrowed), to develop either of them means going back to an earlier stage in the problem-solving process.

It is a good general rule, when developing the Solution Tree, to eliminate any nodes that duplicate earlier ones, since developing them further means taking a step back toward the problem statement. Your direction of movement always should be forward, away from the problem and closer to a solution. Progress to the answer; never regress to the problem. With this in mind we can discount node (iv) which is also equivalent to an earlier node (arrowed).

If you were to break the rule and develop these nodes, you would soon find it impossible to satisfy the conditions laid down by the Givens. You will either create an unsupervised staff combination that had to be avoided or else there are going to be more than five people in the old premises.

The only option left, therefore, is to expand node (i), which immediately makes the final sequence of moves and the solution to the problem apparent.

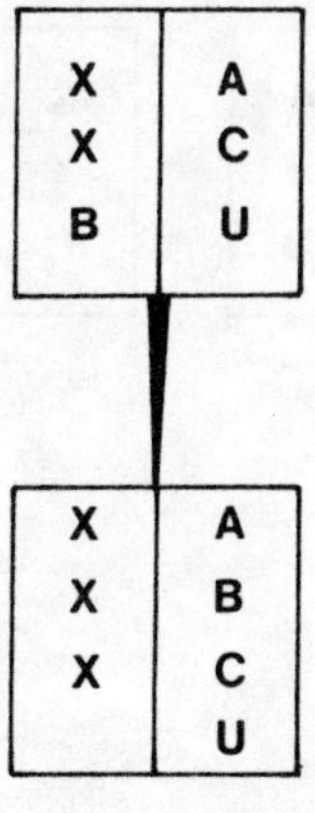

Figure 63F

By using a Solution Tree you have discovered a pathway through the problem which leads directly to the right answer and, at every stage of the journey, it has been possible to maintain a close check on the deductions made to ensure that the conditions of

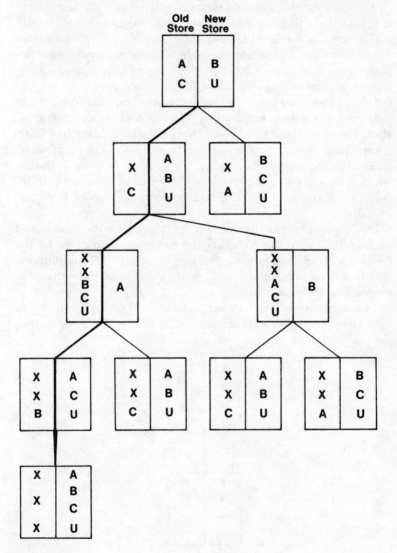

Figure 63G

the task are being met and that the logic applied is faultless. You can therefore feel confident that your solution is not only correct, but also employs the fastest and most efficient sequence of moves available. The only remaining task is to write out the pattern of staff movement by following the pathway created.

The route leading to a solution has been marked by the thicker lines.

Here is how the solution would be presented:

You take Bob to the new store, leaving Al and Chuck to look after business in the old premises. After training Bob, Al is brought over and a new salesman recruited to work in the old store.

You return to the old store yourself, taking Bob with you and leaving Al on his own while another replacement is trained. You then return to the new premises with Chuck and complete his training, leaving Bob and the two new men in the old store.

Finally Bob is brought over to the new store, and the three salesmen are left on their own at the old one.

Now let's return to the node which we left incomplete early on in the Tree building process (See Figure 63E). You may remember that it represented the situation after Chuck had been taken over to the new store to join Bob, having trained a replacement in the old premises:

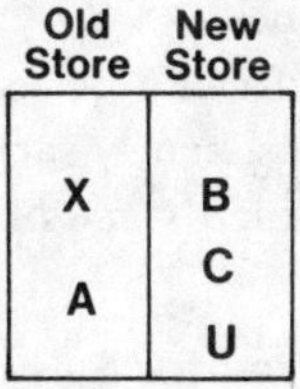

	Old Store	New Store
	X	B
		C
	A	U

Figure 63H

Would this starting point also yield a legitimate solution? To give yourself some practice in Tree building for convergent problems, we suggest you expand this node to see what happens.

Bear in mind that, at all times, forward progress has to be maintained and you must never regress to an earlier level in the solution-seeking process. You should also be careful to prune the Tree as you go along in order to reduce complexity. This will be easiest to achieve, while you gain experience of Tree building, by checking each node you develop against those in the Solution Tree we created.

Once you have completed your Tree, and make certain each node fulfills the conditions laid down by the problem statement, check it against the answer at the end of this section.

As we explained at the start, if your natural problem-solving style is that of the Pathfinder, this type of Solution Tree should seem reasonably straightforward and in line with your preferred approach to finding answers. If your style is that of a Helicopter Pilot, you might feel slightly daunted by the systematic nature of this approach, regard the method as needlessly complex, and consider your more intuitive approach both easier and more effective. You will find, however, that this approach is superior to your current strategies as far as convergent problems are concerned because it eliminates all the weaknesses inherent in your favored approach. The sort of Tree developed in the next section, when we look at divergent problems will probably be more in keeping with your natural style and you are likely to find it easier to adopt than Pathfinders. But we do suggest you acquire these additional skills for convergent problems, just as we will urge Pathfinders to master the divergent Solution Trees since—as we explained at the start of this section—successful problem solving demands that you are equally expert with both approaches.

Solution Trees of this sort can be used for all convergent problems and offer the only consistently satisfactory method for finding the fastest route through each stage of the task.

Alternative Solution Tree for Salesman Problem

As you can see, this also produces a satisfactory solution to the problem. After returning to the old store with Bob, leaving Chuck alone to manage the new premises, you train a second salesman before going back to the new store with Al so that he can gain experience there. Then you travel across town for the last time to train a final novice salesman prior to moving back to the new branch for good with Bob. This sequence of moves meets all the conditions laid down by the Givens and is no more complicated or less direct than the pathway we have already identified.

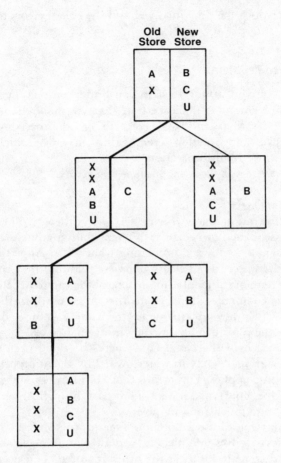

Figure 63I

The fact that there are two effective ways of solving this problem should not come as any surprise, since we have already stressed that although convergent tasks can only have one *correct* answer, there may be many routes to that solution. In some cases a number of these will be equally efficient and there is nothing to choose between them. At other times, however, some may prove more straightforward and consequently both faster and less confusing than the others. Be guided in your choice by the need to eliminate all unnecessary steps between problem statement and answer in order to reduce the time involved and the risk of errors to a minimum.

Practice Problems

Use Creative Carving to help you build Solution Trees to the problems below, but make certain that you have identified the Givens, Operations, and Goals correctly before proceeding. Check your answer and Solution Tree against our own, which can be found at the end of this section.

Now practice your convergent problem-solving skills.

Problem One

The illustration below (Figure 64) shows the situation as three cargo vessels, each owned by a different shipping line, steam up a narrow canal (A) toward unloading wharfs (C). After their ships entered the waterway, the captains were told that they could only tie up or remain stationary in portions of the canal owned by their respective companies. This means they must berth in the reverse order to which they are moving up the waterway. Since there is no room for them to turn about, they must change order by using a second branch of the canal (B), where the same rule about remaining stationary only in water owned by the appropriate shipping line also applies. This means that Ship 1 can only steam as far as Area One, but Ship 3 is allowed to pass through Areas One and Two en route to its stopping position.

We want you to use a Solution Tree to work out the most efficient series of moves by which the captains can resolve their conundrum and come to berth in the order required. You need not attempt to construct a complete Solution Tree for this task since it would prove very extensive and needlessly complicated. You can discover the appropriate maneuvers simply by developing a few parts of the Tree, bearing in mind all that we said about eliminating nodes which either repeat a previous position or take you back toward the problem statement. As with the store and salesmen problem, we suggest that you use some convenient shorthand to represent the vessels and the parts of the waterway. For instance, Ship 3 proceeding from the canal to the docking area (C) could simply be represented as 3–C.

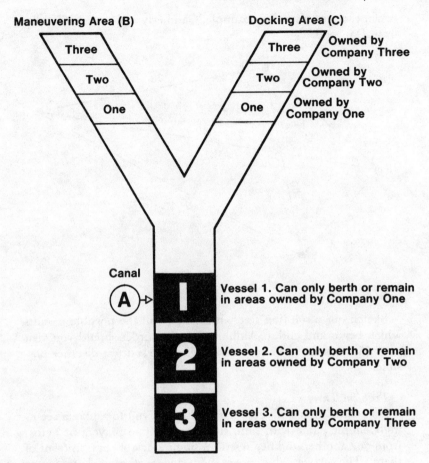

Figure 64

Problem Two

You are about to take an extended holiday and have decided to look up three old school friends. They live in the cities of Brentston, Camberly, and Dalwood. Since these places are somewhat distant from one another, you want to take the shortest route which allows you to visit each friend just once, starting and finishing your trip at your home town, Aldbury. The map below shows the roads connecting the four cities and indicates the distances between each in miles. For example, Camberly is situated 160 miles from Dalwood.

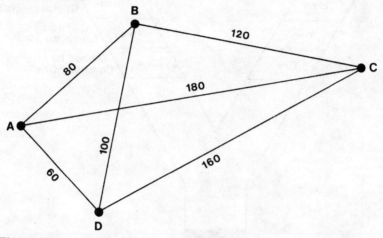

Figure 65

Sketch out a solution tree which shows all the possible circuits which begin and end at Aldbury. In what order should you visit your friends so as to be sure of traveling the shortest distance possible?

Problem Three

An acquaintance of yours has challenged you to a play a seemingly simple game with him. In this game two players sit across from one another and begin with a single stack of coins in front of them. The player who moves first divides the stack into two smaller stacks. These stacks can each contain any amount of coins as long as they are unequal. The second player then divides one of the stacks in two yet again. The two contestants alternate in this manner with each player dividing a stack of his choice until every stack contains either one coin or two and hence can no longer be divided. The first person who cannot play is the loser, and his opponent is allowed to keep all the coins. Since your friend likes to play with fifty-dollar gold pieces, you have decided that a rigorously systematic study of the game is called for. Use a solution tree to analyze the case where two players begin with a stack of seven coins. Is it more advantageous to move first or second? If you play first, which opening move should be avoided? If you are second, how many different sequences result in a win for you? What is the maximum number of moves that could be played in a single game?

Problem Four

Due to its somewhat more extensive structure, the game of "Eights" will give you an excellent opportunity to exercise the solution tree expertise you have developed so far. In Eights, the first player chooses a number from one to three. His opponent then does likewise, and adds the two numbers aloud. Play continues in this manner with each competitor adding a number from one to three to the running total. Only one restriction applies—a player may not choose his opponent's preceding selection. The first player who brings the total to exactly eight is the winner. If a player adds on a number which causes the total to *exceed* eight, he loses. Use a solution tree to analyze this game. Does either player have an advantage? Is it possible to lose by being forced to bring the total to more than eight?

You will find our answers on pages 227–230.

Answers to Convergent Problems

Problem One

The Tree below shows how you can use this technique to find the fastest route to a solution. Although many pathways to a solution exist for the Captains' Conundrum problem, the shortest is seven moves, indicated by the heavier lines. By using a Tree you are able to keep a record of previous blind alleys and inefficient routes taken and can easily avoid making the same mistakes more than once.

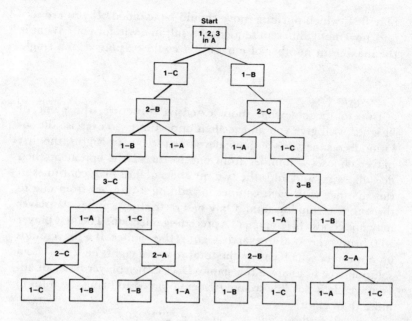

Figure 66

Problem Two

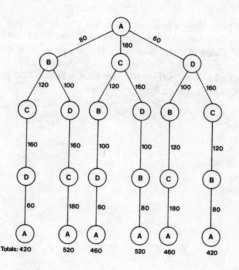

Figure 67

As you can see from the above solution tree, there are two routes which allow you to minimize the distance traveled. These are Aldbury-Brentston-Camberly-Dalwood-Aldbury and Aldbury-Dalwood-Camberly-Brentston-Aldbury. The distance traveled in both cases is 420 miles.

Problem Three

In the tree shown below, the numbers contained in the circles indicate the number of coins in each stack. The column on the left matches two players, A and B, to the moves open to them at each stage in the game. For instance, on the first move, A can choose to create two stacks whose coins number six and one, five and two, or four and three.

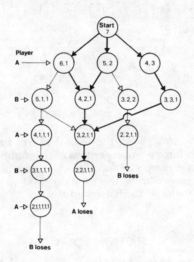

Figure 68

It is most advantageous to play second, since this position makes it possible to force a win regardless of the first player's move. This can be seen by following the heavily shaded arrows. The option to be avoided by the person moving first is that of dividing the coins into stacks of four and three, since this causes B to win automatically. As shown by the shaded arrows, the second player has open to him three winning sequences depending on his opponent's choice of opening move. The maximum number of moves possible is five, as shown by the leftmost branch.

Problem Four

The tree below shows the structure of the game of Eights with illegal moves omitted. The numbers inside the circles represent running totals;

numbers outside the circles indicate the choices available to the players at each stage in the game. Squares represent a winning position.

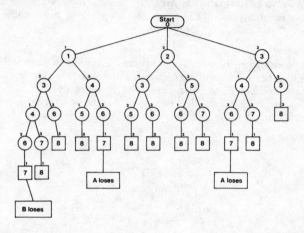

Figure 69

As shown by the tree above, the second player has the advantage since he can always force a win regardless of the numbers chosen by his opponent. There are three positions in which one player can win by forcing his opponent to bring the running total to more than 8, as shown by the rectangles at the bottom of the tree.

SECTION FOUR

How to Handle Divergent Problems

With divergent problems there is never a single correct answer. The key to success lies in finding solutions which break away from the more obvious approaches and often show a high level of creativity. For example, an advertising executive, given a new brand name to promote, must solve the problem of how best to get his client's product established in a highly competitive market. There are clearly any number of ways in which such a campaign might be mounted, and his ability will be judged on both the originality and effectiveness of his ideas. This frequently means being able to go beyond the information given in the task and avoiding the pitfalls, such as functional fixedness, discussed in Section One.

A good example of divergent problem solving in action is the case of the marketing manager whose task was to promote sales of candies for young children. Although the product was of high quality, it was similar to other types of candy on the market and there seemed no easy way to make the brand unique. The solution he found was to ignore the candy and concentrate on the packaging. Realizing that the box in which the candy came could be much more than just an attractive container if the design were slightly modified, he created boxes which could be slotted together to build all kinds of toys. Sales soared as delighted parents found that they were buying not only a tasty treat for their children but a game that provided pleasure long after the candies had been consumed.

Because a methodical approach rarely produces sufficiently creative and original solutions, the broader, more intuitive style of the Helicopter Pilot is favored where this type of problem is concerned. That does not mean, however, that Pathfinders cannot readily acquire the strategies needed to tackle such items with great success.

We are going to illustrate the creation of a Solution Tree for divergent problems by looking at a task which confronted a pioneer in this area of study, Dr. Karl Duncker.[38] When he began to consider the question, some thirty years ago, it was an important clinical problem that was engaging the attention of medical researchers. You do not require any specialized knowledge to produce good solutions, however, since this is primarily a test of the ability to find creative answers to even the most practical of problems.

The Problem of the Stomach Tumor

A patient must be treated for an inoperable stomach tumor. This might be destroyed using radiation but unfortunately the rays which would kill the growth will also do serious damage to healthy surrounding tissue. The problem is to treat the tumor with the rays in such a way that only the growth is affected.

A Tree for the Tumor Problem

The starting point, as with convergent problems, is to state clearly the nature of the task. This constitutes what is called the Problem Stage and consists of a brief but explicit statement of the situation being considered.

Figure 70A

Problem Stage

> **How to destroy a tumor using radiation without harming surrounding healthy tissue.**

The next step is to develop some general notions of how such a problem might be tackled. It is not necessary to worry for the moment about whether the ideas dreamed up are practical, since this consideration is best left to a further level in the Tree.

All you have to do when coming up with proposals for what is called the *General Range* is to produce suggestions that just might prove possible, even if some of them appear far-fetched and unworkable. Where the tumor problem is concerned the two suggestions most often made for the General Range are shown in the developing Tree below.

Figure 70B

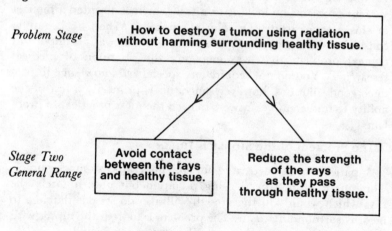

Problem Stage

How to destroy a tumor using radiation without harming surrounding healthy tissue.

Stage Two General Range

Avoid contact between the rays and healthy tissue.

Reduce the strength of the rays as they pass through healthy tissue.

At the third level we look for Functional Solutions. As the term implies, these are methods by which the ideas contained in the General Range might be made to operate. When these are added to the Tree, it expands its branches as follows:

Figure 70C

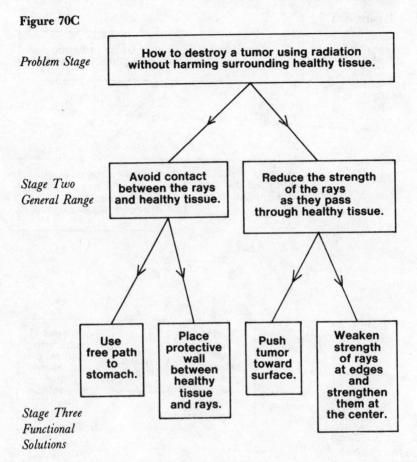

Problem Stage

How to destroy a tumor using radiation without harming surrounding healthy tissue.

Stage Two General Range

Avoid contact between the rays and healthy tissue.

Reduce the strength of the rays as they pass through healthy tissue.

Stage Three Functional Solutions

Use free path to stomach.

Place protective wall between healthy tissue and rays.

Push tumor toward surface.

Weaken strength of rays at edges and strengthen them at the center.

It should be pointed out that these are not the only possible ideas at the General Range stage, nor have we exhausted every potential Functional Solution. We have deliberately restricted the Tree to just two General Range notions and four Functional Solutions in order to keep it reasonably simple.

We have now reached the fourth and final stage of Tree building, the point at which specific methods of applying the functional solutions must be considered. Here the emphasis is on devising

Figure 70D

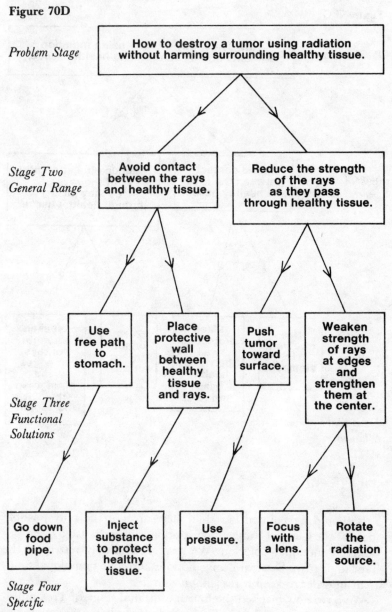

Problem Stage

How to destroy a tumor using radiation without harming surrounding healthy tissue.

*Stage Two
General Range*

Avoid contact between the rays and healthy tissue.

Reduce the strength of the rays as they pass through healthy tissue.

*Stage Three
Functional
Solutions*

Use free path to stomach.

Place protective wall between healthy tissue and rays.

Push tumor toward surface.

Weaken strength of rays at edges and strengthen them at the center.

Go down food pipe.

Inject substance to protect healthy tissue.

Use pressure.

Focus with a lens.

Rotate the radiation source.

*Stage Four
Specific
Solutions*

practical techniques that will enable earlier ideas to be implemented.

The five techniques above are those most frequently suggested but, once again, do not represent a complete list of possibilities.

When we come to consider specific solutions in greater detail it might well be found that some are quite inappropriate, while others would work only with a limited number of patients.

The important thing is to follow this pattern of development when generating ideas, translating general notions into functional solutions, and finally exploring the practicality of the methods evolved. Which is finally chosen will depend on a whole host of factors that need not be taken into account when working on the problem in the first instance.

The proposal to introduce the radiation source via the mouth and food pipe might be found effective only with a patient whose tumor was in a certain location, for example, or else presented insurmountable technical difficulties. Of the solutions that Duncker's problem solvers came up with, the one which finally proved most valuable was a rotating radiation source. Here the rays are turned about the patient's body so that healthy tissue absorbs only a very weak dose as the radiation moves past it, but the tumor, located at the center of the rotation, receives a constant bombardment.

When thinking up ideas at all stages of the Tree, allow your thoughts to flow freely and do not impose any kind of mental editing at this time since it will only inhibit creativity. There will be ample opportunity for eliminating totally impractical proposals when you come to examine the Tree at a later date.

There is no limit to the size of the Tree and, where extremely complex problems are concerned, it may be very large and require gradual development over a period of days or weeks. With relatively simple tasks, however, the expansion is normally fairly modest and will not occupy you for an unreasonable amount of time.

While constructing the Tree, make certain you write down every thought that comes to you, not only because this prevents good ideas from being forgotten, but for the equally important reason that it establishes firm links between various mental concepts and so stimulates the creative processes.

If you are a Pathfinder, this apparently unsystematic approach may leave you feeling slightly uneasy, still preferring to use your normal strategy of exploring each part of the problem methodically instead of allowing your mind to range freely over every aspect of the task. This is an understandable but somewhat misguided attitude, since research, our own and that of other psychologists, has clearly established this procedure as the most effective method available for harnessing creativity and stimulating original ideas. In one of our studies, groups of industrial managers were presented with divergent problems of similar complexity before and after learning how to use the Solution Tree approach. Their suggestions were then rated by a panel of judges in terms of originality and practicality. Those produced after some practice with the Tree procedure were rated, on average, 60 pecent more original and 25 percent more practical than pretraining solutions. In the hard, competitive world of the commercial marketplace, such gains are likely to offer those industrialists a considerable edge over their rivals. We have also taught the procedures to such diverse groups as scientists, teachers, creative directors in advertising, publicists, store managers, and business executives, all of whom were able to report an increase in the volume and effectiveness of their ideas when tackling divergent problems of every kind.

We hope this will convince you of the importance and relevance of this straightforward procedure to your everyday problem-solving ability. If you are a Helicopter Pilot, it will enable you to channel your natural style into the most effective channels; if you are a Pathfinder, it will provide you with the essential additional skills needed to cope with this frequently encountered type of problem.

In order to provide practice with this method we would like you to try your new knowledge on two further problems. At the end of the section you can read the solutions which we came up with, but this does not mean our answers are the only ones or even the best ones available. It could well be that your solutions turn out to be more original and successful than those we devised.

Now practice your divergent problem-solving skills.

Problem One: The Dangerous Defector

The first problem we would like you to think about is that presented to Sherlock Holmes by the intelligence agency. Refresh your memory for the facts by rereading the details on page 189, then see if you can do as well—or even better—than the master sleuth.

You do not have to work out how he managed to crush the defector's skull without leaving any trace of the weapon in the cell, although you might like to see if your Tree produces a possible solution. The main thing is to come up with tactics that allow you to assassinate the man without violating any of the conditions laid down by the problem statement. Be especially careful to observe the one which says the killing has to prove so baffling that it cannot be used as political propaganda.

Problem Two: Saving the Sailor

A sailor, the sole survivor of a shipwreck, is cast up on a remote desert island. During the storm, which drove his vessel onto a coral reef, he was blown far from the shipping lanes so that chances of a ship coming close to the island are remote. Somehow he must signal vessels sailing beyond the horizon and alert them to his plight, but this is easier said than done. The island is generally flat, so there are no suitable locations for a signal beacon and in any event, the amount of firewood available is limited. The main vegetation is bamboo, which can be used to construct a shelter, but would not be suitable for building a boat or raft by which to escape. The mariner's only hope, therefore, is to get a message to the outside world. This is where we want you to help. The flotsam drifting ashore from the wreck included three wooden crates containing soft-drink bottles, a broken mirror from one of the bathrooms, several yards of light canvas, two large balls of twine, and a few dozen pieces of cork. In his possession when he reached the shore, and still in working order, are a watch and several ballpoint pens.

While pondering his fate, the sailor will not go short of food or water since he can easily catch and kill turtles which come regularly to the island to lay their eggs, and there is ample fruit and plenty of fresh water.

What practical ways can you think of for solving the sailor's problem?

Problem Three: Political Prisoners

Six political prisoners escape from a labor camp which lies deep in the snow-covered tundra far from the nearest town. After traveling for several days, with the police and guards never far behind, they arrive at a deep, wide river which marks the frontier between their own country and neutral territory where they will be safe from capture.

There is no bridge or ford and nothing on their side of the river from which to construct a raft or some support for a man in the water. Only one of the six is able to swim and, in his weakened condition, he knows it will only be possible for him to make a single crossing of the river on his own. On the other side of the river, across the snow-covered banks, is a forest which would provide plenty of fallen timber for raft building. But, with their pursuers only thirty minutes away, there seems too little time for one man to construct such a craft and bring it back across the river to rescue them. There are a few small caves in the bank on their side which could provide a temporary hiding place, but any search would lead to rapid discovery and execution. What is their best plan of action?

Problem Four: Trapper's Grain

A trapper arrives at a remote cabin, deep in the snow-clad mountains, to start a season's hunting. Before leaving his hut the previous year, he had stocked up the larder with provisions, the main one being a large sack of grain to sustain him on his next visit.

Unfortunately, during his absence a bear has broken into the cabin and split open several storage sacks. His precious grain has become mixed up with a whole lot of sand left over from building the hut. If he is to have enough to eat he must, somehow, separate the sand and the husks of grain. The most obvious way of doing this would be to use his deep, oblong, prospecting sieve. But the mesh is far too coarse and both sand and husks of grain fall through when he attempts to use it.

In the hut he has a stove, fuel and matches, some small cooking pots, eating utensils, a rifle with ammunition, lengths of rope and a sheet of plastic used for keeping his provisions dry when camping. He also has a hunting knife, sleeping bag and oil lantern. How might he construct some device for separating out the grain and the sand?

There is no need to attempt to solve these problems immediately. It would be better practice to allow yourself time to develop a Solution Tree for each over the next few days so that every possibility is fully explored. Remember, this is just as much an exercise in the use of Trees as it is a test of your skill in finding original, creative answers.

You should now turn to Section Five where we will tell you how to use your mind like a genius by learning how to think without words.

Answers to Divergent Problems

We have not attempted here to reproduce the Solution Trees developed in order to come up with our answers to these problems, as they would occupy too much space and appear confusing to anyone who had not developed them from the Problem Stage. It is very likely that your own Trees are equally complex if you have fully explored every possible pathway to a solution.

From the Trees, we come up with these ideas for each situation:

Problem One: The Dangerous Defector

In order to crush the defector's skull without leaving any trace of a weapon, Holmes had him shot by a marksman using a powerful crossbow and a spear of ice. This struck the man as he stood by the barred window, killing him, but then melting in the heat of the room before it could be discovered.

We explained that it was not necessary to kill him in the way Holmes devised, and there are many other possible methods that might have been adopted. It may well be that your own procedure was far more cunning than the one we came up with.

Problem Two: Saving the Sailor

Our Tree yielded two possible methods for attracting attention that we thought could work well in practice. The sailor might have written messages on scraps of canvas or dried leaves and placed them inside the bottles. To make it more likely these would be found, he could then have attached them to the shells of turtles, using the twine. The creatures might have been made more obvious to hunters by attaching them to buoys made from the cork, with a length of bamboo cane flying a "flag" torn from the canvas.

In addition to casting his messages upon the water, our sailor might also have sent aloft for help by constructing a kite from the bamboo canes and canvas capable of lifting the broken mirror into the air so that it flashed a message over the horizon. By tethering it with the twine, he could have sent SOS signals to vessels on the distant shipping lanes. If he adopted both tactics, our unfortunate castaway could double his chances of being picked up.

Problem Three: The Political Prisoners

Problems 3 and 4 include *snow* because we wanted to see if you were now able to break out of the trap of "functional fixedness." In the first problem the snow is just snow, but the answer we favor in the second question requires you to see snow in a different way!

The best solution we came up with for the prisoners is as follows. The five nonswimmers hide, while the swimmer crosses the river. He clambers up the snow-covered bank opposite and walks into the forest. Then he retraces his footsteps, *walking backwards along a different track* until he is in the water again. Now he emerges for a second time and follows a third trail to the forest, then retracing his path to the water's edge for a fourth time while walking backwards. Finally he goes to and from the forest producing another two pairs of tracks in the snow. Retreating to the safety of the trees for the last time, he steps carefully in a previously made set of footprints. In this way he creates the impression that six men have emerged from the river and made their way across the bank and into the forest.

Before finding hiding places, his companions make matching tracks on their side of the river and then walk along the water's edge, where their footprints are hidden, to a point some distance away. They emerge from the water, smoothing the snow behind them with their jackets so as to cover up their tracks, and hide in the caves.

When the police arrive, they see six sets of footprints leading down to the river and six sets emerging on the opposite bank. This makes them believe that the escapers have got clean away across the frontier and are beyond their reach. They abandon the search and ride away, leaving the men free to escape across the river on a raft constructed by their companion in the forest.

Problem Four: The Trapper's Grain

The problem contains two kinds of *functional fixedness*. Our answer involves seeing snow in terms of *water* and the sieve as a *container* rather than a device for sifting material.

In our solution the trapper constructs a container using the sieve and the sheet of plastic material. This is filled with water obtained by melting show on the stove. By dropping the sand-grain mixture into the water he is then easily able to skim off the husks of grain, which float, while the mineral sinks. He could, of course, have done the same thing using the small cooking utensils, but this would have been a slower and less efficient method.

SECTION FIVE

How to Think Like a Great Genius

In any roll call of the world's greatest problem solvers the name of Albert Einstein must surely come close to the top of the list. His discovery that time and space are relative to the position of an observer shook the very foundations of physics and caused a drastic reappraisal of theories about the nature of matter. For his tremendous contribution to human knowlege, Einstein has justly been termed a genius. But this does not mean that his brain was uniquely different or that he possessed intellectual abilities that must always lie beyond the range of most people. Like so many great thinkers, his performance at school was dismal and only a frenzied bout of last-minute studying, together with extensive coaching from his friends, allowed him to pass his final examinations. As Banesh Hoffman,[39] Professor of Mathematics at the City University of New York, and Einstein's biographer, points out, the father of relativity possessed no special scientific gifts, talents, or technical skills. According to Hoffman, what distinguished him from colleagues with far superior research ability was: "The magic touch without which even the most passionate curiosity would be ineffectual: Einstein had the authentic magic that transcends logic."

The key here is the phrase *transcends logic,* for there are occasions in the quest for answers when logic alone, and the words we employ to formulate logical propositions, prove totally inadequate.

How Words Can Fail Us

Our suggestion that logic is sometimes an ineffective method for solving problems may strike you as remarkable, given our previous emphasis on the need for such highly organized and inherently logical structures as Knowledge Networks for learning, and Solution Trees for problem solving. The contradiction, however, is more apparent than real, for within each system the mind is at liberty to work on the task in any way best suited to its needs. You will remember that the relationships among items in Knowledge Networks were not imposed from the outside but arose from the way you chose to associate different aspects of the study material. It was not important if the links you formed appeared illogical to others, since all that mattered was for them to seem appropriate and helpful to you. Similarly, you will have found when tackling the Solution Tree construction that simply shifting information around in the nodes does not automatically yield answers to either convergent or divergent problems. It is almost always necessary to achieve an insight that goes beyond the information given in the problem statement if you are to be successful. In the salesman problem, for instance, a solution could only be found by realizing that you needed to take men *back* from the store as well as transfer them *to* the store initially. In fact, we deliberately designed the problem to include this twist so that you could not discover the sequence of moves necessary simply by constructing a Tree. We wanted to emphasize the point that convergent problem solving is seldom a purely mechanical task without scope for creative perceptions.

All the techniques we have described are powerful ways of helping your brain achieve more of its total intellectual potential by directing mental activities along constructive pathways, by eliminating needless time wasting, and by reducing confusions in order to decrease any anxiety associated with the task. They provide the vital framework on which to build highly effective problem-solving skills but cannot, of themselves, produce the answers you seek. Being able to identify Givens, Operations, and Goals enables you to clarify complex problems and avoid errors in reasoning which arise out of an initial misunderstanding of the problem's true nature. They can point out the fastest and most direct route to a solution, but your brain must then travel down that mental pathway. However substantially our procedures enhance intellectual performance by enabling you to use your brain in the most efficient manner possible, they do not provide an alternative to thought or a substitute for reason. There are many problems that can be solved through an application of logic alone, but there will be other occasions when, in order to take a giant mental stride into the unknown, it will be essential to follow Einstein's lead and, by transcending logic, to draw on enormously potent forces of the mind that lie outside pure reasoning and beyond the frontiers of conventional thought.

To achieve this mental state, we must jettison the fuel that habitually drives our thought but often serves only as a restraint on the free flight of ideas. We must learn to think without using words.

"The limits of my language mean the limit of my world," wrote the philosopher Ludwig Wittgenstein[40] when speculating on the extent to which ideas may be independent of the language used to express them. It is a problem that has long occupied the attention of psychologists, linguists, and philosophers, since the implications for human thought and perceptions are profound. If words shape ideas, rather than serving only as a means of expressing them, then reality cannot exist independently of the language used to describe it. This means that the world will be conceived differently by people whose languages are not alike and that it is this language structure which creates the different ways of perceiving the world. It also rules out the possibility of effectively translating an idea expressed in one language into any other.

These were the conclusions reached by B. L. Whorf,[41] an American linguistics expert, who, after making a detailed study of American Indian languages, developed what became known as the linguistic-relativity hypothesis. Whorf suggested that we think in ways determined by the language we speak. For example, an Eskimo will perceive snow differently from a non-Eskimo because his tongue contains seventeen different words for expressing variations in snow types that are often too subtle for an outsider even to detect.

Investigating this hypothesis, the psychologist J. B. Carroll[42] looked at the ways in which two groups of young Navajo children sorted objects. Both groups lived on reservations, but one spoke only Navajo and the other only English. A characteristic of the Navajo language is the large number of verbs, eleven of which relate to handling objects. The one used depends on the type of item being handled, with specific verbs for long, flexible objects, square ones, round ones, short ones, thin ones, and so on. The correct word form is known and used even by very young Navajo-speaking children. Carroll wanted to discover whether this larger vocabulary, which emphasizes form in preference to other features, would make a difference in the way children perceived the world.

He asked them to sort out a variety of objects which children of their age would normally have sorted on the basis of color rather than shape. This was, indeed, the way English speakers tackled the task. But those who spoke Navajo sorted for form rather than color at a significantly earlier age, their perception of the environment having been strongly influenced by the nature of the language used to describe it.

The importance of this debate lies not in the way words *influence* ideas, but how they *fail* us. There is often a point in a thought when language no longer serves as a vehicle for mental progess, but becomes a stalled truck blocking the path to insight, understanding, and knowledge.

Language, as the American linguist Noam Chomsky[43] has shown, is essentially a logical structure which must inevitably impose its patterns of logic on human thought. If we are to *transcend logic,* therefore, it is vital to develop the ability to think without using language and to conceive ideas other than in the womb of words. When developing many of his most important theories, including those concerned with relativity, this is exactly what Albert Einstein managed to do.

Einstein's Experiments in the Mind

When asked where his laboratory was, Einstein simply produced a fountain pen and said: "It is here." He might more accurately have tapped his head and made the same comment, for his most significant contributions to science were a product not of the physics laboratory but the result of thought experiments performed entirely in his mind. Without such thought experiments it seems unlikely he could have achieved the insights which produced such a quantum leap in man's understanding of the physical world. For, as Banesh Hoffman has perceptively remarked, one can only properly appreciate the uniqueness of the Theory of Relativity by realizing that there is no *logical pathway to it.* The vision he had of time and space was, of necessity, conceived in what Einstein himself described as "a wildly speculative way." When asked how he had achieved the necessary state of mind for the task, he replied that he allowed his brain to play idly with all kinds of idea and images. It was only when he was later obliged to translate those mental impressions into some kind of symbolic language—mathematical or linguistic—that his problems arose.

Einstein developed this technique of wordless thought to such high levels of perfection that his favored method of investigation was to perform these experiments in the mind.

"When I examined myself and my methods of thought," he once wrote, "I came to the conclusion that the gift of fantasy has meant more to me than my talent for absorbing positive knowledge."[44]

He started using this approach at the age of sixteen when considering the physical properties of light, ideas which would later form the basis of his two theories of relativity. In an attempt to visualize how light might appear, if no longer "blurred" by its tremendous velocity, Einstein imagined himself traveling in a space vehicle alongside the speeding beam. In his mind he constructed a vivid image of how the light would then appear, an image which led to his monumental discovery of photons.

Later in life, when he was trying to solve problems relating to molecular size, a thought experiment, based on the cup of tea he was drinking, provided the insight necessary to make another major breakthrough. In his mind's eye he pictured the tea in the cup before him as a structureless liquid, while the molecules of a lump of sugar he had just dropped into it appeared as numerous small hard balls. This image led him to an understanding of the equations needed to explain exactly how those balls would spread through the liquid and what this would do to its consistency.

In the early 1900s Einstein performed a thought experiment that was to shake the world of physics to its foundations. He had begun to realize that Newton's theory of gravitation, until then the unchallenged dogma, was seriously flawed. To explore the concept he pictured himself as the passenger in an elevator hurtling through the farthest reaches of space at a speed faster than light. He then visualized a slot opening on one side of the elevator cage so that a beam of light was projected onto the opposite wall. This enabled him to realize that if the elevator were moving with sufficient velocity, it would travel a finite distance in the time required for the beam to pass across the cage so that an observer in the cage would see the light beam as curved.

On the basis of such thought experiments, Einstein published a paper asserting that gravity is capable of bending light. Although strongly disputed at the time, his radical theory was later confirmed during an eclipse of the sun. By making very precise astronomical measurements, physicists were able to prove that the light from a distant star was indeed being drawn into a curve by the enormous gravitational pull of the sun.

Einstein was not alone in thinking without words so as to break free from the shackles of the logic which language imposes. After studying the biographies and recollections of scores of the world's most eminent thinkers, such men as the French philosopher René Descartes and the mathematicians Georg Cantor, David Hilbert, and Gottlob Frege, all of whom worked at the very frontiers of human knowledge, we have found that thinking in images rather than with man-made symbols, whether letters or numbers, is an essential strategy for peak mental performance.

But you do not have to be working as a philosopher, mathematician, or theoretical physicist in order to benefit from the power of thought experiments. The same technique that helped Einstein to

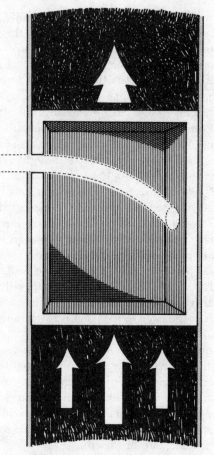

Figure 71

comprehend the laws of the universe can be used equally well for far more mundane mental activities. You can employ exactly the same type of thinking in order to gain insights into problems confronting you at work or at home and, by doing so, produce solutions that might never have occurred to you in any other way.

We have trained people from many different occupations and professions in the thought experiment procedure and then presented them with complex problems which did not yield satisfactory solutions to logic alone. Their suggestions were rated by independent expert judges and compared with the ideas proposed by a matched group of subjects who had received no training. The results showed that by using this easily acquired mental skill experienced thought experimenters were capable of producing three times as many possible solutions. Our judges rated these as being twice as effective and creative as those of untrained subjects.

In this course we have already talked about the power of images to enhance memory, but their value here represents only a small part of their true importance to human thought. By generating images rather than words you can actually gain access to parts of the mind whose frontiers appear to remain forever closed to language.

As is well known, the human brain consists of two separate hemispheres joined by a massive network of connective tissue. Although these hemispheres function as an integrated unit for many tasks, it has long been established that certain activities are localized in one or the other of these cerebral hemispheres. As early as 1861 a Swiss neurologist, Paul Broca, found that when patients suffered damage to a particular area of the left hemisphere they lost the power of speech, although an equal amount of damage to the same portion of the right hemisphere did not lead to any such loss. Studies of people with brain damage from injury or a stroke showed that the comprehension and expression of language is a specific function of the left side of the cerebral cortex, the thick layer of gray cells covering less-developed parts of the brain.

When a surgical technique was devised to alleviate severe epileptic seizures by cutting through the band of fibers (the corpus callosum) connecting the two hemispheres, it became possible to explore the independent functions of each part of the brain more exactly. The so-called split-brain subjects who took part in these studies appeared able to function generally as well as individuals whose hemispheres were still connected, although their performance on specific tasks was very different.

In a typical experiment, the split-brain individual sits before a screen that hides his hands from view while the word "nut" flashes very briefly onto the left side of the screen. With his left hand the subject can easily pick out a nut from a pile of objects hidden from sight behind the screen, but he cannot *tell* the experimenter what word was flashed onto the screen! How can such a strange result be explained?

To understand what is happening in that split-brain person's mind, it is necessary to appreciate two important facts about the way the brain works. The first is that visual information from the eyes is split by the brain so that images received in the left half of each eye go to the right side of the brain and vice-versa. Secondly, we need to know that functions of the left hand are controlled by the right hemisphere of the brain, while the right hand is under the control of the left hemisphere.

When the split-brain subject sees the word "nut" on the left side of the screen, this information is transmitted directly to the right side of the brain which, since it controls his left hand, allows him to pick up the required object. But he is unable to tell the experimenter what the word was because this information cannot be passed across the split to the left hemisphere where language is centered.

The significance to our discussion of thought experiments is that the dominance of the left hemisphere (in right-handed people) and its importance as the language center of the brain are part of the key to the dominance of words over thoughts. It is the left hemisphere which is believed to play a major role in such essentially logical activities as mathematics, scientific experiment, writing, speaking, and deductive reasoning. The right hemisphere, by comparison, is concerned with such processes as music appreciation, fantasy, and artistic expression.

When making use of thought experiments it seems likely that we are able to draw power from this normally nondominant hemisphere. It could also be that left-handed people, because their right hemispheres are usually dominant, have a greater natural ability to use fantasy than most. But, whether you are left- or right-handed, wordless thinking is a skill that can soon be perfected and put to work for any kind of intellectual task.

How to Use Mental Images

If you were asked how many legs a dog has, your immediate response would be *four*. If you were asked the shape of a turtle's tail, you would almost certainly hesitate before replying, unless of course you happen to be an expert on turtles!

The pause for thought was necessary because you employed a rather different method for answering the second question. The reply needed for the first depended on thinking with words. Your brain simply associated dogs with four legs and provided the answer required virtually instantly. What almost certainly happened when you thought about the turtle, however, was that you formed an image of the creature in your mind and mentally examined it to provide a description of the tail. This process took more time and led to the delay between question and response.

It was probably quite easy to conjure up a mental picture of a turtle vivid enough for you to examine it carefully in your mind's eye, but you might have experienced rather more difficulty at this moment in sustaining the image for any length of time or to extending the visual imagery to take in more details of the surroundings in which a turtle might be found.

The point is that almost everyone can conjure up some kind of image on demand and very often hold that picture for a short amount of time. To develop a high level of expertise in thought experiments, therefore, it is only necessary to build on skills which are already present. You need first to practice creating images that are powerful, vivid, and sustained and then learn how to manipulate these in a constructive manner.

We suggest that you carry out at least one thought experiment session per day for the next two weeks in order to perfect the procedure.

Relax by sitting or lying comfortably and loosening any tight clothing. You should remove your shoes, uncross your legs, close your eyes lightly, and keep your breathing regular and shallow. An excellent time for thought experiments is immediately prior to falling asleep, as there is a brief period on the borders between waking and sleeping when especially powerful mental pictures—known as hypnogogic images—can be conjured up.

If you have found the day especially stressful, then spend a couple of minutes unwinding physically before starting the session. You can do this by thinking about each part of your body in turn, starting at your feet and working slowly up the trunk to your hands, arms, shoulders, and face. Seek out any tension in these muscles and then imagine it flowing away, like water pouring down the drain when the plug has been removed. Picture this as vividly as you can in order to bring mind and body into a receptive state.

Now open your mind to images of all kinds and at first make no attempt to exert any influence over them. All you need do at this stage is practice developing each scene as clearly as possible. Notice shapes and colors, and enhance the imagery by adding sounds and scents. If you were picturing a tropical beach, for instance, you should *feel* the warmth of the sand beneath your feet and the hot sun on your back, *smell* the aroma of tropical flowers and salt surf, *hear* the gentle noise of breakers on the shore and the wind in the palms, while *seeing* the scene in every detail of color and form.

Once you have developed the ability to conjure up vividly any scene your mind presents, continue the practice by holding each image for longer and longer periods. At first you will probably find that the brain flashes up a whole variety of scenes during your training sessions, like someone racing through a whole box of projection slides. After a few days, while still permitting your mind to produce whatever picture it wishes, start to exert increasing control over the length of time for which each is presented. Continue with these two basic techniques of developing vivid pictures and holding them for an increasing amount of time for the first week or ten days of training. How long it takes to acquire the necessary amount of control varies among individuals and you must decide for yourself when the moment has arrived to move to the third stage of training.

What you should do now is to order your mind to create the sort of images you wish to see. Begin by looking at familiar scenes, from home or work for example, where it is possible to picture each aspect in clear detail. See yourself as part of the scene, hear the conversations around you, touch and taste the fantasy as appropriate. As well as making the picture as powerful as possible, practice sustaining it in the mind's eye until such time as *you*, rather than your subconscious mental processes, want to switch to another image.

Once you are able to control the scene completely by determining the nature of the images, the vividness with which they are represented, and their duration, you are ready to apply it to practical problems. Here are just three of the ways in which our clients have put thought experiments to work:

1. *For Coping with Personal Problems*

Very often personal problems are the most difficult to deal with because we are too close to them to get an objective view of the various factors to be considered. We cannot be sure what will happen if we decide to take a particular course of action or whether one approach is going to prove more effective than another. Relating these difficulties to the basic building blocks of problems, we can say that our knowledge of the Givens is uncertain (have we interpreted them correctly, have we taken all the essential ones into account?), our thoughts about which Operations to use are confused (which course of action really will prove most successful?), and we may even be unclear about our Goals (what outcome do we really hope for?). It would be pointless to try and construct a Solution Tree, since the information available is too vague, but we can usefully engage in a thought experiment.

Go into the scene where the elements of that problem are present and set up a particular scenario for what is most likely to occur in a given set of circumstances. Hear the words spoken and feel the emotions they will create. See yourself and the other people involved very clearly, observe their reactions to statements you make and your own response to what they are likely to say or do. If you have practiced the mental imagery technique adequately, it should be possible both to participate and stand back from the scene, being simultaneously a part of the action and a detached observer of all that is happening. When an outcome is reached, assess its merits and drawbacks and come to a conclusion about whether the Operations you performed have led to the kind of Goal you desire. If not, then rerun the scene, this time applying different Operations or using different Givens to produce a different Goal.

In some circumstances you may have a Goal clearly in mind from the start, in which case you should use a variation on this approach, which has wide applications to all areas of human achievement.

2. *For Attaining Desired Goals*

It is quite usual for our clients to present us with problems concerned with ways of achieving clearly defined goals. They know exactly where they want to go in life but cannot work out the best way of getting there. Such difficulties may focus on family problems or arise at work. Common ones include problems of asserting oneself; standing up for one's rights; refusing unreasonable demands; asking for a promotion or a raise in pay; speaking in public; questioning the decisions of a superior; presenting one's honest views to a partner; and combating aggression in others.

This type of thought experiment starts with the Goal being successfully accomplished. If you wanted to ask for a promotion or a pay raise, for example, you would begin the scene by picturing yourself making the request to your superior. The response could then be imagined, together with your reply. In this way it is possible to rehearse a wide variety of possible reactions and work out ways of coping with them. It might be that, in the past, you have accepted comments like: "We'll talk about it later . . . ," or been deflected from your goal by signs of aggression. As you use a thought experiment to solve the problem, it is quite easy to think up and use all the retorts and comments that, in the past, you only thought of when it was too late. By establishing clear Operations and rehearsing them during visual imagery sessions, your brain knows exactly how best to respond in the real-life situations. This prevents confusion and allows you to do and say the most appropriate things in that particular circumstance.

It might also be that some Goals, although strongly desired, are associated with such high levels of anxiety that few attempts are made to attain them. Thought experiments can be used to solve this type of problem as well, allowing you to perform any kind of activity without handicapping levels of mental and physical tension.

The procedure for reducing anxiety is similar in most respects to usual thought experiments. You start by imagining yourself, as vividly as possible, carrying out the anxiety-arousing activity. Experience some of the fears which this would produce. Do not try to repress them or pretend that you would cope easily in real life if this is untrue, *but switch off the scene before a high level of anxiety is generated.* As soon as you start to feel mentally or physically tense, stop the image and relax your muscles, using the methods described earlier. As you do this, it is very helpful to conjure up some soothing images that will dispel any lingering mental tension. This scene can be anything that you find restful. Some people enjoy imagining they are sunning themselves on a warm beach; others picture a tranquil country scene or see themselves sitting comfortably at home listening to a favorite piece of music. Whatever scene you select, make sure it is so vivid that you are completely absorbed in it and begin to feel good inside almost as soon as it starts. You can achieve this sense of instant tranquility by finishing each and every session of mental imagery by holding, feeling, and enjoying this special scene in your mind for a few moments.

Once you are physically and mentally relaxed, return to the situation and explore it a little more. Stop as soon as anxiety begins to build up again and banish the fears using mental and physical relaxation as before. It may take a number of thought experiment sessions to achieve, but eventually you will find it possible to to right through that once fear-inducing scene without feeling anything more than the slightest and most easily managed anxiety. At this point you can go into the actual situation confident of your ability to cope effectively.

Use this type of thought experiment to build any Goal you desire up to the point where fantasy can be translated into reality.

3. Finding Solutions to Highly Complex Problems

Mind images can carry your thoughts to realms of discovery they could never reach using other means. If you are confronted by a technical problem which seems so complex that no solution is possible, then stop thinking about it in words and turn on to the power of images.

For many years the German chemist Friedrich Kekule wrestled with the problems of chemical structures, but the discovery he finally made, which has been described as the "most brilliant piece of prediction to be found in the whole range of organic chemistry,"[45] emerged from a thought experiment conducted as he drifted off to sleep.

Into Kekule's mind, as he imagined how the structure of benzene might appear, came a powerful image of a snake chasing its own tail. Such a scene may not seem to bear much relation to benzene, yet Kekule's thought experiment made the connection. He suddenly realized that the atomic structure of benzene, like the snake, must take the form of a ring. Today three quarters of all organic chemistry is directly or indirectly the product of that single insight.

There are many examples in science of the power of thought experiments and they seem to suggest that the key to success lies in *undirected images*. In discussing the ways in which you can use mental imagery for other purposes we have stressed the need to exercise a high degree of control over the scenes produced. But here the exact opposite holds true. You should relax all controls and make no attempt to censure the pictures that flow through your mind. Feed in your problem and then lie back and let your mind do the work, but keep a close watch on the images produced, because one of them may be the clue you need to lead directly to a solution.

When engaged in this type of thought experiment, be sure to keep a note pad and pencil, or better still, a tape recorder beside you. As soon as you get any ideas that might be helpful, stop the experiment and make a note of the thoughts. Never leave this task to the end of the session in the hope you will remember important concepts because it is very unlikely you can hold them in your memory while the thought experiment continues.

When people speak about discoveries that changed the course of their lives, and sometimes the lives of millions of others, you often hear mention of a "flash of inspiration" or a "stroke of genius" that produced the critical idea. What they are really describing is the outcome of a thought experiment which they were probably not even aware was taking place in their minds at the time. Your brain very often works in such a way, especially when sleep liberates it from word domination, which is why if you go to sleep on a problem, you often wake up with an answer.

Now there is no longer any need to rely on the usually haphazard and uncontrollable nature of this process. By making thought experiments part of your daily thinking routine, the normally hidden power of mental imagery can be exploited at will to produce insights, aid understanding, and provide solutions to problems of any kind.

STEP FIVE

Thinking Better
About Decision Making

Would you go out of your way to save $5 on a purchase that normally cost $10? Most people feel such a discount would make the extra trouble worthwhile. But when asked if they would do the same to save $5 on a $500 item, very few thought the amount worth the additional effort. Since exactly the same saving is involved in each case, such a decision is clearly not logical, however sensible it may appear.

Many of the decisions we make are equally illogical, adversely influenced by hidden bias and based on ill-considered options. Because decisions are such a vital part of thinking better we have included them in this training course. We will show you how to enhance your ability to make all types of decisions through the use of mental programs that eliminate bias and allow you to evaluate the information on which to base your choice objectively. You will learn how, as with learning and problem solving, there is a personal style of decision making and you will discover ways of turning this to your best advantage. You will also be able to assess aspects of your personality which play a crucial role in influencing the decisions you reach and how you reach them. Finally, we will be considering some of the common errors and fallacies in the decision-making process that often lead the unwary badly astray.

SECTION ONE

Assessing Your Decision-Making Style

The starting point, as with learning and problem solving, is to find out how your natural thinking style influences the way you make decisions. Our research has shown that this can be accomplished very effectively by the use of a simple questionnaire which asks you to respond to seven situations involving different types of decision.

1. It is early in the morning and you are about to leave for work. Your job is going to take you outdoors a good deal today and, although the sky is clear at the moment, the forecast has warned of rain. Because you have other things to carry, it will be awkward to take an umbrella along and you do not want to wear a raincoat unnecessarily. Which of the following thoughts is most likely to be uppermost in your mind as you prepare to leave the house?

a. Even though the forecast was bad, the sky looks clear to me and that's usually the sign of a fine day. I'll take a chance and leave my umbrella and raincoat at home.

b. It always seems to rain when I leave my umbrella and raincoat at home, so, rather than risk a soaking, I'm going to have to take them along despite the inconvenience.

c. I would feel foolish if I were caught in a downpour without any protection. On the other hand, I shall be annoyed if I burden myself unnecessarily and it doesn't rain. I'll compromise by taking my umbrella and hope this will keep me sufficiently dry if there is a storm.

2. You have saved some money to invest in the stock market and your broker mentions three different types of stock you might buy, providing the following information about each.

There is a very steady blue-chip issue which offers a safe investment but little chance that it will ever bring in a large profit.

There is an extremely speculative mining stock which pundits confidently expect to show a spectacular rise in price shortly. But if this inside information turns out to be wrong, the stock will remain unproductive.

There are shares in a small manufacturing company whose board of directors are considering a takeover by a multinational. If this happens, the stock will rise in price; if not, the price is going to remain where it is.

When deciding which stock to purchase, which of these thoughts is most likely to be passing through your mind?

a. If you never speculate or take a chance, you are never going to get a big profit, so I'll believe the insider information and buy mining stock.

b. With my luck, if there is any possibility of the stock going down, it will. I'll opt for the safe blue-chip investment and a small but steady return.

c. I'd hate to miss out on a good deal. On the other hand, I'll kick myself if I lose money or only break even when there is profit to be made. I'll go for the manufacturing company because, even if the worst happens, I won't feel too bad about my choice.

3. You have been moved by your firm to another part of the country and been obliged to place your home on the market for $80,000. Because you have had to borrow money at a high interest rate to purchase a new house, it is important to sell your old one as quickly as possible. Although your asking price is a fair one, the real estate market is suffering a downturn and properties in your area tend to sell slowly. The day after your house goes on the market a prospective purchaser arrives and offers $70,000 in cash. By taking up his offer at that point you will be badly in the red. On the other hand, if the house fails to sell within the next few months, you will pay more than the difference in interest charges. As you reflect on his offer, which of the following thoughts is likely to be running through your mind?

a. I would be dumb to take $10,000 less than the fair asking price when I might be able to get more later. I'll tell him there is no deal.

b. I'd better take his money even though it is less than I want and below the true value of the property. With my luck and the bad state of the market, it may be a long time before I get anywhere near as good an offer again.

c. If I accept his offer, I shall regret it; on the other hand, if I turn him down flat and nothing better comes along for half a year, I shall feel bad about that decision, too. I will try to keep this buyer interested for a few weeks by stalling and make every effort to sell the house at the price I want in the meantime. If I don't appear too keen, he may up his offer a bit, and, at the worst, I shall have a buyer to fall back on if the price I want is not offered.

4. Your firm's prosperity depends to a great extent on the drive, enthusiasm, and success of its sales force. A rival organization has fired their top salesman and you know that his experience, skill, and contacts could prove a tremendous asset. The difficulty is you cannot find out for certain why he was dismissed. His version is

that there was a personality clash between himself and the new sales director, but the grapevine suggests there might have been other reasons. One story is that he has a drinking problem and is no longer trustworthy; another claims he was caught defrauding the company and only just avoided prosecution. After interviewing him you still do not know the truth, but must decide whether or not to offer him employment. While pondering your decision, would you be most likely to reflect that:

a. It would be worth taking a chance because he could be tremendously valuable, provided the rumors are untrue. The malicious gossip could have been spread by a sales director trying to get back at an awkward ex-employee and one should always trust one's own judgment when assessing staff.

b. It would be foolish to take a risk because where there's smoke there is almost always fire, and even if those stories are untrue, the real reason for his dismissal could be equally serious. It is better to be safe than sorry and accept that if things can go wrong they probably will go wrong.

c. It would be best not to rush into a decision which is likely to give me cause for regret later on. If I employ someone who is dishonest or unreliable, the mistake could be serious; on the other hand, it is foolish to turn his application down flat because, if he is reliable and honest, I don't want to lose him to a rival. My best course of action is to tell him I cannot come to an immediate decision but will let him know by the end of the week. In the meantime I can take steps to check out the allegations more carefully and see if there is any truth in them.

5. After leaving college, John has been confronted by a difficult choice over how best to further his academic career. He could have gone to a prestigous university where finishing a degree would be very tough but would reflect extremely favorably on his intellectual ability. Alternatively, he might have attended a less distinguished academy where a degree would be easier to obtain but lack the same distinction. John decided to take the difficult course and flunked out.

Do you think that:

a. He did the right thing by aiming high because you should always go for the best there is. His failure is unfortunate, but it need not prevent him from trying another university.

b. He only had himself to blame for what happened because overreaching oneself inevitably results in failure and disappointment.

c. His best approach would have been to apply to a wide enough range of universities to avoid a disappointing outcome. By doing so he might have found one that combined a fair amount of prestige with a course better suited to his intellectual abilities.

6. You are owed $6,000 and feel your chances of recovering the money are slender since the debtor seems to have no assets and few prospects of ever obtaining the sum. When you confront him, he frankly admits that he is almost broke but offers you three choices. He will give you all the cash he possesses, some $3,500, in full and final settlement of the debt. Alternatively, being a gambling man, he is prepared to offer a wager based on the toss of a coin. If he wins, you must forget about the debt and give him a letter to that effect. If you win, however, he will part with the only thing of any value he possesses, a solid gold watch which belonged to his father. He had hoped never to part with the heirloom, but now accepts he may have to let it go. After examining the watch you realize it must be worth at least $10,000. When trying to decide what to do for the best, are you most likely to think:

a. I'll take a chance. After all, I shall only really be risking $3,500 since I am never likely to get more out of him than that, and I could almost double my original investment if I get lucky.

b. With my luck I would be bound to lose. It's crazy to risk everything on the toss of a coin. I'd better write off part of the debt, accept his offer of $3,500 and learn not to be so trusting when lending money in the future.

c. I cannot agree to any of his offers because, whatever I decide, I shall end up feeling bad about it. If I win, I will feel I have taken advantage of someone in trouble and profited unreasonably from his misfortune. If I lose, I shall be mad at myself for throwing away all that money. If I accept his settlement, I shall always believe I could have done better. So I'll tell him there's no deal and he must come up with some way of paying me the full amount.

7. You have been given tips on three horses running in different races. As the information comes from a good friend, who is also an experienced trainer, you decide to bet $100 on the first horse,

which romps home at odds of ten to one. With the remaining horses yet to run, would you be most likely to decide:

a. I'll put my money on the second horse and, if that comes in first, transfer those winnings to the third. I would be crazy to pass up this chance to make a really big win.

b. I'll collect my money and go home while I'm still ahead. Nobody knows enough about horses to predict three winners in a row and, with my luck, I'll lose the whole thing.

c. I'll put some of my winnings on the next two tips. I would be annoyed if I failed to bet and they were first past the post. On the other hand, it would be foolish to risk all my gains on the next two races.

To score, simply total the "a"s, "b"s, and "c"s, then see which response appears most frequently. If you have a majority of "a"s, then your personal style of decision making is that of the *Maximizer;* a majority of "b"s, and you are a *Minimizer;* a majority of "c"s indicates that you are a *Protector.*

Each of these styles has certain strengths and weaknesses which need to be appreciated in order to remove a potential source of bias from your decision making. By understanding what motivates you to respond in a particular way, you can ensure that your approach matches the particular situation. It also enables you to identify the tactics being used by others in decision making and, when th is is to your advantage, exploit their weaknesses or appreciate their strengths.

What the Decision Styles Tell You

The Maximizer

This is the style of the entrepreneur who is always willing to take a chance if it looks as if it will pay big dividends. Maximizers are consistently optimistic about their ability to come out on top no matter how adverse the circumstances may appear. When mistakes are made, little time is wasted in regrets; instead setbacks are looked on as valuable learning experiences that can help to prevent similar misjudgments in the future.

They are best at making decisions in situations where, for one reason or another, none of the options seems particularly attractive. This is because the Maximizer is acutely sensitive to any positive features that may be present in a given course of action. The possibilities of good things which *could* happen by adopting a specific option are immediately apparent to such a person, while less attention is paid to negative aspects of the choice.

This style is especially suited to salespersons, people in public relations, publishing, and any activity demanding entrepreneurial flair.

The weakness of this approach is that big gains will often be matched by equally large losses when adverse decisions are taken. The Maximizer's desire to go for broke on all occasions explains why many of them seem to spend their lives spectacularly seesawing from high achievement to near disaster.

The Minimizer

The key feature of this approach to decision making is a desire to minimize the risk of loss. Minimizers take the view that one should always proceed on the assumption that things will go wrong and opt for decisions that lead to the least damaging consequences. It is a style ideally suited to all high-risk situations where there is the possibility of material loss, for instance, when dealing on the stock, property, or currency markets. If the odds are stacked against success, then the Minimizer's decisions are not only going to prove the safest but have the best chance of leading to a steady if unspectacular gain. Minimizers can be trusted to manage big projects or deal in large sums of other people's money because they avoid taking chances, however tempting the potential rewards, and are most unlikely to be interested in an enticing but highly speculative proposal.

Because this style is, in most ways, the complete opposite to the Maximizer, there is always likely to be conflict if they are trying to make joint decisions. As the Minimizer seeks to prevent the worst from happening when things go amiss, the Maximizer will be insisting that real progress can only be made provided risks are taken.

The weakness of this approach is that valuable opportunities may well be neglected and, in attempting to minimize losses, potential gains may never be realized.

The Protector

The major consideration for those adopting this style of decision making is to protect themselves and others from choices which will later be the cause for regret. Unlike the Minimizer, who seeks to reduce the consequences of failure to a minimum, the Protector seeks to safeguard himself or herself against lost chances and missed opportunities.

Of the three styles, those who adopt a Protector approach are most acutely aware of the discrepancy between results actually achieved and what could have been attained had a different course of action been followed. Wasted opportunities are a source of irritation and frustration to the Protector, whose decisions are powerfully influenced by an overwhelming concern to reduce to a minimum the possibility of any subsequent remorse.

Protectors make excellent decisions in situations where there is insufficient information to be certain what to do for the best. If the issues are clouded by doubt and obscured by uncertainty, adopting a middle-of-the-road strategy can often prove the safest and most successful course of action. Should such a decision turn out to be mistaken, then losses are reduced to a minimum; if it proves the right choice, positive gains can still be made.

In the seven situations above, the information was presented in such a way as to illustrate the likely responses of each of these three styles. When it comes to betting money on horses, for example, the Maximizer will be willing to risk all and take a big chance in order to enjoy a big win. The Minimizer, seeking to reduce risks as much as possible, is quite happy to walk away after the first race with a healthy profit on the original stake. For the Protector, however, either decision is likely to lead to regret and will therefore be avoided. By placing a small amount of the initial winnings on the second and third horses, there is always the chance for further gain, but the risk of losing everything is eliminated.

If you scored a near equal total of all three letters, this indicates a useful flexibility in your decision-making style, allowing you to adapt your approach to suit the demands of the situation.

Letter totals of four-two-one show a moderately flexible approach, while a three-two-two sequence reveals an even more closely matched approach. It suggests you are able to identify and use the style best suited to the situation and change it with changing circumstances.

A four-three-zero pattern indicates that your preferred style (total of four) is augmented by a backup style that can be used whenever the first approach seems inappropriate.

If you scored an "a" for the college situation, a "b" for the stock purchase, and a "c" for the raincoat question, you would appear to have a flexible style combined with the ability to switch according to the demands of the task. These situations presented a *conflict choice* best handled by a Maximizer approach; a *condition of high risk* which requires a Minimizer strategy; and a *situation of uncertainty*, where the Protector usually has the best tactics.

It must be emphasized that none of these approaches is necessarily going to prove better or worse than any other, or that by applying the appropriate style to a particular decision task you will be bound to select the correct course of action. All one can say for certain is that you stand the best chance of doing so by matching your style to the demands of the situation.

To demonstrate these styles in action we are going to eavesdrop on a meeting in the office of the managing director of an imaginary cosmetics company which is contemplating the takeover of a rival firm. The director, a brilliant entrepreneur who has built her empire from a back-street business to the status of a major international company, is the driving force behind the bid. A Maximizer, she has pulled off many major coups in the past, often operating with a cool audacity that has horrified her less steel-nerved colleagues. Although she has had her fair share of mistakes and setbacks, she has never let them dent her confidence or her enthusiasm for further expansion. Now she is promoting the takeover against considerable opposition from her fellow directors. The company accountant, a Minimizer, disapproves of the scheme and is prepared to argue strongly against any decision to proceed. He is an experienced and capable director whose careful approach has, on occasion, given the company much-needed stability and saved it from some of the Maximizer's more wildly speculative notions. On other occasions, however, his caution has been responsible for lost opportunities, a fact which the managing director is never slow to point out. In turn, he can list a fair number of projects which went ahead against his advice and cost the firm considerable sums of money.

The third person present, the company secretary, is a Protector, whose approach to all decisions is one of safeguarding his fellow directors against following a course of action they will later regret. In the past, his balanced judgments have proved invaluable, although at times the middle-of-the-road tactics he advocates worry the Minimizer and irritate the Maximizer. It is the company secretary who starts the discussion by outlining the takeover proposal.

Protector: As you all know, Company X has been in financial trouble for many years and seems ripe for a takeover. Most of the plant is outdated, the buildings are in need of repair, they are overstaffed, and their overall efficiency is very poor, factors that have undoubtedly contributed to their current difficulties. However, they do own a number of extremely valuable patents and some of their senior staff, especially in the research and development divisions, are highly skilled. It would certainly be to our advantage to gain these employees and to market some of Company X's lines. The trouble is we would also be spending a good deal of money on antiquated plant and rundown premises.

Maximizer: You well know my feelings on this. It is an opportunity we would be very unwise to miss. The market is suffering from a downturn at the moment, which makes their products less attractive, but when the recession is over I am sure we will see a big upturn in sales on all their lines. If we buy in now, we can acquire skills and patents which might not be on offer again if the company somehow manages to survive their current difficulties. I accept that we will also be taking on an unprofitable plant and buildings, but these can be sold off and the staff we need moved to our own factories and laboratories.

Minimizer: That's fine in theory, but I foresee grave practical difficulties. As you rightly say, we shall be acquiring a great deal of antiquated plant and buildings only fit to be torn down. I'd like to point out that we are not only buying them but also paying a high price for them—a needlessly high price in my opinion. Suppose we can't sell off the premises? They aren't in zones suitable for redevelopment as residential housing and the costs of demolishing and rebuilding would make new factories constructed on those sites prohibitively expensive. I can't see any company, particularly in the current economic climate, being prepared to take them off our hands. So we will continue to pay out on empty buildings that we can do nothing with, that nobody else will want, and that are going to prove a major drain on our resources. As to the plant, most of that is fit only for scrap, so here again we will suffer a loss.

What do we gain apart from the patents? You suggest we can expect to acquire skilled R and D personnel, but what makes you think they will be prepared to work for us? There is a tremendous loyalty within that company and I fear many will regard us as the bad guys who destroyed their old firm. I have been told unofficially that many would refuse any offer of employment we made them, however tempting. Don't forget that the people we need are so skilled they can find work anywhere in the industry. We will be left with buildings we can't use, plant which is worthless, and only those employees whom nobody else wants to employ. I strongly argue that this is a course of action our company should not adopt.

The Maximizer: As usual you have put the worse possible interpretation on things and looked very negatively at my proposals. Okay, we may have trouble with the premises in the short term, but the recession will soon bottom out and when it does, factory accommodation is going to be at a premium. We don't need to demolish and rebuild because sufficient modernization can be achieved at a reasonable cost to turn them into attractive commercial properties. The plant may be old, but much of it is in perfect working order and can be salvaged. As far as the staff is concerned, there is no reason to suppose they will regard us as ogres, provided the terms of the takeover are fair and communication lines are kept open. Our public relations department is skilled at selling deals to all kinds of people and they can sell this one just as effectively. Played right, we are going to get all the staff we want and at a very reasonable price. Don't forget that we are also acquiring patents on a line of products that sold very well in the past.

Minimizer: But now have declined in popularity. You blame the recession, but I think they are old-fashioned and have been overtaken by public taste.

Protector: I agree it seems unwise to miss this chance of buying assets that could be beneficial to our company's prosperity and growth. On the other hand, it seems a little unwise to proceed in the way currently envisaged. Why do we need to buy the whole company in order to get hold of the patents and skilled staff? Since they are in financial trouble and most of their lines have been doing badly recently, might they not be prepared to sell off those patents in order to help themselves out of a hole? As for the staff, it has been pointed out that our public relations people do a fine job in promoting this company's image. Let's use those skills to attract the men and women we need. We can offer more modern laboratories, better recreational facilities, a more secure future, higher pay . . . surely those are tempting enough to bring us the employees we want without having to spend large sums on things we don't want or need.

Maximizer: But all this misses the point. We have to act quickly before somebody else does. Okay, we could try to buy the patents separately or lure away the staff, we could take advantage of their current difficulties ... but we're not the only company interested. While we are playing it safe, somebody else is going to think big, walk in, and grab the whole prize. I say we decide to take them over right away.

Minimizer: I agree that the middle course is not viable because we would be tying ourselves up in long and costly negotiations that could easily come to nothing and, at best, are going to offer negligible gains ... staff whose loyalty is questionable—if they were tempted away by us, what's to stop them being tempted by somebody else—and the patents for products whose commercial viability is open to question. I say we forget the whole thing.

Protector: I still feel both of you are taking too extreme a view. Why go for broke or walk away from the table when there are gains to be made at no real risk to ourselves? If we just ignore the situation we'll be sorry later on, but I am equally certain we would regret a full takeover just as much. I say we proceed modestly and only gain those parts of the company we truly need.

What decision was finally taken, and whether this proved the best course of action, we will never know. But the scenario does make clear the very different approaches to decision making adopted by the three styles. It also illustrates the way in which the styles influence selective attention, causing each member of the group to focus on particular pieces of information and to regard those facts which support their arguments as more significant than the rest.

Bear in mind that your own decision-making style will exert an equally powerful effect not only on the way in which you come to favor a particular course of action but also on how you attend to, assess, evaluate, and select the information on which that judgment is based.

There are, of course, ways in which biases of this type can be eliminated from the decision-making process, and in Section Three we will be discussing these and showing you exactly how to replace subjective judgments with objective assessments. But, before doing so, we need to explore one important factor in any choice situation, the influence of personality on the decisions we prefer to make.

SECTION TWO

How Personality Influences Choice

Whenever we are trying to choose between different courses of action, two factors will always be uppermost in our mind. The first is how *likely* it is that any particular outcome can be achieved and the second is how much we *desire* that result to be attained. These twin elements of probability and desirability exert a powerful influence on any decisions we make and, in the next section, you will learn how to assess them in an objective manner. But it is important to understand, before doing so, the way basic aspects of your own personality are likely to distort and bias estimates of probability and desirability. Only by appreciating the role your feelings about life play in determining how you evaluate outcomes can you expect to assess probability and desirabililty effectively.

At our laboratory in London we have been exploring the ways in which personality and choice interact to make specific courses of action seem more or less probable or more or less desirable. Our findings are generally similar to those obtained by Orville Brim of the Child Study Association in New York,[46] whose research results we will be looking at in a moment.

Before describing these studies and explaining what aspects of personality are important in decision making, we would like you to assess the part played by these traits in the choices you make. Read through the ten pairs of contrasting statements and note the numbers of those which reflect your own approach to decision making. As always in such assessments it is essential to be completely honest with yourself if the results are to prove meaningful.

1. When making up my mind over an issue I rely on my own judgment.

2. When making up my mind on an issue I prefer to listen to and follow advice and suggestions from others.

3. Once I have reached a decision, I usually stick to it.

4. I am always willing to change my views if someone else seems to have a better approach.

5. I consider my judgment is, in general, as good as or superior to other people's.

6. I think that my judgments can often be improved by listening to what others have to say.

7. It would not worry me to take an independent line, even if this were opposed by the majority.

8. I feel more confident my views are right when they are shared by most people.

9. I am more self-reliant than most.

10. I depend on others to a great extent.

11. I think it is unnecessary to listen to others when making a decision.

12. I find it helpful to hear what others have to say before making a decision.

13. I find it easy to let myself go and express my emotions readily.

14. I tend to keep my feelings under tight control.

15. I respond strongly to the mood of those around me, feeling happy if they are happy or sad when they are sad.

16. I do not consider that I am strongly influenced by the emotions of others.

17. I would describe myself as an emotional person.

18. I would not describe myself as an emotional person.

19. I have sympathy with people who allow their true feelings to show.

20. I find it embarrassing when people become emotional in my presence.

What Your Score Reveals

If you ticked *even* numbers for statements 2–12, it indicates a certain dependency on the views of others. If the odd numbers, 1–11, were ticked, then you are more self-sufficient and independent in your judgments. These two aspects of personality should be seen as points on a continuum with extremely dependent behavior at one end and highly independent attitudes at the other.

Since most people lie somewhere between these extremes, it is likely that you scored a mixture of odd and even numbers. A higher score in one direction or the other, however, shows that you have a tendency to be more or less self-dependent when it comes to making decisions. What this implies for the kind of decisions you are most likely to make will be discussed below.

Our research, and that of Dr. Brim, shows that emotionality—itself an important component of personality—also influences decision making. Your position on this dimension was explored by statements 13–20. As you will have realized, *odd* numbers indicate a generally emotional response to life, while *even* numbers show that emotional control is a more dominant trait in your makeup. Once again, these factors can be regarded as points on a continuum where extreme control and extreme emotionality represent poles at each end of the line.

An equal number of odd and even responses reveals an extremely balanced attitude toward life and it is probable that you can change your approach to match the needs of a particular situation. We suggest that you reassess yourself from time to time to try and identify any circumstances likely to tilt you off balance toward one or the other of the extremes. At such times read through our comments below and apply our advice to your decision making.

A higher odd or even score, even if the difference is only one or two points, reveals a *tendency* to react in a way which takes you closer to one or the other of the extremes on the continuum. This is bound to influence your judgments to some extent, although the smaller the difference, the less powerful the overall effect. Nonetheless, you may find it helpful to read through the appropriate categories below so that you can appreciate the ways in which this is likely to affect your choices. The greater the discrepancy between the scores, the more strongly what we have to say applies and the more notice you should take of our cautions.

Dependency and Decision Making

Higher Odd Than Even Score on Statements 1–12

The more independent you are in your decision making, the more ordered and systematic your approach is likely to be. A rather less positive aspect of this personality trait is the amount of pessimism frequently associated with such self-sufficiency. Our research has shown that people who depend on themselves rather than others when making decisions tend to take a generally gloomy view of the probability or desirability of the various options open to them. In the belief that things are more likely to turn out badly than well, they attempt to safeguard themselves against the worst by considering as many possible consequences for their actions as they can. This leads to a confusion of choice and an underestimation of the desirability or probability of every outcome.

In the next section, when we talk about assigning number values to these factors, you will probably find that the logical structuring of decision making we propose appeals to your natural aptitude for rational thought. But you must be on your guard against assigning unrealistically *low* values and avoid trying to consider an unnecessarily large number of possible consequences. Bear in mind the influence of personality over the choices you make, adopt a rather more optimistic attitude toward outcomes, and restrict the range of actions you consider by eliminating any which, while admittedly possible, are actually rather improbable.

Higher Even Than Odd Score on Statements 1–12

Your need for support and reassurance when making decisions ensures that you canvas a wide range of opinions before coming to any conclusion. But it also means that you are frequently overly optimistic about the probability and/or desirability of a particular outcome and this may lead you to consider *too few courses of action.* Dr. Brim's research in the United States, and our own studies in Europe, have shown that dependent people are often so certain what they have decided will work out right for them that they close their minds to equally likely consequences. By focusing too narrowly on one or two choices, it is easy to overlook alternatives that might lead to an even more probable and desirable state of affairs.

We have also found that, unlike the independent decision maker, dependent people tend to use more intuition than logic when evaluating the information on which to base their decisions. They generally prefer hunches and gut reactions to a systematic ordering of the positive or negative features of each option. While feelings certainly have a role, and an important one, to play in decision making they should never be allowed to take control of the situation or to swamp out more reasoned judgments.

In order to increase the number of options being considered you need to take rather more time in thinking about each choice and its probable consequences so as to widen your range of alternative responses. At the same time, you must learn to apply a more objective strategy to assessing the probability and/or desirability of each outcome. In the next section we will explain how this may be achieved so that the acceptance or rejection of a particular course of action is based on an accurate evaluation of the overall situation.

Emotions and Decision Making

Higher Odd Than Even Score on Statements 13–20

If you are one of those people who can express emotions easily and respond readily to the mood of those around you, your decisions are likely to be based on a somewhat extreme judgment of the desirability or probability of a particular course of action. It will either be seen as so certain and desirable as to exclude any other option even being considered, or so uncertain and undesirable that you may be overwhelmed by sensations of helplessness. Equally, it may be seen as highly desirable yet quite unobtainable, a reaction likely to lead to frustration and depression, or highly undesirable and yet very unlikely to happen, a belief which, if wrong, could result in your failing to take appropriate precautions. Extreme judgments, therefore, will frequently lead to the wrong kind of decisions and, in some cases, quite serious errors.

Studies have also revealed that emotional people tend to have a poor sense of time that results in their overestimating or underestimating how long a particular course of action will take to complete. This, too, can lead to faulty decision making since a perfectly satisfactory course of action may needlessly be rejected in the mistaken belief that it will take too long to complete, or an option adopted which turns out to be quite impractical because it can never be completed in the time available.

The higher your score on odd numbers in the second part of the assessment, the more powerful the influence of these emotionally determined factors on the decisions you make.

By regularly using the procedures described in the next section, your assessment of options will become more effective and you will be much less likely to make mistakes over the time needed to complete them. You can reduce an unrealistically extreme judgment about desirability and/or probability by deliberately *underestimating* both when assigning numerical values, a technique described in Section Three.

Higher Even Than Odd Score on Statements 13–20

The higher this score, the more strongly you desire to control emotions and conceal your inner feelings. This personality factor influences decision making by causing you consistently to underestimate the chances that outcomes will prove either probable and/or desirable.

You tend to believe that things are far less likely to happen than is the case and often regard them as less attractive than they are. This leads to poor decision making because you tend not to take advantage of opportunities and to reject courses of action that could prove extremely beneficial.

To compensate for the tendency, you should quite deliberately *overestimate* the chances that something will happen and regard it as *more* desirable that this should occur than you may actually feel at that moment.

In Section Three we will show you how this assessment can be done in an objective manner by assigning number values to particular outcomes. When you practice this technique, bear in mind the need to increase the values slightly in order to compensate for the influences of your personality.

The chart below summarizes the strengths and weaknesses of each personality factor and provides brief guidance as to ways in which adverse influences can be overcome. We suggest that you use this for rapid reference when working through the procedures in the next section.

How to Take Chance Out of Choice

Many of the decisions we make each day require little conscious effort or thought. They are more or less automatic responses to familiar events and we may perform them without being aware that various options have been considered in order to arrive at a particular course of action. When attempting to cross a busy street, for instance, information about road conditions, visibility, the speed and distance of oncoming traffic, and our own fleetness of foot are evaluated by the brain before a decision is made over whether to run, walk, or wait.

When ordering a lunchtime snack in a crowded diner we may have to make decisions quite rapidly from the wide choice available, relying on past experience to guide us most of the time but occasionally trying something new for a change.

In both these cases our minds have computed which course of action is best to follow, using the two key components of decision making described in the last section, *desirability* and *probability*.

Summary Chart of Influences of Personality over Decision Making (Refer to this as you work through Section Three.)

Your Score	Personality Factor Involved	Effect on Decisions	Precautions to be Taken
Higher odd than even score on statements 1–12	*Dependency:* This score shows you to be an independent decision maker.	You adopt a systematic approach to ordering the evidence on which decisions are based.	None. This approach exactly matches the procedures you will use in the next section.
		You are too pessimistic when assessing probability and desirability of particular outcomes.	Adopt a more optimistic approach when assessing these factors. Assign high values rather than low ones in the next section.
		You consider too many courses of action in an attempt to safeguard yourself against adverse consequences.	Limit the courses of action being considered to eliminate those which, while possible, are actually unlikely to occur.
Higher even than odd score on statements 1–12	*Dependency:* This score shows that you tend to rely on others when making up your mind.	You base your decisions on a wide range of views, but still tend to consider too few courses of action because you are overoptimistic about outcomes.	It is a good idea to canvas other people's opinions but widen your range of options. Do not be quite so confident that any single course of action will inevitably work out.
		You use intuition and feelings more than logic when assessing information.	Use feelings to influence your judgments but not to the exclusion of logic.

(*Chart continued*)

Your Score	Personality Factor Involved	Effect on Decisions	Precautions to be Taken
Higher odd than even score on statements 13–20	*Emotionality:* You express your emotions readily and reflect the moods of those around you.	You tend to take extreme views as to the probability or desirability of any course of action.	Be on your guard against adopting extreme views when evaluating information about possible options.
		You are probably rather bad at judging time and working out how long it will take to accomplish something.	The procedures described in the next section will help you to become a better judge of time by allowing your mind to work in a systematic manner when assessing various courses of action.
Higher even than odd score on statements 13–20	*Emotionality:* You prefer to control your emotions and not allow others to know how you feel about things.	You tend to underestimate the desirability and probability of outcomes. This makes it difficult for you to evaluate possible courses of action effectively.	When assigning numerical values to probability and desirability (as explained in the next section) you deliberately overestimate in each case to compensate for this personality factor.

Remember that the higher your score in either direction, the greater the likelihood of the influences described above having an important effect on your decision making. Even if there are only small differences between odd and even scores in each case, bear this tendency in mind when working through the procedures in the next section.

On the sidewalk, as we watch the speeding traffic while waiting to cross, our brains calculate the probability of reaching the other side of the street safely, and only when this is either a certainty or as close to a certainty as possible will we proceed. The desirability of crossing the street will usually be a less significant element of that particular choice. We need to cross to reach a store, office, or apartment entrance, but exactly when or precisely where we do so will normally not be the overriding consideration. There might be circumstances, however, when desirability becomes so crucial that we are prepared to accept a lower probability of crossing in safety. Suppose, for example, that a mother has left her baby in his carriage outside one store while crossing the street to make a quick purchase in another. As she comes out of the shop, she sees a stranger pushing the baby carriage away. In her frantic attempts to prevent the abduction, she dashes out in front of speeding cars, narrowly missing being run down. Her decision to cross at that moment and at that point has been dictated solely by the urgent desire to save her baby, and the probability of reaching the opposite sidewalk safely is given little or no consideration.

Stopping for lunch we decide what to eat by assessing the desirability of a rich but tasty snack in relation to the probability that this will give us indigestion for the rest of the afternoon or add too many extra pounds to our waists. If the probability of either happening is high, this may make us strike the item from the menu even though we desire very much to eat it. On the other hand, the desire might become so powerful that we decide to have it and suffer the increased probability of indigestion or a weight gain.

Because we normally assess probability and desirability more or less automatically, there is a strong tendency to use the same rather unthinking approach when making decisions that really demand a careful examination and evaluation of these two crucial factors. How *probable* is a paticular outcome if we adopt a specific course of action? Have we evaluated the evidence correctly or been misled by subjective bias and selective attention?

How *desirable* is the outcome? Again, have we really thought the situation through or allowed our personal decision-making style to distort an assessment of the consequences?

Objective evaluations, on which sound decision making is based, cannot be achieved in a haphazard manner or by trusting to luck. Instead we need to make use of a special method for analyzing all the available options in terms of their probability and desirability. This technique is called the Decision Tree.

How the Decision Tree Grows

In a Decision Tree all possible choices are made explicit, so that every aspect of the task can clearly be seen. By keeping guesswork, hunches, and subjective influences in check, the Tree also makes it possible for you to employ the style of decision making best suited to the situation, whether this is a Maximizer, Minimizer, or Protector approach. In this way you can significantly enhance the flexibility of your response, matching styles to circumstances as the need arises.

But a Tree is no mechanical device producing decisions by numbers in a sterile way that pays little regard to feelings or intuition. The great advantage of this technique is that these powerful and often valuable emotional components of the task are included in the decision-making process, but *in a controlled manner*. This prevents a flood of emotions or a hunch based on imprecise guesswork from assuming overriding importance in the final decision. You consider emotions, you use them creatively, but you never allow them to dominate your thoughts to the exclusion of more reasoned arguments.

How Hamlet Might Have Built a Tree

To illustrate the growth of a Decision Tree we are going to look at the work of two internationally respected specialists in the area of decision analysis, Desmond Graves and David Lethbridge of the Oxford Center for Management Studies.[47] These British psychologists have used a Tree to carry out an analysis of literature's best-known dilemma, Hamlet's agonized attempts to decide whether it is better "To be or not to be . . ."

What choice should he have made in this situation? We can explore his thinking systematically by noting the options he saw as being open to him and representing them in a diagram as branches sprouting from a single stem:

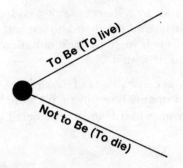

Figure 72

For each course of action there will clearly be one or more consequences, and the next stage in developing this or any other Tree is to write in the possible outcomes. For Hamlet, the results of these choices were either to live and suffer or to die and risk being tormented by dreams:

"For in that sleep of death what dreams may come,
When we have shuffled off this mortal coil,
Must give us pause."

The Decision Tree can be expanded to accommodate these outcomes by the addition of two further lines:

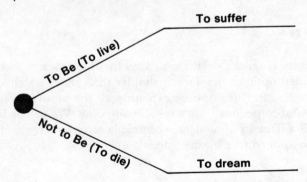

Figure 73

But Hamlet also took the view that in death he might find the peace of mind which was denied him in life:

"To die, to sleep:
No more; and, by a sleep to say we end
The heartache and the thousand natural shocks
That flesh is heir to, 'tis a consummation
Devoutly to be wish'd."

This additional consequence of dying is now added to the Tree and with it the structure is complete. It has included all the options and all the outcomes that Hamlet considered in reaching his decision.

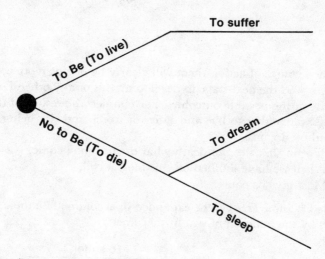

Figure 74

Because Hamlet's decision, as seen by Shakespeare, was based on limited options, the Tree is simpler than those which usually have to be constructed when exploring all the possible courses of action and consequences in a real-life situation. We will be looking at such a Tree in a moment when explaining how the technique may be applied to a business decision.

Evaluating the Outcomes

With the structure of the Tree completed, we now turn our attention to considering the desirability and probability of the three outcomes by assigning each a numerical value.

Assessing Desirability

When making any decisions, we are going to encounter outcomes that are seen as either attractive or disagreeable to various degrees. These can be dealt with in a rating system using positive numbers for desirable and negative numbers for undesirable consequences. The scale devised by Graves and Lethbridge ranges from +6 to −6, with the maximum figures representing outcomes that are regarded as overwhelmingly attractive or entirely unacceptable.

Emphasizing this system, let us see how Hamlet might have applied decision theory to his dilemma. He considered a dreamless death as the best consequence anyone could hope for, regarding it as: "A consummation devoutly to be wish'd." This suggests he would have rated it as +6 on the desirability scale.

What prevented him from immediate suicide was the thought that the death might be made hideous by dreams that would haunt his rest throughout eternity:

"To sleep: perchance to dream: ay, there's the rub:
For in that sleep of death what dreams may come,
When we have shuffled off this mortal coil,
Must give us pause."

It seems he could consider no worse fate than this and would probably have assigned it a −6 rating. Hamlet appeared to regard living and enduring his sufferings as preferable to the possibility of nightmares of the dead:

"But that the dread of something after death,
The undiscover'd country from whose bourn
No traveller returns, puzzles the will
And makes us rather bear those ills we have
Than fly to others that we know not of?
Thus conscience does make cowards of us all."

It was, however, an option less to be desired than a dream-free death:

"To die, to sleep:
No more; and by a sleep to say we end
The heartache and the thousand natural shocks
That flesh is heir to, 'tis a consummation
Devoutly to be wish'd . . ."

Balancing these components of his thoughts we might give life a rating of −3, indicating moderate undesirability.

These outcomes may now be rated according to their desirability, or otherwise, to produce this table:

Options	Outcomes	Desirability
To be	To suffer	−3
Not to be	To dream (purgatory)	−6
	To sleep (death without dreams)	+6

With desirability evaluated, we can now turn our attention to the likelihood of each outcome arising.

Assessing Probability

As it is seldom possible to know precisely how likely it is that a particular result will occur, we can only make an educated guess when estimating this factor. The most useful method to adopt is one in which you rate each outcome on a scale from 0 to 1.

Where an outcome is certain, it gets a score of 1. If you estimate there is a 50/50 chance that it will occur, then give it .5. Where the probability seems very low indeed, it gets a .2 or .1 rating.

Using this system with Hamlet's Decision Tree, we see that he considered that living must produce only one outcome, continued suffering. If he remains alive, he must go on enduring "The slings and arrows of outrageous fortune." Therefore, this result gets a 1.

Considering the possible consequences of suicide, we must weigh the chances of absolute death against the risk of purgatory. Part of his dilemma stemmed from the fact that Hamlet had no idea of the probabilities involved in either outcome and seems to have regarded them as equally likely. He must have felt there was a 50/50 chance of either dreaming or merely sleeping, which gives each a rating of .5.

The final listing of Desirability and Probability for the three outcomes produces the following:

Options	Outcomes	Desirability	Probability
To Be	To suffer	−3	1
	To dream	−6	.5
Not to Be	To sleep	+6	.5

If Hamlet had taken a more favorable view of his past life and considered his behavior virtuous, he might well have rated his chances of escaping purgatory more highly, in which case the probability score might have been .3 rather than .5. Since the total score for all outcomes which result from a particular course of action must always equal 1, the reduced likelihood of enduring the hell of dreaming would have led to an increase in his chances of experiencing a dreamless death. The Probability score here would have been increased from .5 to .7. However, the observation that: "Conscience does make cowards of us all" suggests he felt incapable of adopting anythng but the most gloomy view.

In order to calculate the most favorable course of action, all one needs to do is multiply the desirability and probability scores together and produce a final rating which is known as the Decision Value. The higher this value, the wiser it would be to adopt that particular option. Hamlet's Tree produces the following Decision Values:

Options	Outcomes	Desira-bility $\times$	Proba-bility	= Decision Value	Total
To Be (To live)	To suffer	−3	1	−3 total	−3 −3
Not to Be (To die)	To dream	−6	.5	−3	−3
	To sleep	+6	.5	+3 total	+3 0

From this it is clear that Hamlet's most logical course of action has to be suicide. The worst that might happen after death is to dream (−6), but this is no worse than remaining alive and suffering because, although the desirability of this outcome is somewhat greater (−3), its probability is much larger and this gives us an equivalent Decision Value. Remember that we are dealing with subjective impressions of the desirability and probability of each occurrence, and Hamlet seems to have been very strongly of the opinion that dreaming and sleeping were equally likely after suicide. Because of this and the far greater desirability of a dreamless sleep (+6), we get the most favorable Decision Value of the three options.

You will see that the consequences of suicide, a +3 and a −3, total zero and such a neutral value indicates that the outcome can be considered neither particularly desirable nor undesirable.

How might our three styles of decision making have coped with the result of this Tree? The ratings which each style produced would probably have been different because of their aptitude for focusing on particular aspects of the situation and perceiving them in a highly individual way.

The Maximizer would probably have viewed the available evidence from the perspective of an optimist who expects things to work out: "I'll probably go to heaven despite my transgressions." He might have the comforting reflection that "After all, my life was not all wicked. I did many kindly things too." Because of this he or she would probably have rated "dreaming" as a less likely outcome, giving it a value of, say, .2, while seeing a dreamless death as a greater certainty and rating it up to, say, .8. Transferring this assessment into Decision Values we get the following:

Options	Outcomes	Desirability ×	Probability	= Decision Value	Total
To Be	To suffer	−3	.5	−1.5	−1.5
Not to Be	To dream	−6	.2	−1.2	−1.2
	To sleep	+6	.8	+4.8	+4.8 +3.6

Here again the logical decision is suicide, with the Maximizer— given only the options which Hamlet was allowed to consider— seeing death as an even more favorable method for avoiding the sufferings of life.

A Minimizer would be likely to consider purgatory a more probable outcome than dreamless sleep, but this still makes suicide a better outcome than living since the desirability of dreamless rest is rated so highly:

Options	Outcomes	Desira-bility $\times$ Proba-bility		= Decision Value	Total
To Be	To suffer	−5	1	−5	= −5
Not to Be	To dream	−6	.8	−4.8	−4.8
	To sleep	+6	.2	+1.2	+1.2
					= −3.6

The Protector, similarly, although his powerful drive to avoid regrets could cause him to assess the desirability of each outcome rather differently, is still going to conclude that death offers the best answer to life's suffering.

Options	Outcomes	Desira-bility $\times$ Proba-bility		= Decision Value	Total
To Be	To suffer	−2	1	−2	= −2
Not to Be	To dream	−6	.5	−3	−3
	To sleep	+6	.5	+3	+3
					0

There is, of course, a fourth choice, which we have not looked at so far because Shakespeare did not allow Hamlet to regard it as an option, that is, to live without such suffering. The decision whether or not to kill oneself would then depend on how desirable and probable life without suffering was considered.

Options	Outcomes	Desira-bility $\times$ Proba-bility		= Decision Value	Total
To Be	To suffer	−3	.5	−1.5	−1.5
	Not to suffer	+6	.5	+3	+3
					= +1.5
Not to Be	To dream	−6	.5	−3	−3
	To sleep	+6	.5	+3	+3
					0

Here the decision is to stay alive in the expectation that things will get better. Since Hamlet did not take his own life, he must have entertained these thoughts, only Shakespeare did not bother to tell us about them! Alternatively, of course, he could have been a great writer but an unskilled decision analyst!

The notion that Hamlet kept back some of his feelings is consistent with modern research which has shown people frequently make decisions on the basis of feelings, beliefs, and opinions they are unwilling to state openly. This is a point to keep in mind when constructing your own Decision Trees, and since they will be a completely private creation, always be frank and include *everything* that is going to influence your decisions, even if these are feelings you would normally keep to yourself.

When forming the branches try to envisage as many courses of action as possible, and always aim for at least *four* options per Tree, even if only some of these are realistic and practical. By increasing the range of possibilities, especially if you have a tendency toward self-sufficiency in decision making, it becomes easier to place those which are truly viable in perspective. If you are dependent in your decision making, there should be no difficulty in envisaging a large number of options and, in this case, your task may be to eliminate the truly bizarre or clearly unworkable courses of action.

To illustrate the Tree working in a real-life business decision we are going to look at a task confronting the manager of a small import company who has purchased a large number of electronic toys which he hopes to market through major stores. You will find that, although this decision may seem slightly easier than Hamlet's heart-searching dilemma, the Tree it produces is considerably more involved and seemingly complex. As you work through its development with us, however, you should find that this ordered method for presenting and considering every aspect of the task resolves difficulties and confusions quickly and effectively, leading toward the most rational of all possible decisions. As you follow the construction of this Tree, make certain you understand the thinking behind each stage of development, especially when it comes to assigning values for desirability and probability to the various courses of action. Although this Tree analyzes a business transaction, exactly the same method and approach can be used when considering any type of decision in your personal or professional life.

Dilemma in Toyland

The problem facing Eric, sales director of an import–export company, was how best to market a large number of electronic toys which he had imported at the peak of a boom and now saw himself in danger of being stuck with as the market started to decline. He knew that the only way of disposing of the quantity he had available was to make sales to one of two major retail chains. Having done business with them in the past, he knew the buying managers personally and felt he could persuade one of them to help him out, but both stores would not be willing to carry the same line. Company A, whose buying manager was Alison Martin, was his first choice because similar lines he had sold them proved popular and their outlets were in the sort of neighborhoods where sales of such a sophisticated and costly electronic toy had a better chance of success. On the other hand, he was on friendlier terms with Alan Peters, the chief buyer for Company B. Eric knew that he would have to tread with great care in his negotiations, since by offering to one buyer, he was making it far less likely he could subsequently offer to the other if he received a rejection. Alison and Alan had long been bitter rivals and either would be annoyed at not being given first refusal on any new line. Eric expressed his dilemma like this: "I think I could make the best deal with Alison because her store would promote the line hard, they have a good track record with me, and are likely to reorder, provided their original deal was a success. The difficulty is, I think Alan is more likely to agree to take the goods, even though he may place a smaller order initially and then be reluctant to reorder because sales have been poor recently. Word gets around quickly in our business and whichever company I approach first, the other is bound to learn about it.

"I have done some good deals with Alison in the past and it's just possible that if I go to Alan first and get a rejection she might still be willing to consider my proposals, but I think the chance is less than even. On the other hand, Alan dislikes Alison so much that if I go to her first and get nowhere, it is even less likely that I can go back to him and secure a contract. If I make the wrong decision and fail to sell to either of them, I am going to have a hard job disposing of these toys at a realistic price and I'll stand to lose a considerable sum. There are no other outlets large enough and specialized enough to take this product in the numbers I have available, so I must try to make a deal with either Alison or Alan."

This kind of decision is typical of those that confront people in business since it contains considerable uncertainty and a fair amount of risk. The Decision Tree does, however, provide the best technique for reducing that uncertainty to a minimum, bringing the risks involved into a more objective perspective and identifying the most effective options.

Eric assigned a desirability rating to each outcome, as his first step in constructing a Tree, as follows:

Options	Desirability
Sell to Alan	+5
Sell to Alison	+6
Sell to neither	−6

His next task was to evaluate the probability of acceptance or refusal by each buyer. This took some careful thought but, based on his previous dealings with them, he estimated his chances in each case like this:

Options	Probability		
First Choice	Accept	Reject	Total
Try to deal with Alan	.7	.3	1
Try to deal with Alison	.6	.4	1

(Remember, the probability ratings for acceptance and refusal by each buyer must total 1.)

Finally Eric had to work out his chances of persuading either Alison or Alan to buy his goods when each knew the other had been approached first and turned down the proposition. He made an educated guess, based on past experience, that the likelihood would be as follows:

Options	Probability		
Second Choice	Accept	Reject	Total
Try to deal with Alan	.2	.8	1
Try to deal with Alison	.3	.7	1

He then constructed the Decision Tree shown below (Figure 75) and added on his ratings. The structure is more extended than the first one we looked at because Eric, unlike Hamlet, could be faced with a second choice after learning the outcome of his first option.

To obtain the final probability rating of the outcomes of these second choices, Eric only needed to perform a simple multiplication. Let us consider, for example, the chances of his failing to make any sale at all because, having been turned down by Alan, his proposals are then rejected by an angry Alison (shown on the top branch of the Tree).

This value can be calculated by multiplying the chances of a turn-down by Alan (.3) and the probability of Alison refusing to make a deal with him subsequently (.7).

This gives us a value of .21, which is written at the top of the Probability column on the Tree. Similarly, given that the chances of Alison refusing a deal if asked first (.4) and the probability of Alan being willing to give him a contract after he had been turned down by his rival (.2), we get an overall probability of Alan signing a contract if asked second of (.2 × .4) or .08. Finally Eric calculated that there would be a .32 probability of his missing out on the deal entirely if he asked Alan after being refused by Alison—her likelihood of refusal is (.4 × .8) = .32.

To obtain the final Decision Value, Eric used a calculator to carry out some rapid multiplications, followed by a little simple addition. As you can see from the Tree, the total of the three possible outcomes when he puts the deal to Alan first gives a Decision Value of 2.78. This falls to 2.08 when Alison is contacted before Alan.

On the basis of this analysis, Eric concluded that his best course of action was to offer the toys to Alan first, even though he had originally favored Alison.

It is impossible, of course, to be 100 percent certain that Eric made the correct choice since Alison might well have taken his toys and done better for him if asked first, and Alan might not have turned down the deal even if contacted second. In each and every decision there is always going to be an element of uncertainty, but using the systematic procedures of the Decision Tree you stand the best possible chance of making the best possible choice for four important reasons.

1. The mental task of fixing number values to each aspect of the decision focuses attention on specific issues and prevents your attention from being distracted by more general and less essential

Figure 75

Decision Tree for Dilemma in Toyland

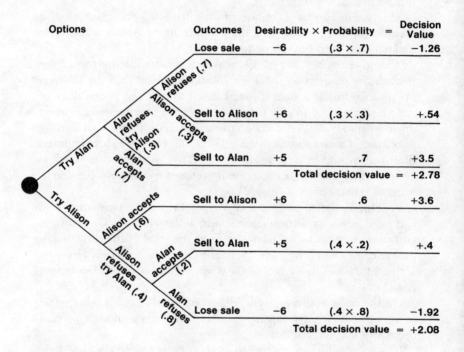

considerations. This process clarifies the key elements that will have to be considered, allows you to make a more objective assessment of their true significance, and, by providing a clearly structured procedure to follow, reduces any anxiety associated with the decision.

2. By constructing the Tree you make explicit all the possible options and outcomes, recording these on paper rather than trying to retain and manipulate the variables in your memory. As we have already explained, the capacity of short-term or working memory is limited, and if you overload the system, you are more likely to become confused, forget important points, and produce a decision based on incomplete consideration of the available information.

3. Constructing a Decision Tree stimulates the flow of ideas and enables you to discover original courses of action or identify the less obvious options far more easily than when thinking about the situation in an unstructured manner.

4. The Tree, while allowing you to take into account personal preferences and your emotional response to the situation, does not allow feelings to overwhelm more reasoned judgments. By assigning numbers to the desirability and probability of outcomes, you do not eliminate the spontaneity from choice, but you can be more confident that decision making remains under intellectual rather than emotional control.

You might still feel guesswork is a preferable tactic, either because it seems a less time-consuming way of making decisions or because the Decision Tree technique strikes you as too mechanistic. You might also argue that in many instances choice stems from personal preferences that cannot ever be quantified. We may, for example, decide to play Mozart rather than rock, choose salami instead of cream cheese as a sandwich filler, and like one person more than another without really being able to explain or justify such a choice. Because points like this are sometimes raised as objections to the Tree technique, we will discuss them briefly.

One cannot deny that tossing a coin in order to decide is a lot quicker than constructing a Tree, and leaving everything to luck is a lot easier than assigning numerical values to each option. If the choice has little real significance, then there is no purpose in carrying out a careful analysis of consequences. But where the decision is important and involves issues that could have a significant effect on your happiness or success, then it is obviously preferable to pause for a while and analyze your choices objectively than to waste time, effort, and energy at a later date in an attempt to correct the damage caused by a hasty, badly judged course of action.

To investigate the effectiveness of Decision Trees, we asked several top managers attending some of our workshops to keep a record of their more important decisions for a period of some six months. They were requested to continue using their normal strategies for the first half of this period and then to switch to the Tree whenever confronted by a major decision. The success of each approach was measured in several ways, including the number of options generated, the effectiveness with which information was assessed, the extent to which undesirable bias influenced the final outcome, and the degree of success which each decision produced.

Even in those instances where managers were convinced their decision making was already highly efficient, some significant improvements were noted when comparing results over the two periods. These were especially noticeable in situations where the task contained a great deal of uncertainty, where the information on which to base the decision was confusing, or when there was a strong emotional component to the task. In the first case, the Tree led to a wider range of possible options being considered; in the second, to a faster understanding of key aspects of the information, and in the last case, to a far more objective appreciation of the true situation. One industrialist explained how he had applied the Tree to a decision of whether or not to close down a no longer productive branch of his factory:

"In the first three months I made the decision not to shut down despite heavy losses. I had convinced myself that this judgment was based on the notion that it could somehow be made viable, or not wanting to sack staff, and a belief that in a more buoyant market we could use the plant productively. When I applied the Tree to the same decision a few weeks later, I quickly realized that my earlier decision arose from what was mainly an emotional response. When my father started the company he ran it from those premises. I simply hadn't appreciated before what this meant to me. The Tree plainly showed me it had to be closed down, but I was also able to discover courses of action that minimized the effect on my workforce and gave me the option of expanding again when the market picked up."

The Decision Tree is a powerful tool whenever you are faced with a choice that is difficult to make and important to your future. Practice on fairly trivial, straightforward decision tasks at first so as to understand the structuring process completely before applying the technique to major decisions. When using it, bear in mind the comments we made about the influence of personality over choice and consider which of the three styles is best suited to that particular task. It will also be useful to be on your guard against common pitfalls and fallacies surrounding decision making. These are easily overlooked when making a choice and invariably lead to faulty decisions. You will learn what they are and how to avoid them in the next section.

SECTION THREE

The Hidden Hazards of Decision Making

Most people assume that groups make more cautious decisions than individuals. That old joke about a camel being a horse designed by a committee reflects the widely held belief that although decision makers working on their own are enterprising and audacious, initiative vanishes and caution replaces daring as soon as they come together in a group. Until the late 1960s this was a view that most psychologists would have shared. Then came a series of epic experiments in group decision making by James Stoner at the Massachusetts Institute of Technology[48] and these popular assumptions were shown to be hopelessly wide of the mark. The effect he discovered, which has been found among all kinds of groups during the past fifteen years, came to be known as the *Risky Shift*. It is a component of collective choice that all concerned with group decisions should be aware of and on their guard to avoid. No one knows for sure why the Risky Shift occurs, but its influence on the judgments made when people gather together to decide some issue are profound. Instead of being prudent and cautious, groups have been found to advocate proposals involving far greater degrees of risk than the members of those groups would dare to put forward if making decisions on their own.

In Dr. Stoner's studies, subjects were first asked to make individual decisions about what to do about imaginary characters in different stories. A group of options was suggested that varied according to the amount of reward and risk involved. In every case, however, the greater reward was associated with a far higher degree of risk. After deciding alone what course of action the characters should follow, the subjects were brought together in a group to make a joint decision for the same set of characters in identical situations.

While deciding alone, most subjects chose a middle-of-the-road option that combined modest rewards with moderate degrees of risk. When the same kind of decisions were made in a group, however, their judgments shifted in the direction of far greater risk, most subjects now being willing to abandon caution and opt for a choice that offered high levels of rewards at higher levels of risk. James Stoner found that the group choice was almost always the greater gamble, with decisions ranging from the slightly rash to the downright foolhardy.

If you are involved in group decision making, where the risk of outcomes must be a consideration, then safeguard yourself against this hazard by taking the following steps:

• Warn members of the group about Risky Shift.

• Try to get each of them to come to a decision on his or her own. Then ensure that they are not swayed too far from their original positions when the same choice is debated in the group.

• Finally, prepare yourself for group discussion by thinking out your own decision in advance of the meeting. Use the Tree to come to the most rational and realistic course of action and do not subsequently allow yourself to be persuaded that an option you have already rejected because of the high degree of risk involved is somehow justified or desirable. Always keep in mind that the views put forward by a group may be unrepresentative of the decisions that the individual members of that group would have reached on their own.

Avoid the Gambler's Fallacy

Because gambling requires a constant series of quick decisions involving considerable risk and a great deal of uncertainty, it tends to bring bad decision-making habits into open view more readily than any other human activity.

Let's look in on a typical Las Vegas casino to watch the most important of these bad habits in action. Called the *Gambler's Fal-*

lacy, it may be found not only around the roulette wheels but any-where that decisions are being made.

Mark has been playing the wheel for the last couple of hours. As he has lost a fair bit, he has stopped betting for a few turns to study the trends of the winning numbers. Black numbers have come up on the past eleven spins of the wheel and Mark is reasoning as fol-lows: "That was a long run of black. The chances against another black number coming up must be greatly increased. I'd better get some money down on a red number for the next spin."

Although all roulette players must lose in the long run, due to the way casinos pay out on the game, Mark is actually going to get through his money faster than the average if he persists with this type of decision making. Why that should be so we will consider in a moment, but, before doing that, let us examine such a strategy more closely to understand why it is based on entirely incorrect as-sumptions.

The roulette wheel, having no memory, keeps no tally of how many times it has rewarded one color against another. The odds of red coming up after a run of eleven black numbers, or eleven hun-dred, or eleven thousand, or any number, is exactly the same as it was before the wheel ever began to spin. In theory, it should be 50/50; in practice, the chance is deliberately made slightly less to ensure that the house always makes a profit. It is the same with tossing a coin, a chance situation we will be looking at later, where you can come up heads a million times, yet the likelihood of that coin landing tails upward on the millionth and first toss will still be no more than 50 percent.

You may feel that by avoiding gambling you will never come across this kind of faulty decision making. But this is not so, as psy-chologists have observed variations of the Gambler's Fallacy in a wide range of decisions containing risk and/or uncertainty. Con-sider, for example, the businessman who says: "I've lost money on the last four projects, so I've just got to get lucky on this one!", or the inexperienced cook who remarks: "I burned the last three din-ners cooked on this new stove, so I must be about out of bad luck."

Both are falling into the trap of the Gambler's Fallacy. Rather than trying to analyze their actions and look for some realistic rea-son to account for the failures, they are trusting to lucky breaks. Perhaps that sounds all too obvious, and maybe it is when looked at away from an actual decision-making situation. But if you are honest, we think it likely you will be able to remember at least one occasion when you told yourself: "Things can't go on being this bad. I must be due for some good luck soon." If so, then the Fallacy has been undermining your decisions by distracting you from taking a more objective look at what might have been going wrong.

Be Aware of the Guesser's Disadvantage

Professional gamblers have long been convinced that the person doing the guessing in a game of chance is at a disadvantage and will always lose more often than the individual who controls the gambling. They claim, for example, that if you have one man tossing a coin and another placing bets on whether it will come down heads or tails, the coin tosser is going to have the best chance of winning.

If this idea is right, it obviously has important implications for all kinds of decisions that involve a high degree of risk or uncertainty since, merely by forcing the other person to make a decision, you will be more likely to come out on top.

To find out if the notion of *The Guesser's Disadvantage* had any scientific basis, psychologists studied coin tossing using a computer programmed to present either the word "heads" or the word "tails" on a TV screen. By using a computer, rather than simply tossing a real coin, they were able to eliminate bias and ensure that the presentation of words was truly random. Subjects who sat before the screen had to anticipate what word the computer would present by pressing one of two buttons immediately prior to it being flashed up on the TV.

If you were to toss a coin a very large number of times, you would find that it came down heads as often as it came down tails. Anyone betting on the outcome in a random fashion could therefore be expected to guess correctly 50 percent of the time. Indeed, if their score were significantly higher or lower than that predicted by chance, one would immediately know that their decision making was non-random: that is, it included a bias which, for some reason, made them more or less accurate in their guesses than could be explained on the basis of chance alone.

The computer program ensured that the word "heads" or "tails" appeared in a truly random fashion and subjects who were able to match this by guessing randomly would have been right half the time. But that was not what the scientists found in practice because all their subjects guessed significantly below the predicted rate of success. Although they knew that in order to be right 50 percent of the time they must press the buttons randomly and attempted to do so, a pattern was always present in the decisions they took and this distorted the results. No matter how hard they tried to distribute their guesses evenly between heads and tails, one or the other was consistently favored.

Now it might be argued, in view of what we know about Gambler's Fallacy, that this was sufficient explanation for the effect. The idea that, given a run of heads, for example, it was more likely that tails would turn up could well impose a pattern on the distribution of guesses. Certainly Gambler's Fallacy does involve a patterning of decision making, and it probably plays a role in the Guesser's Disadvantage. But this is not the only factor involved. When psychologists controlled for the Fallacy phenomenon, subjects continued to guess at below-chance levels. In other words, their thinking was patterned and their decisions other than random.

To understand why such patterns occur, try this simple experiment. For the next thirty seconds sit still and try *not* to think of the word "wolf." You will find it quite impossible.

The computer can produce random events because its "thoughts" can be switched on and off at will. We cannot at any moment of our waking life (and this probably applies to sleep as well), turn off the flow of thoughts that floods the mind. It is this tumult of ideas, this powerful current of mental activity, that shapes and directs the course of decision making. We may think we are picking heads or tails at random, plucking the choice from empty air, but such beliefs are illusions. The guesswork is not what it seems, a random selection from alternative options. Rather it is the outcome of a pattern of intellectual responses operating below the level of normal awareness.

Like most gambling effects, the Guesser's Disadvantage has something to tell us about many types of decision making. It may lead to a series of similar choices being made in the face of common sense and experience. Take, for example, the case of a woman who marries a brute, frees herself at last from the ruinous entanglement only to become involved with another man who is just as much of a rogue as the first. And so the pattern of choice may be continued, causing one desperately miserable love affair to be followed by others no less distressing.

In business it is not uncommon for an otherwise clever and perceptive individual to go into partnership with people who turn out to be idle, incompetent, and dishonest. No sooner have they picked up the pieces of that shattered enterprise than they embark on further associations which are likely to be just as disastrous.

So be aware of the effects of the Guesser's Disadvantage whenever you have to make a decision. Understand that forces are at work within your mind of which you may well remain unaware. If you have experienced a run of bad decisions recently, do not be tempted to fall into the trap of Gambler's Fallacy and put the blame on ill fortune. Look for the underlying pattern which has shaped your choices, then work to adopt more productive and effective strategies in the future. In the same way, a series of "lucky" decisions should not be attributed to your passing through a period of good fortune. Once again, the realistic and most rewarding approach is to identify the underlying mental strategies which led to those choices being taken and the favorable courses of actions followed.

Taking Chance Out of Choice

Some uncertainty must always remain in many of the decisions you make. How much depends on the degree of control you are able to exert over events and the amount of accurate knowledge available on which to base your choice of options. But, in all circumstances, chance can be taken out of choice to a very great extent by adopting the techniques we have explained here:

• Start by understanding your preferred decision-making style. Identify the type of choice being made and, if your natural style is not the most suitable for that particular situation, switch to one that is.

• Construct a Decision Tree so that you can evaluate all the options and their likely outcomes, then assign numerical values to the probability and desirability of each in order to gain an objective and rational perspective on the courses of action open to you.

• When making decisions with the Tree, take the biasing factors of your personality into account and adjust outcome values accordingly.

• Be on your guard against the Risky Shift when making decisions as one of a group, and avoid the traps of Gambler's Fallacy and the Guesser's Disadvantage at all times. Remember that in a situation of risk and/or uncertainty, the person making a decision is often disadvantaged by hidden thought patterns which should be identified and turned to your advantage.

These simple, straightforward tactics will ensure that any decision you have to make stands the best chance of proving successful. They will enable you to maximize advantages, minimize risks, and only very rarely end up wishing "If only I had done that instead."

This concludes our Five-Step training course. You now have programs designed to enhance every major aspect of intellectual activity. You cannot hope to remember all the procedures described, nor to use them all at once. We suggest that you adopt a few of the key strategies from each of the five steps and begin to introduce these into your regular thinking processes whenever the opportunity arises. Once you have mastered them successfully and make use of them consistently, you can start using a few more until you gradually incorporate all of them into your routine mental procedures.

To help us in our continuing research into intellectual enhancement, we would greatly appreciate your views on this training program, especially by hearing about any ways in which the techniques have been helpful in everyday problem solving, decision making and learning tasks. Please write to us at *The Mind Potential Study Group*, 22 Queen Anne Street, London W.1. UK.

Footnote References

1. Neisser, U., *Cognition and Reality* (San Francisco: W. H. Freeman, 1976).
2. Rosenthal, R. and Jacobson, L., *Pygmalion in the Classroom: Teacher Expectancy and Pupils' Intellectual Development* (New York: Holt, Rinehart & Winston, 1968).
3. Penfield, W., "Consciousness, Memory, and Man's Conditioned Reflexes," *On the Biology of Learning*, ed. Pribram, K. (New York: Harcourt Brace Jovanovich, 1969).
4. Reiff, R. and Sheerer, M., *Memory and Hypnotic Age Regression* (New York: International University Press, 1959).
5. True, R. M., "Experimental Control in Hypnotic Age Regression," *Science*, 110 (1949): 583–584.
6. Walker, N., Paper presented at American Psychological Association conference (1976).
7. Luria, A. R., *The Mind of a Mnemonist* (New York: Basic Books, 1968).
8. Stratton, G. M., "Retroactive Amnesia and Other Emotional Effects on the Memory," *Psychological Review*, 26 (1919): 474–486.
9. Diamond, M., Study reported in *Psychology Today* (British), November (1978).
10. Naylor, G. and Harwood, E., "Old Dogs, New Tricks: Age and Ability," *Psychology Today* (British), April (1975): 29–33.
11. Study, *Human Behavior*, May (1979): 58–59.
12. Maslow, A., *The Farther Reaches of Human Behavior* (New York: Viking Press, 1971).
13. Young, J. Z., *Programs of the Brain* (Oxford, England: Oxford University Press, 1980).
14. Michaels, W., Lecture presented at the Mind Potential Study Group, London, England (1980).
15. Mulholland, T. M., Pellegrino, J. W., and Glaser, R., "Components of Geometric Analogy Solutions," *Cognitive Psychology*, 12 (1980): 252–284.
16. Sternberg, R. J., "Compotential Investigations of Human Intelligence," *Cognitive Psychology and Instruction*, ed. Lesgold, A. M. et al. (New York: Plenum Press, 1978).

17. Jacobs, P. J. and Vandeventer, M. "Evaluating the Teaching of Intelligence," *Educational and Psychological Measurement,* 32 (1972): 235–248.
18. Linn, M. C., "The Role of Intelligence in Children's Responses to Instruction," *Psychology in the Schools,* 10 (1973): 67–75.
19. Penrose, L. S. and Raven, J. C., "A New Series of Perceptual Tests," *British Journal of Medical Psychology,* 16 (1936), part two.
20. Jacobs, P. J. and Vandeventer, M., loc. cit., reference 17.
21. Whitely, S. E. and Dawis, R., "The Effects of Cognitive Intervention on Estimates of Latent Ability Measured from Analogy Items," *Technical Report,* No. 3011 (Minneapolis: University of Minnesota, 1973).
22. Willner, A., "An Experimental Analysis of Analogical Reasoning," *Psychological Reports,* 15 (1964): 479–494.
23. Miller, G. A., "The Magical Number Seven Plus or Minus Two: Some Limits on Our Capacity for Storing Information," *Psychological Review,* 63 (1956): 81–97.
24. Thorpe, C. and Rowland, G. "The Effect of 'Natural' Grouping of Numbers on Short-Term Memory," *Human Factors,* 7 (1965): 38–44.
25. Frankel, Al and Snyder, M. "Poor Performance Following Unsolvable Problems: Learned Helplessness or Egotism?" *Journal of Personality and Social Psychology,* 36 (1978): 1415.
26. Pellegrino, J. W. and Schadler, M., *"Maximizing Performance in a Problem-Solving Task,"* (Paper developed at the University of Pittsburgh Learning Research, and Development Center, 1974). Cited in Resnick, L. B., *The Nature of Intelligence* (New York: John Wiley & Sons, 1976).
27. Ace, M. C. and Dawis, R. V., "Item Structure as a Determinant of Item Difficulty in Verbal Analogies," *Education and Psychological Measurement,* 33 (1973): 143–149.
28. Flaubert, G., *L'Educacion Sentimentale* (Paris, 1869).
29. Pask, G., "Styles and Strategies of Learning," *British Journal of Educational Psychology,* 46 (1976): 128–48.
30. Collins, A. M. and Quillian, M. R., "How to Make a Language User," *Organization of Memory,* eds. Tulving E. and Donaldson, W. (New York: Academic Press, 1972).
31. Atkinson, R. C., "A Stochastic Model for Rote Serial Learning," *Psychometrika,* 22 (1957): 87–95; *idem,* "Ingredients for a Theory of Instruction," *American Psychologist,* 27 (1972): 921–931.
32. Erdelyi, M. and Kleinbard, J., "Has Ebbinghaus Decayed with Time?: The Growth of Recall (Hypermnesia) Over Days," *Journal of Experimental Psychology,* 4 (1978): 275–289.
33. Atkinson, R. C. and Raugh, M. R., "An Application of the Mnemonic Keyword Method to the Acquisition of a Russian Vocabulary," *Journal of Experimental Psychology: Human Learning and Memory,* 104 (1975): 129–133.
34. Guilford, J. P., *The Nature of Human Intelligence* (New York: McGraw-Hill, 1967).

35. Wickelgren, W. A., *How to Solve Problems: Elements of a Theory of Problems and Problem-Solving* (San Francisco: W. H. Freeman & Co., 1974).
36. Duncker, K., "On Problem-Solving," *Psychological Monographs,* 270 (1945).
37. Interview with George Miller, *Psychology Today* (British), January (1980).
38. Duncker, K., loc. cit, reference 36.
39. Hoffman, B., *Albert Einstein: Creator and Rebel* (New York: New American Library, 1972).
40. Wittgenstein, L. J., *Tractatus Logico—Philosophicus* No. 5.6 in Korner, Stephan, *Fundamental Questions in Philosophy* (London: Allen Lane, The Penguin Press, 1969).
41. Whorf, B. L., in Carroll, J. B., *Language and Thought.* (Englewood Cliffs, NJ: Prentice Hall, Inc., 1964).
42. Carroll, J. B., *Language and Thought* (Englewood Cliffs, NJ: Prentice-Hall, Inc., 1964).
43. Chomsky, N., *Aspects of the Theory of Syntax.* (Cambridge, Mass.: M.I.T. Press, 1965).
44. Ghiselin, B., *The Creative Process* (New York: New American Library, 1952).
45. Kekule, F. A. in Japp, F. R., "Kekule Memorial Lecture," *Journal of the Chemical Society* (1898).
46. Brim, O. C. et al., *Personality and Decision Processes* (Stanford: Stanford University Press, 1962).
47. Graves, D. and Lethbridge, D., "Could Decision Analysis Have Saved Hamlet?" *Journal of Management Studies,* 12 (1975): 216–224.
48. Stoner, J., "Risky and Cautious Shifts in Group Decisions: The Influence of Widely Held Values," *Journal of Experimental Social Psychology,* 4 (1968): 442–459.

Bibliography

Anastasi, Anne, *Psychological Testing* 4th ed. (New York: MacMillan, 1976).

Anderson, John R. and Bower, Gordon H., *Human Associative Memory* (Silver Spring, Md.: V. H. Winston & Sons, 1973).

Baddeley, Alan, *The Psychology of Memory* (New York: Harper & Row, 1976).

Bransford, John, *Human Cognition: Learning, Understanding and Remembering* (Belmont, California: Wadsworth, Inc., 1979).

Brinkers, Henry, *Decision-Making: Creativity, Judgement and Systems* (Columbus, Ohio: Ohio State University Press, 1972).

Cattell, Raymond, *Abilities: Their Structure and Growth* (Boston: Houghton Mifflin Co., 1971).

Davis, Gary, *Psychology of Problem-Solving: Theory and Practice* (New York: Basic Books, 1973).

Eysenck, Hans, *The Structure and Measurement of Intelligence* (New York: Springer Publishing Co., Inc., 1979).

Ferguson, Marilyn, *The Brain Revolution* (London: Davis-Poynter, 1973).

Gagne, Robert, *The Conditions of Learning* (New York: Holt, Rinehart and Winston, 1977).

Glass, Arnold; Holyoak, Keith; and Santa, John, *Cognition* (Reading, MA: Addison-Wesley, 1979).

Hilgard, Ernest, and Bower, Gordon, *Theories of Learning* (Englewood Cliffs, New Jersey: Prentice Hall, 1966).

Hofstadter, Douglas, *Gödel, Escher, Bach: An Eternal Golden Braid* (New York: Basic Books, 1979).

Horowitz, E. and Sahni, S., *Fundamentals of Data Structures* (London: Pitman, 1976).

Kramer, Edna, *The Nature and Growth of Modern Mathematics* (New York: The Hawthorn Press, 1970).

Lee, Wayne, *Decision Theory and Human Behaviour* (New York: John Wiley and Sons, 1971).

Lesgold, Alan; Pellegrino, James; Fokkema, Sipke; and Glaser, Robert, *Cognitive Psychology and Instruction* (New York: Plenum Press, 1978).

Lindsay, Peter, and Norman, Donald, *Human Information Processing* (New York: Academic Press, 1972).

Marx, Melvin, *Learning: Theories* (New York: MacMillan, 1970).

Milner, Peter, *Physiological Psychology* (New York: Holt, Rinehart and Winston, 1970).

Newell, Allen and Simon, Herbert, *Human Problem-Solving* (Englewood Cliffs, New Jersey: Prentice Hall, 1972).

Nilsson, Lars, *Perspective on Memory Research* (Hillsdale, New Jersey: Lawrence Erlbaum, 1979).

Nilsson, Nils, *Problem-Solving Methods in Artificial Intelligence* (New York: McGraw-Hill, 1971).

Norman, Donald, *Memory and Attention: An Introduction to Human Information Processing* (New York: John Wiley, 1976).

Prather, R. E., *Discrete Mathematical Structures in Computer Science* (Boston: Houghton Mifflin, 1976).

Resnick, Lauren, *The Nature of Intelligence* (Hillsdale, New Jersey: Lawrence Erlbaum, 1976).

Rumelhart, David, *Introduction to Human Information Processing* (New York: John Wiley, 1977).

Tarpy, Roger, and Mayer, Richard, *Foundations of Learning and Memory* (Glenview, Il.: Scott, Foresman, 1978).

Wason, Peter and Johnson-Laird, Philip, *The Psychology of Reasoning* (London: Batesford, 1972).

Weizenbaum, J., *Computer Power and Human Reason* (San Francisco: W. H. Freeman, 1976).

Winston, Patrick, *Artificial Intelligence* (Reading, MA: Addison-Wesley, 1979).

Wulf, William; Shaw, Mary; Hilfinger, Paul; and Flon, Lawrence, *Fundamental Structures of Computer Science* (Reading, MA: Addison-Wesley, 1981).

Index